LITERARY CRITICISM AND CULTURAL THEORY

OUTSTANDING DISSERTATIONS

Edited by

William E. Cain
Professor of English
Wellesley College

A ROUTLEDGE SERIES

LITERARY CRITICISM AND CULTURAL THEORY

WILLIAM E. CAIN, *General Editor*

Dead Letters to the New World

Melville, Emerson, and American Transcendentalism

Michael McLoughlin

Routledge
New York & London

Published in 2003 by
Routledge
270 Madison Avenue
New York, NY 10016
www.routledge-ny.com

Published in Great Britain by
Routledge
2 Park Square
Milton Park, Abingdon
Oxon OX14 4RN
www.routledge.co.uk

Routledge is an imprint of the Taylor & Francis Group

Transferred to Digital Printing 2005

Copyright © 2003 by Taylor and Francis Books, Inc.

Library of Congress Cataloging-in-Publication Data
McLoughlin, Michael.
    Dead letters to the new world : Melville, Emerson, and American transcendentalism / by Michael McLoughlin.
        p. cm. — (Literary criticism and cultural theory)
    Includes bibliographical references and index.
    ISBN 0-415-96784-8
    1. Melville, Herman, 1819–1891—Criticism and interpretation. 2. Emerson, Ralph Waldo, 1803–1882—Influence. 3. Sea stories, American—History and criticism. 4. Melville, Herman, 1819–1891—Philosophy. 5. Transcendentalism in literature. 6. Fate and fatalism in literature. 7. Transcendentalism (New England) 8. Philosophy in literature. I. Title. II. Series.
PS2387.M356 2003
813'.3—dc21   2003006145

To my mother, Mary Ann McLoughlin,
for keeping me true to the dreams of my youth

Contents

Acknowledgments

I WISH TO THANK ROBERT NEWMAN, WILLIAM RICHEY, GRETA LITTLE, AND William Rivers for the financial support that has allowed me to complete the research necessary for this book. I also wish to thank the staff and faculty of USC's English department for all their help and encouragement — most notably, Modestine Redden, Lisa Saxon, professors Ezra Greenspan, William Richey, Don Greiner, and in particular, Joel Myerson. Thanks go to Jerry Wallulis for reading and commenting on an initial draft of this book. I'm also grateful to professors Maureen Hood, Brenda Wineapple, Frank Gado, and Trevor H. Howard-Hill for their mentorship early in my education.

I would like to thank Mila Tasseva-Kurktchieva for her long-standing friendship and for shouldering my former professional responsibilities with aplomb and competence at the time when this book most required my attention. Thanks to Sammantha Bremer for flowers upon my grandfather's death and many happy memories. Thanks, too, to my uncle Joe Schultz, Seabrook Wilkinson, Ray Soulard, Jr., Michael Powelson, and Tate McLoughlin, who, through their friendship, have helped to remind me what matters most. I'm grateful to Kelly Smith for a memorable walk on the beach, WFO motorcycle rides high in the North Carolina mountains, and one of the best home-cooked meals I've ever had. Thanks go to my dear friend Barbara Brannon for her help and guidance early in my academic career, as well as her many contributions to this project. Also, I would like to recognize Laura Pleicones and the rest of her family for their support during the composition of this book and for many years of precious friendship. Thanks to Karen Verch and the Murphy family for always making me feel welcome. I'm grateful to Ron Perez, Jr. for a lifelong friendship of truly Melvillian proportions.

I'd like to acknowledge some of my many Microsoft friends who have helped me along the way, including—but by no means limited to—Megan Kennedy, John Weston, Pat Hayes, Keith Combs, Diane Swingen, Kai Axford, Tiffany Towb, Jennifer Turvold, Shawn Henry, Michael Lytle, Stephen Cracknell, Don Roessler, Dave Kane, Susan Powitzky (thanks again for the cake!), Diane Jackson, and Bret Rohloff.

Lastly, for their profound and inveterate sacrifices on my behalf, I would like to thank my parents, Richard and Mary Ann McLoughlin, and my grandfather, Frank B. Schultz, who value education and learning above all things.

Michael McLoughlin
April 15th, 2003
Columbia, SC

Introduction

I F Melville's literary career had ended in 1851 with the publication of *Moby-Dick*, the Transcendental currents in his early novels would probably be as easily discernible to contemporary readers as they were to some critics of the late 1840s and early 1850s. Evert Duyckinck's reviews of *Mardi* and *Moby-Dick* in *The Literary World* referred to Emersonian qualities in Melville's language and philosophical speculation. In a review of *Mardi* dated April 21, 1849, Duyckinck observed, "There is a world of poetical, thoughtful, ingenious moral writing in it which Emerson would not disclaim."[1] On the other hand, Duyckinck in his review of *Moby-Dick* on November 22, 1851, criticized portions of the book that attacked conventions with "the conceited indifferentism of Emerson, or the run-a-muck style of Carlyle."[2] Melville apparently had become too much of a literary nonconformist to suit his New York publisher friend. In contrast, George Ripley, the Transcendentalist reviewer, praised *Moby-Dick* without reservation in the December 1851 issue of *Harper's*. "Beneath the whole story," Ripley said,

> The subtle end imaginative reader may perhaps find a pregnant allegory, intended to illustrate the mystery of human life. Certain it is that the rapid, pointed hints which are thrown out, with the keenness and velocity of a harpoon, penetrate deep into the heart of things, showing that the genius of the author for moral analysis is scarcely surpassed by the wizard power of description.[3]

What was not apparent then, except perhaps to a few readers, is that *Moby-Dick* represents an important transitional moment in Melville's art, dramatically altering tendencies inherent in the novels from

Typee onward. If the early critics could not agree on the quality of Melville's work, they were able, nevertheless, to sense the underlying affinity between Melville and Emerson. However, in contrast to Melville's blithely exciting and largely optimistic first six novels of the sea, Melville's later works—beginning with his pivotal epic *Moby-Dick*—assume a much darker and increasingly anti-Transcendental philosophical position.

The disillusionment permeating these later works probably stems from a combination of depressing events in Melville's life during the months leading up to the publication of *Moby-Dick*. First of all, Elizabeth Melville did not make a normal recovery following the birth on October 22, 1851, of the couple's second child, Stanwix.[4] Dr. Amos Nourse wrote to Lemuel Shaw, Melville's father-in-law, the following February 18 that he had "heard indirectly from time to time of Elizabeth, that she was feeble, and did not regain her strength after confinement as at the birth of her first child."[5] Melville's granddaughter, Eleanor Melville Metcalf, observes, "Melville, exhausted by his recent intensive labor on *Moby-Dick*, settled down to a fall and winter less social, but no less demanding in every way."[6]

Worried about Elizabeth and sensing from the mixed reviews that *Moby-Dick* would not be a financial success, Melville plunged immediately into writing another novel, *Pierre*, completing it in approximately five months, as compared to the year and a half spent on *Moby-Dick*.[7] "Yet he must go on writing," Metcalf comments, "Where else will bread and butter come from?"[8]

In the meantime, Melville was apparently attempting to sustain the high emotional pitch of his friendship with Hawthorne, which began in the summer of 1850 with Melville's enthusiastic admiration of Hawthorne's self-reliant artistry in "Hawthorne and His Mosses." During 1851, Melville not only exchanged visits with Hawthorne in nearby Lenox, but also wrote six letters to him, the last one dated November 17, 1851, in response to Hawthorne's praise of *Moby-Dick*.[9] The elation Melville displayed in this letter is phrased in Transcendental references to pantheism, immortality, and even the "*One*," which in this passage Melville describes as a divine magnet uniting his and Hawthorne's genius:

> P.S. I can't stop yet. If the world was entirely made up of Magians, I'll tell you what I should do. I should have a paper-mill established at one end of the house, and so have an endless riband of foolscap rolling in upon my desk; and upon that endless riband I should write a thousand—a million—billion thoughts, all in the form of a letter to you. The divine magnet is on you, and my

magnet responds. Which is the biggest? A foolish question—they
are *One*.[10]

Such unrestrained exuberance could not last. For Melville, emotional exhaustion and the failure of *Moby-Dick* to bring financial security and fame comparable to Hawthorne's undoubtedly contributed to
the mood of black despair that appears in the later novels without
the compensatory spark of hope for the individual self that characterizes Melville's art in the period before 1852.

Hawthorne moved away from Lenox in late November of 1851 at
approximately the time Melville began to write *Pierre*.[11] Randall
Stewart observes that Hawthorne's dislike of the climate, the inconveniences of "the Red House" in Lenox, and his desire to rejoin his
Concord friends motivated the change.[12] Melville, however, reacted
to the move with a correct politeness and detachment that indicate a
basic change in attitude not only toward his friend, but also toward
Transcendentalism. After the letter of November 17, Melville apparently did not write again directly to Hawthorne for eight months. In
his next known communication on July 17, 1852, approximately
three months after the completion of *Pierre*, Melville acknowledged
receipt of Hawthorne's new novel, *The Blithedale Romance*, and cour-
teously refused an invitation to visit Hawthorne in Concord:

> Said my lady-wife, "there is Mr. Hawthorne's new book, come by
> mail." And this morning, lo! on my table a little note, subscribed
> by Hawthorne again.—Well, the Hawthorne is a sweet flower;
> may it flourish in every hedge.
>
> I am sorry, but I can not at present come to see you at Concord
> as you propose.—I am but just returned from a two weeks'
> absence; and for the last three months and more I have been an
> utter idler and a savage—out of doors all the time. So, the hour
> has come for me to sit down again.[13]

It was actually Sophia Hawthorne who first wrote to Melville one
month after the Hawthornes moved from Lenox. In her letter to
Melville dated December 29, 1851, she praised *Moby-Dick*. Melville's
reply on January 8, 1852, was cordial, but surprisingly fatalistic, in
contrast to his earlier references to the Transcendental "One."
Although he admitted that *Moby-Dick* "was susceptible of an allegoric
construction," which Hawthorne had apparently recognized, Melville
denied that he had meant to spiritualize nature.[14] Melville also rejected the Transcendental ethic of self-reliance in a reference to his continuing admiration of Hawthorne:

and so we see how true was that musical sentence of the poet when he sang—

"We can't help ourselves"

For tho' we know what we ought to be; and what it would be very sweet and beautiful to be; yet we can't be it. That is most sad, too.[15]

The especial poignancy of this remark, which suggests the theme of *Pierre*, is that it is addressed to a Transcendentalist. Melville concluded his letter with a description of the helplessness of the individual, who is swept along by currents beyond his power to control:

Life is a long Dardenelles, My Dear Madam, the shores whereof are bright with flowers, which we want to pluck, but the bank is too high; and so we float on and on, hoping to come to a landing place at last—but swoop! we launch into the great sea: Yet the geographers say, even then we must not despair, because across the great sea, however desolate and vacant it may look, lie all Persia and the delicious lands roundabout Damascus.

So wishing you a pleasant voyage at last to that sweet and far countree—[16]

Except for the complimentary conclusion—perhaps a belated farewell to his departed friends—Melville's letter anticipates the pessimistic tone of his remaining pre-Civil War fiction.

Two reliable observers expressed their concern for Melville's health during the trying period during which he composed *Pierre*. Family friend Sarah Morewood entertained the Melvilles at Christmas dinner and then reported in a letter to George Duyckinck, dated December 28, 1851, that "Mr. Herman was more quiet than usual," but still a pleasant companion. "It is a pity," she continued,

that Mr. Melville so often in conversation uses irreverent language—he will not be popular in society here on that account. . . . I think he cares very little as to what others may think of him or his books so long as they sell well. I hear that he is now engaged in a new work [*Pierre*] as frequently not to leave his room till quite dark in the evening—when he for the first time during the whole day partakes of solid food. He must therefore write under a state of morbid excitement which will soon injure his health. . . .[17]

Another observer was Dr. Nourse, who wrote again to Judge Shaw on March 1 about Elizabeth Melville's recovery of health, and added: "Her husband I fear is devoting himself to writing with an assiduity that will cost him dear by and by."[18]

Melville's new novel, which he ironically alluded to as a "rural bowl of milk" in his letter to Sophia Hawthorne, strongly hints at his growing pessimism;[19] the subtext—or "little lower layer"—of this comment, of course, lies in the work as a negation of the absolute Transcendental moral values in the preceding novels.[20] In his introduction to *Pierre*, Henry A. Murray calls the novel a "prodigious by-blow of genius whose appearance is marred by a variety of freakish features and whose organic worth is invalidated by the sickness of despair."[21]

Adverse public reaction to *Pierre* resulted for Melville in the loss of an audience that anticipated sequels to *Typee* but tolerated the complex mixture of philosophy and whaling in *Moby-Dick*. Hugh W. Hetherington adequately states the critical consensus of the 1850s that *Pierre* "was morally vicious, stylistically monstrous, incomprehensibly Transcendental, and violently mad."[22] Melville's remaining fiction of the pre-Civil War period received relatively little public recognition, despite the arguably increased brilliance of his work.

In perspective, Melville's professional career as a novelist falls into two major phases corresponding to the growth and shift in his art. In the developmental phase, from 1845 to 1850, Melville wrote his five Transcendental novels of the sea in which he defended self-reliance, attacked conformity, and learned to employ Transcendental symbols of increasing complexity. This phase culminates in *Moby-Dick*, with its remarkable matching of Transcendental idealism with tragic drama influenced by Hawthorne. After the departure of Hawthorne in the winter of 1851, Melville endeavored to find new ways to express himself and to re-envision human experience philosophically. In this period of transition, he wrote anti-Transcendental fiction attacking self-reliance as well as conformity and substituting fatalism for Emersonian optimism. In terms of representative characters, the two phases are as different from each other as buoyant Jack Chase of *White-Jacket* is from inert Bartleby, both of whom are portraits of self-reliance.

Despite the profound influence Transcendentalism had on Melville and Emerson's key role in shaping the movement in America, only one book-length study has explored the Emerson-Melville relationship—John Williams's 1991 *White Fire: The Influence of Emerson on Melville*.[23] Williams discusses *Mardi, Redburn, White-Jacket,* and *Moby-Dick* to demonstrate Melville's interest in

Emersonian self-reliance and to argue that these works derive their force from the "white fire" of Transcendentalism. I engage and continue Williams's exploration of this important connection in the ensuing pages.

In chapter one, "Correspondent Colorings: Emerson and Melville," I outline the critical history of the Emerson-Melville relationship and discuss the European origins of American Transcendentalism. Chapter two, "American Transcendentalism and Its Discontents," considers Transcendentalism in detail and provides critical commentary on Emerson's major works. Chapter three, "Deeper Shadows to Come: The Transcendental Underpinnings of Melville's Early Works," treats Melville's early exposure to Emerson and explores the Transcendental dimensions of Melville's fiction leading up to 1850. Chapter four, "Defying Nature: *Moby-Dick* and the Limits of Emersonian Affirmation," examines *Moby-Dick* as both a Transcendental *and* an anti-Transcendental work that marks Melville's transition away from idealism. Chapter five, "A Hell-Fired Rural Bowl of Milk: Melville's *Pierre* and Transcendental Rebellion," considers *Pierre* as the quintessential expression of Melville's dissatisfaction and disillusionment with Transcendentalism, along with an exploration of Melville's marginal notations in his copies of Emerson's *Essays*. Chapter six, "Naked Nature Aboard the *San Dominick*: 'Benito Cereno,' Emerson, and the Gothic," analyzes "Benito Cereno" as a reactively Gothic anti-Transcendental work attacking Emersonian optimism. Chapter seven, "The Endless, Winding Way: Melville's Engagement with Emerson in *The Whale's* Wake," locates Melville's later works—"Bartleby, the Scrivener," *The Confidence-Man*, and *Billy Budd, Sailor*—in the continuum of his relationship as an artist to Emerson and Transcendentalism. Finally, the appendix collects, annotates, and assesses secondary works treating the Emerson-Melville relationship.

DEAD LETTERS TO THE NEW WORLD

Chapter One

Correspondent Colorings: Emerson and Melville

IN THE LATE SUMMER OF 1837, WHEN HERMAN MELVILLE WAS AN EIGHTEEN-year-old man about to begin a short, unsuccessful engagement as a teacher in Pittsfield, Massachusetts, Ralph Waldo Emerson addressed the students and faculty at Harvard.[1] Though Melville did not hear Emerson's Phi Beta Kappa oration, "The American Scholar," his future father-in-law, Lemuel Shaw—Chief Justice of the Massachusetts Supreme Judicial Court and Fellow of the Harvard Corporation—was present.[2] Shaw had been a friend and legal advisor of Melville's father, who died in 1832, and Herman was a frequent visitor in the Shaw home in later years. Through Shaw or otherwise, Melville surely became familiar with Emerson's celebrated portrait of the self-reliant scholar as "Man Thinking," which led Oliver Wendell Holmes to characterize this speech as "our intellectual Declaration of Independence."[3]

Emerson's theme was partly traditional. In 1809, for example, Dr. J. S. Buckminster of Boston had delivered the Phi Beta Kappa oration on "Dangers and Duties of Men of Letters," and in 1818, Edward Tyrrel Channing, a Harvard teacher of rhetoric, spoke on "Independence in Literary Pursuits." Likewise, in 1824, clergyman, educator, and diplomat Edward Everett spoke on "The Peculiar Motives to Intellectual Exertion."[4] Emerson's plea for an independent national literature, however, nevertheless shocked his scholarly audience with its bold assertion that the growing mind is influenced fundamentally by nature rather than by educational systems, and that "books are for the scholar's idle times."[5]

Of all American writers who developed in the twenty years following this address, Melville best fits Emerson's description of the great achiever whose vitality is derived primarily from savage nature. Emerson said:

> Not out of those on whom systems of education have exhausted their culture comes the helpful giant to destroy the old or to build the new, but out of the unhandselled savage nature; out of the terrible Druids and Berserkers come at last Alfred and Shakespeare.[6]

Among the acknowledged inheritors of the Transcendental philosophy that Emerson's speech proclaimed, Henry David Thoreau and Walt Whitman had relatively limited encounters with savage nature. Thoreau, two years older than Melville, was a Harvard-educated rebel whose residence on Emerson's property at Walden Pond from 1845 to 1847 was interrupted by occasional visits from friends, walks to nearby Concord, and a day's imprisonment for his refusal to pay a poll tax because of his objection to the Mexican War. His brute neighbors were the small creatures close at hand, such as the ants among chips in his woodpile and the pickerel in the pond. Whitman, who was the same age as Melville, grew up in Brooklyn and abandoned a newspaper career there in 1855 to exalt in poetry the commonplaces of life, the miracle of leaves of grass, the dignity of the simple, separate person whose individuality merges with the whole of nature.

Melville, on the other hand, turned to the sea in his early twenties. The three whalers and the U.S. Navy frigate on which he served during 1841 to 1844 were, as he later indicated, his "Yale College and his Harvard."[7] His elemental experiences of harpooning whales, jumping ship, and living for nearly four months among savages in the Marquesas Islands provided raw materials for his romances of the sea, the best of which illustrate Emerson's intuition with their savage vitality.[8] With the publication in 1846 of his first book, *Typee*, which he dedicated to Chief Justice Shaw, Melville became known as "the man who lived among cannibals."[9] His masterpiece, *Moby-Dick*, completed in the summer of 1851 when he was thirty-two, is appropriately characterized by Henry A. Murray as "of one substance with himself, a wild Everest of art, limit of governable imagination."[10]

In addition to prophesying the emergence of a literary giant like Melville from the primitive forces of nature, Emerson described the polarity that would typify his art. The scholar or artist who lives an active life in contact with nature, Emerson said, has nature's elemental rhythms as a powerful resource:

But the final value of action, like that of books, and better than
books, is that it is a resource. The great principle of Undulation in
nature, that shows itself in the inspiring and expiring of the
breath; in desire and satiety; in the ebb and flow of the sea; in
day and night; in heat and cold; and, as yet more deeply in-
grained in every atom and every fluid, is known to us under the
name of Polarity,—these 'fits of easy transmission and reflection,'
as Newton called them, are the law of nature because they are
the law of spirit.[11]

For Melville, the "great principle of Undulation" was central to
his art. Shortly before his death in 1891, Melville summed up his conception of the artist's task in these lines from his poem, "Art":

What unlike things must meet and mate:
A flame to melt—a wind to freeze;
Sad patience—joyous energies;
Humility—yet pride and scorn;
Instinct and study; love and hate;
Audacity—reverence. These must mate
And fuse with Jacob's mystic heart,
To wrestle with the angel—Art.[12]

Though Melville's statement is not great poetry—his imagination was
too untamed for the discipline of poetic form—his portrayal of the
artist wrestling with the paradoxes of nature and the spirit is in harmony with Emerson's more eloquently expressed ideas.

Despite the abundance of scholarship on Melville during the past
seventy-nine years, there has ironically been no thorough study of
the impact of the American Transcendental movement, of which
Emerson was the principal spokesperson, on Melville's art. As mentioned in the Preface, John B. Williams published *White Fire:
Emerson's Influence on Melville*, but his 1991 book disappointingly concludes with its treatment of *Moby-Dick*, arguably omitting the most
intellectually fertile period of Melville's career.[13] I believe this is attrib-
utable to the frequent dismissal of Melville's works after *Moby-Dick*—
with perhaps the exceptions of "Bartleby, the Scrivener" and *Billy
Budd, Sailor*—as markedly inferior to Melville's earlier publications.
Despite the lack of scholarship seeking a pattern of Emerson's influence on Melville—rather than focusing on particular texts in isolation—there is undeniably a critical tradition dating back to the
Melville revival that connects Melville to Emerson, which is detailed
in the Appendix. To be sure, Raymond Weaver's *Herman Melville,
Mariner and Mystic*,[14] the first important biography of Melville, sug-

gests the subject; but the references to Melville's mysticism are vague and inconclusive. With few exceptions, later critics have stressed the obvious contrast between Melville's pessimism and Emerson's optimism. For example, even though Vernon L. Parrington in *Main Currents of American Thought* acknowledges Melville's "transcendental craftsmanship," he observes that it is "something very different" from that of Emerson and Thoreau. He says:

> Transcendentalism in Concord village and at Walden pond was one thing. Emerson's infrequent anger at the folly of men was soothed by the perfect art with which he phrased it, and never seriously ruffled his temperamental placidity. Thoreau's mystical communings were with the young god Pan; he was too wise to seek to domesticate a woodland nymph . . . . But transcendentalism in the forecastle of the *Acushnet*, transcendentalism that drove fiercely into the blood-red sunsets of dwarfing seas, transcendentalism in the hot and passionate heart of a man whose vast dreams outran his feet—this was something very different from the gentle mysticism of cooler natures and unembittered hearts where no Promethean fires were raging.[15]

Parrington's impressionistic comments, which do not define Transcendentalism, form the basis for a sharper distinction between Melville and Emerson in F. O. Matthiessen's *American Renaissance*, still the most comprehensive treatment of the pre-Civil War literary revival. Matthiessen has set forth the direction of much subsequent scholarship on Melville's relation to his times with the comment, "You might judge that the era least likely to have produced a tragic vision of life would have been dominated by Emerson's doctrine of 'the infinitude of the private man.'"[16] Emerson's theory of expression, Matthiessen writes, "was that on which Thoreau built, to which Whitman gave extension, and to which Hawthorne and Melville were indebted by being forced to react against its philosophical assumptions."[17] Melville and Hawthorne differ from Emerson and his followers in having a sense of

> tragedy, which Matthiessen relates to the practice of both Shakespeare and Milton. The one common denominator uniting the Transcendental and tragic writers, according to Matthiessen, is their devotion to the possibilities of democracy.[18]

A more recent contrast between Melville and Emerson, which is indebted to Matthiessen's classification of the two writers, is Charles Feidelson's *Symbolism in American Literature*. In this study, Melville and Emerson are characterized as being at the opposite poles of the mid-nineteenth-century movement toward Symbolism. "Between them," Feidelson observes, "these two ran the gamut of possibilities created by the symbolist point of view. Emerson represented the upsurge of a capacity, Melville the relapse into doubt. Emerson was the theorist and advocate, Melville the practicing poet. Emerson embodied the monistic phase of symbolism, the sweeping sense of fusion; Melville lived in a universe of paradox and knew the struggle to implement the claims of symbolic imagination."[19]

Among the studies that have emphasized the common ground shared by Melville and Emerson, Robert A. Spiller's chapter, "Democratic Vistas," in *Literary History of the United States*, recognizes the decisive influence of American Transcendentalism on the literature of the period in which the two wrote. Spiller presents his thesis as follows:

> For, by reawakening—even among its critics—an interest in the great problems of human nature and destiny, Transcendentalism conferred upon American literature a perspective far wider and deeper than that proposed by its own formulated doctrines, the perspective of humanity itself. This perspective it is which gives common purpose and meaning to the otherwise divergent achievements of Emerson, Thoreau, Hawthorne, Melville, and Whitman, to predecessors like Irving and Bryant whose interests were less profound and more superficially literary.[20]

Although Spiller restates Matthiessen's argument that Melville and Hawthorne were in reaction against Transcendentalism, he identifies four concepts underlying the writings of Emerson, Thoreau, Hawthorne, Melville, and Whitman: man as spiritual center of the universe, the need for self-realization, the importance of intuition, and the primacy of the metaphorical and didactic in literature.[21] Because Emerson was the first of these writers to gain prominence, Spiller implies that Emerson served as an important source for the ideas they have in common. Perry Miller is explicit in developing this relationship in his essay "Melville and Transcendentalism," in which he reasons that Emerson was the incubus for Melville's art and that both writers were "aware of a configuration of ideas which, popularly identified with Germany, challenged the regnant ethic and esthetic of nature."[22]

None of these studies, however, has adequately accounted for the controlling fact of change, both in the nature of American Transcendentalism from a religious to a philosophical and literary

..ent and in Melville's attitudes towards the Transcendentalists
..j their theories. Neither Melville nor Emerson was static in his
assumptions and practices. Melville especially was aware of shifts in
mood within the passing moment. For example, after completing
Moby-Dick, he wrote to Hawthorne on November 17, 1851:

> In me divine magnanimities are spontaneous and instanta-
> neous—catch them while you can. The world goes round, and the
> other side comes up. So now I can't write what I felt. But I felt
> pantheistic then—your heart beat in my ribs and mine in yours,
> and both in God's.[23]

At this point, Melville suggests the polarity inherent in the structure
of his novel with the paradoxical comment, "A sense of unspeakable
security is in me this moment, on account of your having understood
the book. I have written a wicked book, and feel spotless as the
lamb."[23] In the conclusion of his letter, he displays an extraordinary
sensitivity to change, or as Emerson called it, "Undulation":

> This is a long letter, but you are not at all bound to answer it.
> Possibly, if you do answer it, and direct it to Herman Melville, you
> will missend it—for the very fingers that now guide this pen are
> not precisely the same that dust took it up and put it on this
> paper. Lord, when shall we be done changing?[24]

This sense of change is more than the nervous vacillation of an
exhausted author. In the context of this letter, change is equated with
growing. Melville is caught up for the moment with a conception of
an even greater accomplishment in a passage that associates the
incoherence of his shifting attitudes with truth:

> My dear Hawthorne, the atmospheric skepticisms steal into me
> now, and make me doubtful of my sanity in writing I you thus.
> But, believe me, I am not mad, most noble Festus: But truth is
> ever incoherent, and when the big hearts strike together, the con-
> cussion is a little stunning. . . . Lord, when shall we be done grow-
> ing? As long as we have anything more to do, we have done
> nothing. So, now, let us add *Moby-Dick* to our blessing, and step
> from that. Leviathan is not the biggest fish;—I have heard of
> Krakens.[25]

Melville's frank confession of inconsistency when "big hearts strike
together" is in harmony with Emerson's aphoristic comment in "Self-
Reliance":

> With consistency a great soul has simply nothing to do. He may
> as well concern himself with his shadow on the wall. Speak what
> you think now in hard words and tomorrow speak what to-mor-
> row thinks in hard words again, though it contradict every thing
> you said today.—'Ah, I so you shall be sure to be misunder-
> stood.'—Is it so bad then to be misunderstood? . . . To be great is
> to be misunderstood.[26]

Emerson applied this principle to his own writing, which he said con-
veyed more of himself than he knew:

> [L]et me record day by day my honest thought without prospect
> or retrospect, and, I cannot doubt, it will be found symmetrical,
> though I mean it not and see it not . . . . We pass for what we
> are.[27]

Clearly, any accurate consideration of the Transcendentalism in
Melville's art must ultimately account for the dynamic nature of literary influence, which moves through time in patterns of attraction
and repulsion, ranging in emphasis between the poles of original
interpretation and critical reaction. To deny or ignore such a relationship between Melville and the American Transcendentalists is to
assume his indifference to the most influential literary movement of
the period in which he wrote. Such a position is inconceivable in
light of Emerson's stature as philosopher and poet in the 1840s and
1850s and Melville's voracious reading habits and keen interest in the
people and ideas of his time. Melville easily fits Henry James's characterization of the writer as one on whom nothing is lost.
    During the 1830s, when Melville was an adolescent living with
his widowed mother in upstate New York, the American
Transcendental movement was emerging as a revolt of young
Unitarian clergymen and intellectuals against what they considered
to be the stagnant rationalization, empty ritualism, and social complacency of Boston Unitarianism. The nucleus of the movement was
an informal organization in Boston and Concord, whose members
reluctantly allowed themselves to be called "The Transcendental
Club."[28] Of the twenty-six people who became most active in the
group, seventeen were Unitarian ministers; the oldest was Convers
Francis, forty-one at the time of the first meeting called on September
19, 1836, in the home of George Ripley, a Boston clergyman.[29]
Members of the club opposed the doctrinaire practices of the church
essentially by reasserting a native religious tradition of "inward communication" and of "the divine symbolism of nature" that originat-

ed in the older New England Puritanism and continued in Quakerism with the concept of the "inner light."[30] They were stimulated by the enthusiasm and intuitionism in post-Kantian idealism, which they received largely second-hand through the writings of Coleridge and Carlyle, both of whom Emerson had visited on his European tour in 1832 and 1833 after resigning from the ministry. In addition, they drew upon such varied other sources as Plato, Neoplatonism, Swedenborg, and Oriental philosophy.[31] As a result, the youthful "protestants" were as much aware of their inconsistencies as of their underlying agreement in principle. James Freeman Clarke remarked that the group was called "the Club of the Like-Minded" because "no two of us thought alike."[32]

An early sign of this eclecticism was the reluctance of the members at first to accept the label "Transcendental" that their neighbors and the public applied to them. The term unfortunately suggested a greater agreement in technical philosophy than they actually shared. Bronson Alcott referred to the club as "The Symposium" and Orestes Brownson tried to popularize the label "Eclecticism." Other names tried out without success included "Disciples of the Newness" and simply the "New School." Occasionally, members referred to themselves as "Hedge's Club," after the Reverend Frederic H. Hedge, who originally proposed the idea for the group in a letter to Emerson.[33]

The term "Transcendental" as used in this period had at least two distinct classes of meanings. Popularly, the word suggested "any view that is 'enthusiastic,' 'mystical,' extravagant, impractical, ethereal, supernatural, vague, abstruse, lacking in common sense."[34] The Transcendentalists themselves occasionally used the term in the popular sense. For example, Theodore Parker in a letter to George Ripley dated October 29, 1859, wrote: "You remember the stuff which Margaret Fuller used to twaddle forth on that theme ('absence of art' in America), and what transcendental nonsense got delivered from gawky girls and long-haired men."[35] Similarly, Melville, who was not a member of the nucleus organization, wrote in a letter to his friend Evert Duyckinck, dated March 3, 1849, his admiring reaction on hearing Emerson speak:

> I was very agreeably disappointed in Mr. Emerson. I had heard of him as full of Transcendentalisms, myths and oracular gibberish; I had only glanced at a book of his once in Putnam's store—that was all I knew of him, till I heard him lecture. To my surprise, I found him quite intelligible, tho' to say truth, they told me that night he was unusually plain.[37]

In contrast to this uncomplimentary use of the term is a cluster of more or less technical definitions asserting the primacy of intuition over logic as an interpreter of experience. These ideas derive indirectly from the philosophy of Immanuel Kant, who employed the term in his *Critique of Pure Reason* to refer to knowledge which is not derived from experience but which is inherent in the mind and essential for an understanding of experience. "I call all knowledge transcendental," Kant wrote, "which is occupied not so much with objects, as with our a priori concepts of objects."[38]

Kant's "Transcendental philosophy" was in part a reaction to the extreme empiricism of John Locke, whose *Essay Concerning Human Understanding* denied the existence of innate qualities of the mind and took the position that all knowledge derives from particular sensory experience or combinations of experiences, which are formed into concepts through reflection. In addition, the empiricist David Hume had drawn the further conclusion that if knowledge depends entirely on sensory perception and reflection, then conceptions of God, the soul, and total nature are beyond human reason because they cannot be demonstrated through the senses. Although Kant agreed with this emphasis on sensory experience as a source of knowledge, he proposed that the mind itself has inherent concepts and forms of pure intuition, such as causality, time, and space, which serve as a patterned screen to give structure to experience.[39]

Kant further distinguished between these "Transcendental" forms of Pure Reason and "Transcendent" ideas that derive from Practical Reason or the moral consciousness. Such concepts as God, freedom, and immortality are extensions of empirical knowledge abstracted from experience, he reasoned, because they have the practical purpose of guiding moral action. These Transcendent ideas differ from Transcendental patterns already in the mind because they refer to a level of reality that goes beyond both sensory experience and the limits of human comprehension.[40] In other words, the Transcendent cannot be scientifically described through the application of the forms of pure reason on the faculties of sense perception. Immortality, for example, is an implication of experience that cannot be reduced to the measurement of time.

Kant's careful discrimination between the properties of Pure Reason and Practical Reason, which properties restrict the scope of comprehension, led to efforts by successors in Germany to unify his conception of Reason and thereby extend the limits of knowledge. Their search for an absolute principle by which all things would be knowable led to expansive systems of knowledge in which ultimate reality lay in supersensual, or Transcendental, processes of thought.[41]

Among the earliest revisers of Kant's philosophy, the poet J. G. Herder proposed the unity of soul-life, with the faculties of thought, will, understanding, and sensation depending on one another and springing from a common source. God is revealed in the soul and in nature, particularly in religion, art, and history, which are evolving toward humanitarian ideals of harmony and fullness of growth. H. F. Jacobi asserted that faith and feeling are intuitive sources of knowledge of God and freedom.[42]

The most important successors of Kant—Gottlieb Fichte, Freidrich Wilhelm Schelling, and G. W. F. Hegel—devised complementary philosophies that found their way into the American Transcendental movement largely through Coleridge and Carlyle.

Fichte proposed that basic reality is will, or ego, which intuits its own activity as Universal Reason and rises above space and time. This Transcendental ego produces nature and expresses itself in moral law. Furthermore, the individual's inward sense of duty or moral consciousness is an expression of this absolute purpose. Schelling agreed with Fichte's conception of Reason as will, but broadened it to include the unconscious. In other words, reality is creative energy, and all nature is an expression of this purposeful spiritual force trying to realize itself with the aid of time in matter. Schelling reasoned that this energy is organic and evolutionary in expression and is moving toward the goal of perfect self-expression and consciousness. Accordingly, man is capable of imagining better things than he knows. Thus, his highest stage of self-realization is in art, which serves to reveal nature's own art. The unity in Schelling's philosophy is derived in part from his theory of correspondences between matter and spirit, which provide the basis in nature and art for the reconciliation of the apparent opposites of form and substance.[43]

Hegel, the most prominent of the post-Kantian idealists, rejected Schelling's notion of an undifferentiated absolute energy, which he described as "the night in which all cows are black."[44] The universe, he wrote, is basically logical and moves through space and time in the triadic pattern of thesis, antithesis, and synthesis. God is the Idea, the ultimate synthesis or timeless totality of all processes of evolution, who reveals himself in religion, philosophy, and art. Hegel's conception of the logic of nature resulted in greater emphasis on change and contradiction than Schelling had placed, although both proposed that unity is the result of the reconciliation of opposite qualities in art and in nature.[45]

These core ideas of German post-Kantian idealism reached the American Transcendentalists through three main avenues. In the first place, Emerson and his circle read the German philosophers, either in the original or in translations. Records of Emerson's withdrawals from libraries, for example, indicate a continuing interest in the philosophy of Herder, whose concept of the soul-life suggests Emerson's Over-Soul. In 1829 Emerson checked out of the Harvard College Library a translation of Herder's *Outlines of a Philosophy of Man*; three years later, he borrowed this work on two occasions from the Boston Athenaeum. In addition, Emerson withdrew from the Boston Atheneum in 1837 two volumes of Jacobi's *Werke*.[46] His extensive personal library contained Kant's *Critique of Pure Reason*, Fichte's *The Nature of the Scholar and Its Manifestations*, and several volumes by Hegel, including *Vorlesungen über die Aesthetic*.[47]

Of greater significance, however, was the broad avenue to German thought through German romantic literature, which was permeated with post-Kantian idealism. By 1836, for example, Emerson had read most of his fifty-five-volume set of Goethe's works in German, which he apparently had purchased during his first trip to Europe.[48] The general interest of the American Transcendentalists in German authors is readily demonstrated in the twenty articles and poems about German literature in *The Dial*, the Transcendental publication issued in sixteen volumes between 1840 and 1844.[49] As Stanley Vogel says, "These New Englanders preferred Herder, Wieland, Schiller and Goethe to Kant, Fichte and Schelling. When the iron regulations of Calvinism began to hem them in, the Transcendentalists turned to these German literary men and not to the philosophers for inspiration."[50]

The third and perhaps most important route by which German idealism reached the American Transcendentalists was through the writings of Coleridge and Carlyle. Although neither author redefined the term Transcendental, both accented particular aspects of the German philosophical systems, which resulted in oversimplifications that appealed to the Americans, who were not trained in technical philosophy. Drawing largely on Schelling's philosophy, Coleridge stressed the distinction between intuitive Reason and cognitive Understanding and an evolutionary theory of natural-spiritual correspondences. Coleridge's conception of the creative imagination as the shaping power of the mind is a variant of his idea of Reason. In a celebrated passage in his *Biographia Literaria*, which anticipates Emerson's doctrine of polarity and Melville's conception of paradox, Coleridge points out that the poetic imagination is activated by the will and "reveals itself in the balance or reconciliation of opposite or discordant qualities: of sameness, with difference; of the general, with the concrete; the idea, with the image; the individual, with the representative."[51] Carlyle, on the other hand, made pronounced use of

Fichte's assertive Transcendental ego, the individual soul merged with the spirit that encompasses and transcends external nature.

Emerson's personal meetings in 1833 with Coleridge and Carlyle, who are credited with stimulating Emerson's interest in German literature and philosophy, were supplemented by extensive reading of their major works and by a lifelong friendship with Carlyle. During the period from 1825 to 1836, Emerson's journals indicate a pervading interest in Coleridge's philosophical and critical writings, including *Aids to Reflection, Biographia Literaria, The Friend, Statesman's Manual*, and *Church and State*.[52] Furthermore, in 1836 Emerson wrote an appreciative preface to the American edition of Carlyle's *Sartor Resartus*, a spiritual autobiography disguised as the life and opinions of a German Professor of Things in General, who acquires a positive philosophy in which he sees nature as the "Living Garment of God."[53]

The impact of post-Kantian idealism on the American Transcendental movement is perhaps most clearly illustrated by Emerson's definition of the term "Transcendental" in this passage from his lecture "The Transcendentalist":

> It is well known to most of my audience that the Idealism of the present day acquired the name Transcendental from the use of that term by Immanuel Kant, of Königsberg, who replied to the skeptical philosophy of Locke, which insisted that there was nothing in the intellect which was not previously in the experience of the senses, by showing that there was a very important class of ideas or imperative forms, which did not come by experience, but through which experience was acquired; that these were intuitions of the mind itself; and he denominated them *Transcendental* forms. The extraordinary profoundness and precision of that man's thinking have given vogue to his nomenclature, in Europe and America, to the extent that whatever belongs to the class of intuitive thought is popularly called at the present day *Transcendental*.[54]

Instead of limiting the term to Kant's a priori forms and intuitions in Pure Reason of causality, space, and time, Emerson broadened its denotation in the manner of Fichte and Schelling to include supersensual ideas that Kant had declared were beyond human comprehension.[55] Intuitive thought was for Emerson, but not for Kant, the basis for Transcendental knowledge of God, total nature, and immortality. "Nature is Transcendental," Emerson said, "exists primarily, necessarily, ever works and advances, yet takes no thought for the morrow."[56]

Emerson observed that the Transcendentalist adopts the whole connection of spiritual doctrine. He believes in miracle, in the perpetual openness of the human mind to new influx of light and power; he believes in inspiration, and in ecstasy. He wishes that the spiritual principle should be suffered to demonstrate itself to the end, in all possible applications to the state of man, without the admission of anything unspiritual.[57]

Other Transcendentalists offered similar definitions stressing the reality of spirit over sensory experience. For example, George Ripley made this comment in his letter of resignation as pastor of the Unitarian Church in Purchase Street, Boston:

There is a class of persons who desire a reform in the prevailing philosophy of the day. These are called Transcendentalists, because they believe in an order of truths which transcends the sphere of external sense. Their leading idea is the supremacy of mind over matter. Hence they maintain that the truth of religion does not depend on tradition, nor on historical facts, but has an unerring witness in the soul.[58]

The value of post-Kantian idealism to the American Transcendentalists, however, was not in offering a ready-made philosophical system that would suit their initial purpose of church reform, but in confirming the faith of the Americans in the presence of God in nature and in the integrity of the individual conscience. These ideas were implicit in the stern Calvinistic theology of the colonial period, which interpreted acts of nature as the providences of God and considered the soul as having a being that transcends the body. Though Emerson admired the European writers and thinkers, he and his friends denied that the primary sources of American Transcendentalism were from abroad.[59] They believed instead in the power of their own intuition to rediscover old truths which had been obscured rather than preserved by tradition. "How impossible to find Germany," Emerson reminisced in his journals:

Our young men went to the Rhine to find the genius which had charmed them, and it was not there. They hunted it in Heidelberg, in Gottingen, in Halle, in Berlin; no one knew where it was; from Vienna to the frontier, it was not found, and they very slowly and mournfully learned, that in the speaking it had escaped, and as it had charmed them in Boston, they must return and look for it there.[60]

American Transcendentalism, then, was essentially a native movement, reinforced though not initiated by ideas from abroad. One inevitable result of the stimulus of post-Kantian idealism and other philosophies on members of the "Transcendental Club" was the early extension of their interests beyond the narrow limits of religious controversy. In his history of the movement, O. B. Frothingham observes that "the ideas entertained by the foreign thinkers took root in the native soil and blossomed out in every form of social life."[61] Although the club met infrequently for a period variously estimated at between four and twelve years, the energies of members found diversified expression in such secular activities as lecturing, literary criticism, poetry, and experiments in communal living.[62] In other words, the Transcendental priest gave way to the poet and reformer in what Charles R. Metzger has described as the "delayed secularization of New England thought."[63]

Ideally, the unifying "spiritual principle" of Transcendentalism should have provided a single common denominator for the extended interests of the members, harmonizing their "Transcendental faith" or intuition of the true with their conceptions of the good and the beautiful. These ideas derive in part from the philosophy of Plato, who reasoned in *The Republic* that ultimate reality consists of the idea of the good, the apprehension of which provides knowledge of absolute truth and beauty.[64] Frothingham comments, "The Transcendentalist believed in man's ability to apprehend absolute ideas of Truth, Justice, Rectitude, Goodness; he spoke of The Right, The True, The Beautiful, as eternal realities which he perceived."[65]

Actually, however, the shift in emphasis within the movement accented inconsistencies: the impulse that led to the Utopian experiment in collective living at Brook Farm also resulted in Thoreau's demonstration of individualism at Walden Pond. No Transcendentalist expected or received unanimous agreement with his views. Even Emerson, who represents the broadest range of Transcendental thought in America with his clerical background and his activities as a lecturer, essayist, and poet, did not enjoy complete rapport with the other Transcendentalists. Although his first volume, *Nature*, published in 1836 shortly before the first meeting of the club, was accepted with enthusiasm as a manifesto of the movement, most of the members scrupulously avoided in their own writings his tendency toward pantheism.[66] Furthermore, Emerson appeared to detach himself from the movement, referring in his lecture, "The Transcendentalist," to "this class" and "these children'" who have held themselves aloof because "they feel the disproportion between their faculties and the work offered them."[67]

On the other hand, despite the lack of a systematic philosophy to which all members could agree, the movement represented a community of loosely related thought, which must be summarized under headings that agree with the changing emphases that produced the priest, the reformer, and the poet. These three overlapping categories—representing the Transcendental religion, ethic, and aesthetics—offer the most realistic way of accounting for Melville's turning away from Emerson's optimism and Transcendental conceptions of metaphysical truth.

Chapter Two

Shadows in Eden: American Transcendentalism and Its Discontents

MELVILLE AND EMERSON WERE BOTH PRODUCTS OF MID-NINETEENTH-century America, where culture was on the brink of a great change. The period from 1830 to 1860 was simultaneously marked by disintegration and fulfillment. Democracy in government became for the nation and for most of the states a fact as well as a theory. Canals, turnpikes, steamboats, and railroads multiplied, revolutionizing transportation. Print culture exploded and spread rapidly throughout the country. The industrialization and consequent urbanization of the Northeast progressed with startling rapidity, and the advance of the Western frontier continued. The enervating spirit of independence and technological amelioration pervaded the air.

The new scene stirred the American intellect. During this period inventive genius was stimulated and literary production rose to unprecedented heights.[1] In an age in which people believed intensely in the capacity of humankind for improvement, one nevertheless could not fail to become increasingly aware of the evils with which it was afflicted, and to seek for remedies. The rapid advance of the factory system presented the country with a serious labor problem. As the number of employees under a single management grew, the gulf between the two classes widened. The influx of immigrant labor that accompanied the industrial revolution saw the advent of overcrowded slum areas. During these years the very word "reform" had an almost irresistible appeal for multitudes of Americans, and the mere adoption of that label was sufficient to secure a following. Reformers attacked, with cheerful enthusiasm, all manner of evils, confident that America was, at last, on the brink of "true" democracy.

From the confident optimism that pervaded the land, Emerson arose as the spokesman for individualism. What the statesmen had ready accomplished in the sphere of politics, Emerson applied to culture through his radiant exhortations. Always professing confidence in the infinite possibilities of man, Emerson found a firm basis for his reasoning in the society he saw around him. Americans were accomplishing new things, building a new civilization, and material progress must be matched by spiritual progress. Emerson realized that American thinkers, like American men of action, must strike out for themselves along original lines. "Why should not we also enjoy an original relation to the universe? Why should not we have a poetry and philosophy of insight and not of tradition and a religion by revelation to us?"[2] He exhorted the people to demand their own "works and laws and worship."[3]

Other young Americans of this generation, inspired by Emerson's stirring appeals, joined in a mild revolution against the narrow confines of orthodox religion and conformist society. This group of people considered to be radical and anarchic by many, became known as Transcendentalists. The underlying philosophical ideas of this movement are probably older than Plato or Buddha, but as stated in the previous chapter, the immediate impulse came from the philosophers of Germany, through many agents, conspicuously Coleridge and Carlyle.[4] Beginning as a speculative philosophy only, it struck in New England upon very ardent moralists and very practical-minded men, among whom had already been sown the seeds of liberalism, and who, dissatisfied with their old forms and creeds, caught up this attractive philosophy and proceeded at once to erect it into a kind of gospel and guide of life. At the base of it lay what is called idealism—the reliance, as the word implies, upon ideas, or the world within, as the only sure testimony we can have of matter or the outside world. Transcendentalism, as understood in New England, referred to the belief that within the mind are certain intuitions that rise above all experience. The philosophy of the eighteenth century was, as a rule, skeptical and materialistic; it was concerned with this world chiefly; it was doubtful of God and even of the human soul. It alleged that all knowledge and all ideas depend solely upon matter and sense, upon what we can see and touch. In this it carried forward the theory of the English philosopher Locke, who taught that the mind is essentially a *tabula rasa*, a blank sheet, on which knowledge is inscribed only by experience.[5] The idealists of the nineteenth century, in contrast, were radically opposed to such a view of man and of the universe. They taught that the human mind has a knowledge of its own, independent of the senses or of the material world; that certain ideas—of right and wrong, of good and evil, of God, duty, freedom, immortality—are innate in the soul, and that such ideas transcend or go beyond experience. It was because Emerson and his peers exalted this innate knowledge that they were called Transcendentalists.

The Transcendental movement, however, was not of a nature to attract the masses. It differed radically from the temperance and abolition movements of the time in that these, being more definite "causes," could be fought out on the platform or by the people at the polls. Although stripped of emotional and popular elements, however, Transcendentalism was nonetheless a wave of sentiment and reform. It had a significant element of religion in it. Nothing could lightly shake the moral earnestness of the New Englanders, deepened as it was by more than two centuries of persecutions, hardships, and wars. The Unitarianism that came to divide the old church was altogether reverent and serious. And when new doctrines came to the wide bonds of Unitarianism, there was still never any thought of giving up the fundamental principles of morality and religion. As Herbert W. Edwards and Rod W. Horton point out, because Concord had once been Puritan, the stamp of Puritanism was always deep and lasting. They even go so far as to suggest that "transcendentalism was Calvinism modified by the assumption of the innate goodness of man."[6] At any rate, the men of this group no longer concerned themselves about special schemes of salvation. But they were all the more deeply concerned about right living and thinking; and their doctrines emphasized high thought and simple living. As Thoreau puts it: "I went to the woods because I wished to live deliberately, to front only the essential facts of life, and see if I could not learn what it had to teach. . . ."[7] His statement indicates the Transcendental doctrine of becoming wisely familiar with Nature for its own sake, as well as for its spiritual values and revelations.

But despite whatever foreign influences may have inspired American Transcendentalism, the doctrines of it quickly assimilated into an idiosyncratically national product, for it grew out of the fusion of two fundamental American qualities: religious mysticism and the love of nature. Whenever it appeared in literature it had two subjects, nature and man. Nature was regarded as an open book of the Lord. Man was seen not as a poor creature enslaved by the senses, but as an immortal and divine being. While Transcendentalism was not particularly attractive to the masses, it held a strange fascination for many of the New England literati, and through such persons as Emerson, Thoreau, Hawthorne, Fuller, Channing, and Alcott, it came to have a broad effect upon the nation as a whole. The first Transcendentalist meeting, or "Symposium," met in Boston in 1836 and, though never definitely organized, the group came to be known in time as the Transcendental Club. In 1840 *The Dial*, a quarterly magazine, was established as the organ of the movement. The editorship was held by Margaret Fuller for two years and then passed to Emerson for two years more, at which time the paper died for lack of support.

While the magazine necessarily remained on an idealistic plane, it was instrumental in the formation of the Brook Farm experiment, which was one of the more practical outcomes of the New-World attempt to bring philosophy down from the heavens to the earth. In 1840 George Ripley, later known as a literary editor and critic, resigned from the ministry and purchased a farm at West Roxbury, Massachusetts, persuading a number of others to cooperate with him in establishing there an agricultural association. Their object was to see whether the brain and hand could not be made to work advantageously together, whether the same individual might not be both thinker and worker, and thus find for himself a simpler, freer, and happier life. They proposed also to conduct for the younger members a school in accordance with these idealistic principles. Ripley and small band of associates, including Hawthorne and Charles A. Dana, moved to the farm in the spring of 1841 and set to work enthusiastically. Hawthorne recorded his disillusionment with the experiment in his *Journals* and later based his novel, *The Blithedale Romance*, on his experiences there. Despite the high hopes with which it was begun and the modicum of success it enjoyed for a few years, the enterprise was dissolved in 1847 and generally regarded as a failure.

At this period, when reform was in the air, there were many who probably expected too much of human nature. They fancied that wonderful revolutions could be brought about in a day, and many of the methods proposed were extravagant. "Some," says James Russell Lowell in his essay on Thoreau, "had assurance of instant millennium so soon as hooks and eyes should be substituted for buttons."[8] Like most complex movements, Transcendentalism developed the usual "lunatic fringe" to be found on the outskirts of any new and liberal mode of thought. Two elements contributed to bring it into disrepute. The first, which was inherent in Transcendentalism as a system of thought, related to the doctrine of innate ideas. Because a man may have knowledge that transcends experience, shallow minds jumped to the conclusion that experience was unnecessary. Because an individual may be in touch with the divine source of knowledge, enthusiasts felt free to disregard the saints and sages. It was inevitable, therefore, that this doctrine should tend to extremes and vagaries. As Lowell saw it, "every possible form of intellectual and physical dyspepsia brought forth its gospel."[9] The second disruptive element was the same spirit of agitation that troubled our politics. Just as state problems of the hour were used by extremists to keep the country in turmoil, so the new philosophy was demoralized by zealots. Every unbalanced enthusiast took it up; visionaries snatched leadership away from the wise and prudent and went forth to preach the gospel of individualism, proclaiming that every man was his own and only source of wisdom and authority. To quote Lowell again:

> Everybody had a mission (with a capital M) to attend to every-body-else's business. No brain but had its private maggot, which must have found pitiably short commons sometimes. . . . All stood ready at a moment's notice to reform, everything but them-selves.[10]

While the common man had little understanding of the basic tenets of Transcendentalism, the people found its sentiments to be noble and rewardingly democratic. To a young country just begin-ning to enjoy its independence and vigorously expanding in all direc-tions, this style of thinking was natural and satisfying. Many Americans believed that anything could be accomplished; thus, the Transcendentalists merely confirmed what they already felt to be true. It is easy to give intuition authority over experience in a young country, where there is a dearth of national history and culture. But of all the espousers of this concept, one figure still maintains promi-nence today, continuing to be echoed from soapbox to pulpit—Ralph Waldo Emerson. Even Lowell, who felt little kinship to the Transcendental movement, could not resist the power of Emerson's oratory, nor withhold his admiration of Emerson's importance to his generation:

> . . . there is no man to whom our aesthetic culture owes so much. The Puritan revolt had made us ecclesiastically, and the Revo-lution politically independent, but we were still socially and intel-lectually moored to English thought, till Emerson cut the cable and gave us a chance at the dangers and the glories of blue water. No man young enough to have felt it can forget, or cease to be grateful for, the mental and moral *nudge* which he received from the writings of his high-minded and brave-spirited country-man. That we agree with him, or that he always agrees with him-self, is aside from the question; but that he arouses in us some-thing that we are the better for having awakened, whether that something be of opposition or assent, that he speaks always to what is highest and least selfish in us, few Americans of the gen-eration younger than his own would be disposed to deny.[11]

Arguably the most distinguished of the New England Transcendentalists, Emerson was the son of a devoted but impecunious Unitarian minister. In keeping with his heritage, Emerson also trained for the ministry and served in that capacity for a short time. Probably his one really dramatic and decisive public action was his resigning of his Unitarian pastorate at the Second Church because of scruples of conscience over praying in public and because of his inability to believe in the sacramental significance of the Lord's Supper.[12] But despite his doctrinal differences with the church, the influence of the Unitarianism beliefs had an abiding effect upon Emerson's later philosophical thought, and much that is thought of as Transcendental can be traced to its original source in Unitarianism. Because Unitarianism served as a bridge between Calvinism and Transcendentalism, an understanding of the basic beliefs of this group is helpful in the consideration of Emerson's later ideas.

The pervasive spirit of the Enlightenment, with its doctrine of the natural rights of man, made itself manifest not only in the intellectual and political trends of the eighteenth century, but in the field of orthodox religion as well. Here, even more than in secular matters, the rationalistic temper revived and gave added force to certain "heretical" departures from authoritarian interpretation of the Scriptures that had plagued the church fathers almost from the beginning. One of the most persistent of these heresies had been that Adam's fall did not involve the whole human race, and that, though men are prone to sin, they are capable of effecting their own salvation by faith alone. From this small beginning the breach widened more and more. The doctrine of the Trinity was soon openly attacked and, while the political ferment of the Revolution drew thoughts largely away from theological questions, Unitarianism quietly spread in eastern Massachusetts.[13]

As originally formulated, Unitarianism was extremely rationalistic. It had little of the old "hellfire and brimstone" doctrine that had made Calvinism so stimulating to the emotions but, instead, it attempted to approximate the spirit of scientific inquiry in its approach to the Bible as the word of God. Unitarians, in addition to denying the threefold nature of God, hold that Jesus was a man, and therefore not divine, and that Christianity is not a series of creeds or definitions, but a way of life. They speak of "statements of faith" rather than of doctrines, and they believe in five such statements: (1) the Fatherhood of God; (2) the Brotherhood of Man; (3) the Leadership of Jesus; (4) Salvation by character; and (5) Progress of mankind onward and upward forever.[14]

Other ideas of Unitarianism follow naturally, almost necessarily. The Bible was written by men, and is, therefore, not infallible. There are no states of absolute salvation or damnation; instead, man is a progressively spiritual creature who may continue to develop even after death. Jesus was a man, although a great and unusual one, for otherwise his life would be impossible for other people to imitate. Although his greatness as a leader is stressed, his death on the cross is regarded as the inevitable outcome of the implications of his teachings and life work, and not as a sacrifice for the sins of mankind. The fatherhood of God is emphasized over his sovereignty, and since he is the universal Father, all men are brothers.

On the point of salvation, Unitarianism maintains its consistency. Sin is not an offense against God but, rather, a matter of morality, involving human relationships. The Bible is not inspired, but is only one of many possible avenues to truth, and is read for ethics rather than for theology. Because God has made man in his own image, man also partakes of the Divine goodness, and the greatest moral force here on earth is to be found in the example of the lives of noble men. The sacrament of baptism and the Lord's Supper are regarded simply as memorials, without the overtones of vicarious atonement.[15]

With these ideas, then, as his heritage from his ancestors, Emerson found the step over into Transcendentalism a logical progression of his growing liberalism. He was encouraged in his liberal direction by a visit to Europe in 1833. Returning by way of England, he met Coleridge, Wordsworth, and Carlyle,[16] whose influence he had already felt. After his stay in Europe, Emerson returned to Concord, where he married again, bought a home, and settled down for the rest of his life. From his study in this quiet little town, Emerson ventured forth to deliver occasional lectures, to walk on the shores of nearby Walden Pond, and to commune with nature in the Concord woods. He saw no need to go beyond Concord to find the true beauties of the world: "we can find these enchantments without visiting the Como Lake, or the Madeira Islands."[17] After all, "in every landscape the point of astonishment is the meeting of the sky and the earth, and that is seen from the first hillock as well as from the top of the Alleghanies."[18] Nature is nature, no matter from what spot it is seen, and since "every shell on the beach is a key to it,"[19] it matters little on what beach the shell is found.

In the year and the month in which the Transcendental Club came into being, September 1836, Emerson published his first book, the slow growth of three years or more of meditation. He entitled it *Nature*, showing already his liking for brief titles, which allow a wide latitude of treatment. Although it was a small book—eight short chapters in all—almost every sentence had the weight of a lecture: "Nature always wears the colors of the spirit";[20] "The eye is the best of artists" (14); "Beauty is the mark God sets upon virtue" (16); "Every natural action is graceful" (16); "A work of art is an abstract or epitome of the world"(18); "All things are moral" (28); "A man is a god in ruins" (45).

In the introduction to *Nature*, Emerson issues a stirring call for American men to shake loose the shackles of the past and to behold "God and nature face to face" (7) as did their forefathers. He exhorts man to cease groping "among the dry bones of the past" (7) and to find his own unique relationship with the world by consulting Nature as to the unanswered riddles of the universe. In the introduction he states, perhaps unintentionally, the problem of duality that he never quite resolves:

> Philosophically considered, the universe is composed of Nature and the Soul. Strictly speaking, therefore, all that is separate from us, all which Philosophy distinguishes as the NOT ME, that is, both nature and art, all other men and my own body, must be ranked under this name, NATURE. (8)

While Emerson continually strives to absorb the Not Me into the Me, he admits his inability to do so when he says of the dualism in traditional idealistic philosophy: ". . . let it stand then . . . serving to apprise us of the eternal distinction between the soul and the world" (41). He is not content, however, to let it stand, and in a later essay he tries to dissolve or merge it into an all-inclusive monism which he stresses as the working of the Over-Soul throughout Nature and man. In this introduction he strives for clarity by defining the distinction between "natural" Nature and "improved" Nature: "Nature, in the common sense, refers to essences unchanged by man; space, the air, the river, the leaf. Art is applied to the mixture of his will with the same things" (8).

Although Emerson's philosophy was not a system it had something of a plan in the way he developed it. His attitude toward life was based on his love of nature, as is stated in his first book. In Section I, he establishes a romantic thesis, reminiscent of Wordsworth's "Intimations of Immortality," when he states that "few adult persons can see nature. . . . The sun illuminates only the eye of the man, but shines into the eye and the heart of the child" (10). He goes on to develop the idea by establishing the fact that the true lover of nature is "he whose inward and outward senses are still truly adjusted to each other; who has retained the spirit of infancy even into the era of manhood" (10). One cannot help being reminded of Wordsworth's infant, "trailing clouds of glory." One is also reminded of the Biblical admonition to become as a little child. When we view nature, then, with the proper blending of both "inward and outward senses," we can go into the woods and "return to reason and faith" (10, 11). In this section Emerson makes his first of several statements concerning the Transcendental mystical experience:

> Standing on the bare ground—my head bathed by the blithe air and uplifted into infinite space—all mean egotism vanishes. I become a transparent eyeball; I am nothing; I see all; the currents of the Universal Being circulate through me; I am part or parcel of God. (10)

He also, inadvertently perhaps, refers in Section I to one of the apparent fallacies of his philosophical theory when he says, "Nature always wears the colors of the spirit" (11). This concept is reiterated several times throughout the body of the essay, and in the final paragraph he says, "What we are, that only can we see" (48). He has described Nature as "the universal tablet" (39) and an "open book" (25) from which man may read the messages of God, for, as he points out in Section VII:

> ... the noblest ministry of nature is to stand as the apparition of God. It is the organ through which the universal spirit speaks to the individual, and strives to lead back the individual to it. (40)

The fallacy, then, becomes apparent with his admission of the fact that what a man reads in nature is not so much the word of "the universal spirit" as it is the reflection of his own transient mood or particular turn of mind.

In the course of this essay, Emerson implied that science, by assuming the independent existence of matter for technical reasons and thus ignoring the spirit, cannot reach ultimate Truth. Religion, he suggests, ignores matter and limits its speculation to spirit, and therefore also falls short. Emerson worked for an Ideal Theory that takes account of both matter and spirit and assumes that man and nature, or spirit and matter, are wedded, harmonized or fused. Despite its logical flaws, *Nature* becomes a noble and inspiring rhapsody, representing a great emotional experience for Emerson and inspiring an emotional response from its readers. One cannot help responding to his radiant presentation of the idea that Nature is not mechanical but vital, that the universe is not dead or inanimate but radiantly alive, and that God is not remote but ever-present. Emerson saw Nature as a medium of the Transcendental Being's appearance to man, to show the latter some aspects of ultimate reality. According to him, every natural fact is trivial until it takes on symbolical or moral significance.

Emerson aimed to formulate an all-inclusive monism: the Over-Soul transcends all and is omnipresent—that is, the spirit manifests itself in material forms. The spiritual universe envelopes, fuses with, and unifies the world of sense and science. Emerson adheres to the microcosmic theory that each particle reflects all of the spirit that transcends all natural phenomena. There is a unity of man and Nature, which is also a unity with God. The "currents of the universal being circulate through me; I am part or parcel of God." The poet, who "animates nature with his own thoughts and proposes Beauty as his main end" is the spokesman for other men; "the perception of real affinities between events . . . enables the poet . . . to make free with the most imposing forms and phenomena of the world; and to assert the predominance of the soul" (36). Herein lies the nucleus of Emerson's later essay, "The Poet."

Emerson speaks of Nature as the medium between God and man—the three (God, Nature, Man) being akin because of the spiritual element or divinity in Nature and man. The main purpose of the essay is to present the theory that the secret of Nature will be unraveled by no man who divorces Nature and man, but only by him who perceives their spiritual harmony or unity—through Over-Soul, as developed in his essay by that name. The doctrine of evolution is used to confirm Emerson's optimistic hopes for man's betterment. He believes the future of the constantly evolving human race is glorious to contemplate, and that the eventual "kingdom of man over nature" will be "a dominion such as now is beyond his dream of God" (49).

This essay is of particular importance because of its function as a preview of many of his later essays, in which Emerson developed fragmentary ideas that appeared in this first work. As he points out in section VIII, "We learn to prefer imperfect theories, and sentences which contain glimpses of truth, to digested systems which have no one valuable suggestion" (45). This statement might be a formula for Emerson's unsystematic system of presentation. Since, in later years, Emerson tried to perfect his "imperfect theories" and expand some of the "glimpses of truth" set forth in *Nature*, it serves as a basis for many later essays.

If we think of *Nature* as a preview of Emerson's later ideas, we might well think of "The Over-Soul" as the cornerstone of his whole doctrine. In this essay he attempted to formulate the basic idea on which his theories were to stand. Not content with the God-as-father, Man-as-brother idea of Unitarianism, Emerson sought to bring about an even closer relationship. He wanted to bring all men into a monistic relationship which could only be achieved through some unitizing master-scheme. He sets forth his new-view when he says: "Man is a stream whose source is hidden. Our being is descending into us from we know not whence" (385). Man, thus, is not a static, finite creation, but a part of a constantly flowing stream into whom being is continuously descending—"that flowing river, which, out of regions I see not, pours for a season its streams into me" (385). This source of being is "that Unity, that Over-Soul, within which every man's particular being is contained and made one with all other; that common heart of which all sincere conversation is the worship" (385–386). He explains that

> . . . the soul in man is not an organ, but animates and exercises all the organs; is not a function, like the power of memory, of calculation, of comparison, but uses these as hands and feet; is not a faculty but a light; is not the intellect or the will, but the master of the intellect and the will; is the background of our being, in which they lie—an immensity not possessed and that cannot be possessed. From within or from behind, a light shines through us upon things and makes us aware that we are nothing, but the light is all. (386–387)

This essay reveals Emerson as a seer who perceives truth through intuitive revelation—man's happiness or serenity lies in placing himself in harmony with the Over-Soul or in finding truths which are manifest in the universe. Emerson also emphasizes the world of cause and effect, in which goodness and truth predominate positively. The world is essentially beneficent to man; it is a world in which joy is not only eminently possible, but is, in fact, a natural condition of man. Evil is an insignificant part of the "All," and has no reality, *per se*. The truths come to man in moments of insight; the assurance of beneficence in the world accompanies these insights; the spirit of prophecy is innate in every man; the soul in man is not a faculty but a spiritual light; the soul is not intellect or will, but is the master of intellect and will. This soul is the potential perceiver and the revealer of truth. The simplest person who worships God with sincerity becomes a part of God; he discovers the absolute oneness of all things. He experiences the law of love, which is spiritual harmony within himself and with the Over-Soul. There is one mind common to every mind, and history is a revelation of God in the domain of freedom. The whole of history is necessary to reveal the whole of the Soul—as each individual expresses but a part of himself, so does each historical event. Man can best comprehend history through his own life, since history is a revelation of the Over-Soul, and each individual has the key in himself.

This idea that everyone has divinity in his or her nature and thus can commune directly with the Over-Soul, provides a foundation for Emerson's famous essay "Self-Reliance"—his most dynamic and vigorous declaration of the meaning of the Over-Soul: through intuition everyone can perceive ultimate truth; consequently, each person should have implicit faith in his own spiritual perceptions, and thereby attain self-reliance. This essay strongly urges people uncompromisingly to follow their spiritual impulses: "To believe your own thought, to believe that what is true for you in your private heart is true for all men,—that is Genius" (259). It is natural for man to behave with a certain nonchalance and to disdain dependence. According to Emerson, men should not pay lip service to traditions or be weakly charitably; should not act merely to appease popular conscience; should not have political affiliations; should avoid a terrified adherence to consistency (especially to social traditions which are customarily overcautious; to social usages that restrict freedom of action); should resist convenient (foolish) conformity.

He preaches a definite, defiant independence—but *not* rugged individualism, which relies too much on the lower self. He urges the inner law against outer legislations—and individual control and mastery as against the supine or blind acceptance of the mass (reform should come from within and cannot be legislated.) Essentially, Emerson is practicing a higher "lawlessness," which only the small minority can master without anarchy. Emerson is aware of the responsibilities, even when he states: "What I must do is all that concerns me, not what people think" (263). He considers himself as a worthy individual in a worthy society and, therefore, his responsibility is to perfect his behavior and attitudes so that he can promote the best humanitarian motives.

In this essay, again, we discover one of the flaws of Emerson's theoretical idealism—or perhaps it would be more accurate to call it a limitation. When reading Emerson, it is imperative that we recognize his reluctantly admitted social snobbery, or personal caste system. He never directly expounds it, but he inadvertently suggests it in the body of his writings. In "Self-Reliance" he describes the masses as "the unintelligent brute force that lies at the bottom of society" (265). He disavows any concern for charity for the masses, for they are not his. He attaches himself only to a small group of like thinkers, and for them he "will go to prison, if need be" (262). Although his Over-Soul theory is based on the natural divinity of *all* people, and he espouses the value of intuition in *all* people, in actuality it becomes apparent that he is really only applying his theories to a small, elect group.

If we keep in mind what his intention really was, one clearly sees that the numerous socio-economic criticisms of his idealism are simply not applicable. Nevertheless, the majority of his followers in the period considered him the great spokesman for democracy and accepted his teachings at face value. An example of his reputation with the common man is indicated in a story repeated by Tremaine McDowell: "Do you understand Mr. Emerson?" Mrs. Hoar inquired of a scrubwoman who always attended Emerson's lectures in Concord. "Not a word," the scrubwoman replied, "but I like to go and see him stand up there and look as though he thought everyone was as good as he was." A Concord farmer boasted that he had heard all of Emerson's lectures at the Lyceum and "understood 'em, too."[21]

It is doubtful, however, whether a rough and rugged farmer of the period would have realized that Emerson's ideal of self-reliance is quite difficult to attain or practice because it involves religiously following the dictates of highest Reason or Self, and Emerson assures us that Reason is a rigorous taskmaster. He does not endorse rugged individualism—reliance on the lower self or the sense-loving Understanding—but he endorses the truly affirmative individualism which is the emergence of the individual Self in conscience from the unthinking mass of people. It is the intimate and spiritual consciousness of the Divine Presence within a person—it is the true reliance on the divine within us, and is, therefore, an essential part in the code of conduct for a Whole person.

That Emerson believed in and acted upon his own ideas of self-reliance is obvious. One need only consider his "Divinity School Address" at Harvard University in 1838 to be thoroughly convinced of how radically independent this "mild" scholar could be. In this address to the graduating class of the Divinity School, Emerson inveighed against the formal and uninspired style of pulpit addresses and disputed the true value of historical Christianity. This criticism of the ministry and religious thought met with indignant opposition among the clergy. Emerson was branded an atheist, and he was no longer welcome in pulpits and on lecture platforms for which he had previously been sought. This essay deals with religious tradition versus real divinity and emphasizes that man should directly contact the Over-Soul, not go through a mediator. He boldly enumerated the weaknesses of church doctrine, criticizing the church's denial that Christ was a man and worship of him as a demigod, scoffing at the church's belief that the age of miracles was past, and noting the lack of power in the uninspired preaching of his day. This address was, predictably, enthusiastically received by the students, but the faculty members were understandably in disagreement.

Their reaction to this address was far different from the spirit with which they had received his Phi Beta Kappa address, "The American Scholar," just a year before. At that time Emerson's emphasis had been upon how the nation as a whole could achieve independence from European literary traditions, and told of the part that scholars, philosophers, and men of letters could play in developing self-reliant nationhood. Emerson's faith was dynamic, and that was why he seemed to the young people of his time to be the great cultural liberator. He was always on the side of imaginative exploration. In "The American Scholar" he said that the sole use of books is to inspire: "One must be an inventor to read well" (59). The scholar's preoccupation with bookish learning seemed moribund to him. He urged the scholar to become a man of action and learn directly from life: "Life is our dictionary. Years are well spent in country labors; in town—in the insight into trades and manufactures; in frank intercourse with many men and women; in science; in art; to the end of mastering in all facts a language by which to illustrate and embody our perceptions" (61–62). These ideas, which were radical for his time, were well received by the scholars and gentlemen of Harvard. Lowell, in his essay on Thoreau, declared that it was an "event without any former parallel in our literary annals."[22] However, when this same form of creative criticism was leveled against the religious institutions of the day, the officers of the school found it so objectionable that they publicly disclaimed any responsibility for it. Nearly thirty years passed before Emerson was invited again to speak at Harvard after his "Divinity School Address." Oliver Wendell Holmes described him as "an iconoclast without a hammer, who took down our idols from their pedestals so tenderly that it seemed like an act of worship."[23]

While Emerson's ideas follow in many respects those of the Unitarian church, he could not allow himself to be stultified by even a mildly theological explanation of the universe. Based on the conception he formulated of the Over-Soul, which by definition is good, it follows that the universe is necessarily moral. In his essay "Compensation," Emerson proceeded to the logical (based on his original premise) conclusion that if the Over-Soul is all powerful and at the same time good, then evil does not exist. With one stroke he removed the knotty problem of evil over which his Puritan forefathers had brooded so intensively: evil is negative, the opposite of good, and as such is powerless to effect anything, either in this world or the next. All temporary unbalance is redressed by "compensation"—that is, every "evil" deed is offset by a corresponding "good" one, and every apparent "gain" carries with it the price tag of a corresponding "loss." Nor is this adjustment of the balance postponed to the uncertainties of the life beyond the grave. Emerson was not at all impressed with the church's attitude toward a materialistic form of reward and retribution in the hereafter: "The legitimate inference the disciple would draw was—'We are to have *such* a good time as the sinners have now';—or, to push it to its extreme import,—'You sin now, we shall, sin by and by; we would sin now, if we could; not being successful we expect our revenge to-morrow'" (286). According to Emerson's view, the forces in the universe flow forever in the direction of the good, and ultimately shape all things to their benign will—even though the individual man may not see within his own experience the full working out of this principle. Thus the thief steals only from himself, the man in high office suffers from the care and calumny that accompany his position, and even sorrow and bereavement have their compensating factor in the deepening of the character of the one undergoing these trials.

To support this theory Emerson drew heavily upon his view of nature as exhibiting a constant unity-in-dualism. Every act or occurrence must have its counterpart somewhere in the universe. To the obvious objection that such a view of morality would lead either to fatalism or complete irresponsibility, Emerson replied that man's highest duty is to demonstrate by the fullness and goodness of his daily life the beauty and perfection of the Over-Soul, and that to fail to do so was simply to negate oneself. And against those wicked ones who wilfully persisted in negating themselves, he could always invoke his law of compensation and prove that the universe, by its very nature, will "make all things work together for good for those who love the Lord," in spite of those who do not.[24]

Upon careful perusal of Emerson's essays, one discovers that there is a unity—not of structure or form—but of intuited or spiritual attitude in his essays. This unity becomes apparent when the reader realizes that each of the poems and essays focuses upon some one of the concepts which, taken together, make up Emerson's belief. In the notes to the complete works, Emerson's son has pointed out that the first series of essays derive from a plan set down in the journals:

> There is one soul.
> It is related to the world.
> Art is its action thereon.
> Science finds its methods.

Literature is its record.
Religion is the emotion of reverence that it inspires.
Ethics is the soul illustrated in human life.
Society is the finding of this soul by individuals in each other.
Trades are the learning of the soul in nature by labor.
Politics is the activity of the soul illustrated in power.
Manners are silent and mediate expressions of soul.[25]

In the overall view, one might summarize Emerson's outlook as emphasizing the spiritual nature of reality, the primary importance of self-reliance, the existence of a unifying Over-Soul that harmonizes all life, the supreme significance of character, and the obligation or necessity of optimism.

Likewise, some of the major ideas of Transcendentalism, as derived from the basic concepts, could also be stated in condensed form. Every man (as well as Christ, in a higher degree) has, in his nature, something of the divine, is himself part of the Over-Soul. As a result he has, within himself, and himself is, the measure of all things. Further, man is capable of establishing a direct relationship with the universal spirit by means of his spiritual intuition. Transcendentalists believed that every man is capable of attaining a receptive harmony with the Over-Soul and of spontaneously perceiving the highest truth; man, thus, becomes the concrete media of the Divine. Also, Nature is another part of the same manifestation of the world or universal soul—thus Nature is the most closely related to the central reality of man—and partly through contact with the central reality of man—and partly through contact with Nature and partly through his inner promptings man communicates with the Over-Soul and perceives true knowledge. Transcendentalism, which is profoundly idealistic, emphasizes the instinctive-intuitive-mystical approach to truth and believes in the essential beneficence of the world. This belief, which is a sort of spiritual insight, consists in accepting the spontaneous affirmation of the human soul between the finite mind and the infinite mind—between man's changeable reasoning and his divine aspiration for ultimate principles. The doctrine teaches that one mind, one law, governs the universe and all things are essential reflections of a primarily beneficent design. All ideas are essentially *one* idea; all religions are basically the same; all poets sing the same music of the same world, chanting throughout the ages the recurrent theme: God is the slayer and slain and the creator. For the Transcendentalists, the ugly and the beautiful, the evil and the good, are contained in the universal mind. There is an organic identity of moral and physical laws—in the negative of evil and the positive endurance of good. He has, therefore, an enduring belief in the infinite capacity of creativeness in the individual and in the beneficent potentiality in human life. Finally, Emerson insisted on an eternally living God—an omnipresent God, rather than a mystical or absentee God. Eternity, he believed, is here and now.

There is little doubt that the views of the Transcendentalists served as an ethical guide for many in nineteenth-century America. Their doctrine appealed to the optimistic side of human nature and, expressing confidence in the divine spark in all men, was a clarion call to throw off the shackles of custom and tradition, and go forward to the development of a new and distinctly American culture. In its insistence on the essential worth and dignity of the individual it was a powerful force for democracy, and at the same time it preached— and practiced—an idealism that was greatly needed in a rapidly expanding economy where opportunity too often became mere opportunism, and the desire for "success" obscured the moral necessity for rising to spiritual heights.

On the other hand, the weaknesses of Transcendentalism were grave. Logically, it failed to do all that Emerson had hoped for it. Indeed, it has been said that the greatest success of Transcendentalism was its ability to take refuge in a fascile mysticism whenever the demands of logic became too insistent.[26] But the most serious criticism of the movement in the overall view is that, as applied by people who did not possess Emerson's purity of nature and moral idealism, Transcendentalism became a rationale for the pressure toward expansionism that was already shifting to the conquest of the West. Emerson's injunction to "hitch your wagon to a star," coupled with Horace Greeley's "Go west, young man," resulted more frequently in rampant individualism than in the ideal democracy of mutual helpfulness and equal opportunity. His confusion of natural and moral law, and his belief in compensation as the balance wheel of the universe, led to the shallow optimism which makes impossible the tragic view of life and stultifies at one stroke all human suffering and anguish.

Outside the small, select group in Concord, the simple logic of the common people distilled out of Emersonianism merely those elements that served to justify their acquisitiveness, and left it up to the principle of compensation to balance the rest of the account. While Emerson lived long enough to see the full tide of post–Civil War exploitation and private and public corruption, he never publicly acknowledged that his own teachings were, from a certain perspective, partly responsible. Nor would the Sage of Concord have believed that his tranquil communing with the Walden pines would eventually have led, through Hegel and Nietzsche, to the "supermen" of the German Reich. Nevertheless, Emerson's teachings had a significant impact on succeeding generations of scholars and philosophers.

In this world of magnified good and minimized evil, Herman Melville grew to young manhood. Although he was born in New York City, he had access to the advantages of the rural life so strongly recommended by Emerson, through the wealthy Dutch landholders on his mother's side. He was reared in the typical upper-middle-class atmosphere of the period, which placed more stress on external and material values than it did on the internal, spiritual aspects of life. When his father died, bankrupt and insane, young Melville found himself cast out into a world unlike the one in which he had been prepared to live. The financial reverses of the family made it impossible for him to continue his education beyond the Albany Academy, and he was forced to take a menial position in the commercial world. The material comforts which his family had taken for granted were no longer his, and his spiritual resources, unlike those of Emerson, had not been developed sufficiently to compensate for this loss. His whole scale of values had suddenly been inverted, and he felt compelled to seek a new standard of values to replace the old. In order to escape the drab life which stretched before him, he shipped out as a sailor; thus began the search for meaning that was to occupy him for the rest of his life.

To Melville, schooled in the American ideals of independence and individualism, the brutal facts of life-at-sea came as a harsh awakening. Life was not at all as he had thought it to be. He had suddenly become a nonentity, at the mercy of a stern and occasionally unjust sea-captain. He was naturally idealistic, as demonstrated by his early attraction to Emerson, and he sought to compromise his inborn idealism with the painful realism of his experiences. Melville's problem, then, became much the same as the one which had confronted Emerson. Although both men started with the same problem—the merging of the spiritual with the natural world—their methods of approach caused a distinct divergence in their final opinions, which would be pronounced in Melville's later works. Where Emerson solved the dilemma, to his own satisfaction, by bringing the individual, along with all other things, into the perspective of the divine Over-Soul, Melville sought to bring all things into the perspective of the individual. Thus Emerson's universe was God-centered, while Melville's universe was man-centered.

Emerson attempted to view the whole vast panorama of human history from the perspective of God. From this height the mountains and the canyons of human experience—the triumph and the grandeur, the bloodshed and the misery—all leveled out into one gently undulating plain of compensated balance. Melville, however, surveyed the scene from the viewpoint of the man who is involved in the turmoil, actively experiencing the vast heights and the great depths. Although a man in this position might agree that the overview from the perspective of God is indeed noble and inspiring, such noble inspiration would bring him little consolation in his day-by-day grapplings with a reality fraught with hardships and suffering. Such a man, aspiring to the heights and yet unable to change his viewpoint, might very well become embittered toward another man who had succeeded in lifting himself beyond the human level of experience. As a youth, Melville saw much that was noble in the doctrines of Emerson, but after his epiphanic meeting with Hawthorne and his careful reading of Shakespeare, he would come to see more that became unacceptable to him.

Chapter Three

Deeper Shadows to Come: The Transcendental Underpinnings of Melville's Early Works

THE HIGH HOPES WITH WHICH MELVILLE HAD LAUNCHED *MARDI* INTO THE literary world soon foundered under the storm of criticism that issued from the marketplace upon the novel's publication. His masterpiece, as he had considered it, went unappreciated by the critics and the general reading public. Melville found himself hardpressed for money and forced to return to writing the romantic sea novels that his public expected from him, the man who had "lived among the cannibals," but that he considered incompatible with his present ambitions. Growing increasingly disillusioned and embittered, he wrote *Redburn* and *White-Jacket* in an attempt to recapture the readers he had alienated by the ill-fated *Mardi* and to satisfy his unhappy publisher's demands for another "successful" novel. It was during the interim between *White-Jacket* and *Moby-Dick* that Melville discovered Hawthorne, who became one of the major influences on his philosophical development. His friendship with Hawthorne was the only really close mentoring relationship Melville ever experienced, and he felt that in Hawthorne he had found his alter-ego; here he found affirmation of his own growing awareness of the limitations of optimism, and during the months when their relationship was at its most intense, Melville underwent an immense change in attitude—especially toward Transcendentalism.

At the time that he wrote *Mardi*, Melville had been attracted to such Emersonian ideas as the repetition of great thoughts throughout the centuries, the mystical revelation of truth, and Nature as a microcosmic theologian. He also agreed with the necessity for "aloneness" in the search for meaning, the failure of the Christian doctrine as practiced in the world, and the limitations of science in ascertaining metaphysical truth. Finally, Melville clearly recognized the subjectivity of religion and believed that real religion is found within man, rather than without.

During the interval between *Mardi* and *Moby-Dick*, however, many of Melville's formerly rather vague criticisms of Transcendentalism had crystallized into very definite objections. On the basis of his comments in *Moby-Dick*, *Pierre*, and "Benito Cereno," along with the annotations in his copy of Emerson's *Essays*, the major points on which Melville disagreed with Emerson become apparent. These comments and annotations reveal Melville's disagreement with the concept of the mystical revelation of absolute truth, the unimportance of circumstances, and the equality of a man's ambitions and his powers. Likewise, Melville was clearly questioning the poet's ability to reconcile man to the deepest mysteries, the necessity for plain living, and the negative quality of evil. Melville had come to have serious doubts about the beneficial tendency of the universe and Emerson's law of compensation as well. There were influences at work in Melville's life during this period which contributed to his changing viewpoint, all of which must be taken into consideration— but probably one of the most important was the dismal failure of *Mardi*.

When *Mardi* appeared in the literary world, following quickly after *Typee* and *Omoo*, the critics were faced with a puzzling problem. They scarcely knew what to make of this book, which bore so many similarities to Melville's earlier works, and yet, at the same time, so many dissimilarities. Some of the critics skirted the issue, while others bluntly described *Mardi* in such terms as "one of the most grotesque volumes we have met with for a long time. . . . The very idea of the work is one that we scarcely know whether to admire of condemn."[1] A critic in *The Examiner* said of *Mardi*:

> From the first to the last it is an outrageous fiction; a Transcendental Gulliver, or Robinson Crusoe run mad. A heap of fanciful speculations, vivid descriptions, satirical insinuations, and allegorical typifications are flung together with little order or connexion.[2]

Remarkably reminiscent of these opinions about *Mardi* are the opinions later expressed by the critics concerning *Pierre*. *The Athenaeum* says that *Pierre* is "one of the most diffuse doses of Transcendentalism offered for a long time to the public."[3] In *Putnam's Monthly* of February, 1853, Fitz-James O'Brien, reviewing Melville's achievements as an author, had this to say: "*Typee*, his first book, was healthy; *Omoo* nearly so; after that came *Mardi*, with its excusable wildness; then came *Moby-Dick*, and *Pierre* with its inexcusable insanity."[4]

Upon reading the contemporaneous critical reviews of Melville's works, one becomes aware that critics of the era seemed to regard Melville as a sort of Jekyll-Hyde character. For the most part, they were pleased with *Typee*, *Omoo*, *Redburn*, *White-Jacket*, and, in some instances, *Moby-Dick*. *Mardi* and *Pierre*, however, with their probings into philosophy and theology and with their unveilings of the imperfections of an eternally imperfect world, showed not only a dark side of Melville's nature that the critics felt would be better off unrevealed, but also pointed out a dark side of a glittering Gilded Age that was not at all in keeping with the tenor of the times. As one critic said: "if one does not desire to look at virtue and religion with the eye of Mephistopheles . . . he had better leave 'Pierre of the Ambiguities' unbought on the shelves of the bookseller."[5] In much the same vein, an English critic commented concerning *Mardi*:

> We cannot but express our profound regret that a pen so talented, and an apparatus so fascinating, as those which the author of *Mardi* commands, should have been made use of for the dissemination of skeptical notions. To introduce the Saviour of mankind under a fabulous name, and to talk down the verities of the Christian faith by sophistry, the more than irreverence of which is but flimsily veiled, is a grave offence, not against good taste alone.[6]

That such criticisms had a telling effect on Melville is indicated by his letter to Evert Duyckinck in December of 1849 concerning the reviews of *Mardi*:

> What a madness & anguish it is, that an author can never—under no conceivable circumstances—be at all frank with his readers.—Could I, for one, be frank with them—how would they cease their railing—those at least who have railed.[7]

There is little doubt, however, that Melville not only recognized the Jekyll-Hyde quality in himself but also was concerned about it. In a letter written to Richard Bentley, he says, after commenting upon the disappointing reviews of *Mardi* in England:

> You may think, in your own mind that a man is unwise,—indiscreet, to write a work of that kind, when he might have written one perhaps, calculated merely to please the general reader, & not provoke attack, however masqued in an affectation of indif-

ference or contempt. But some of us scribblers, My Dear Sir,
always have a certain something unmanageable in us, that bids
us do this or that, and be done it must—hit or miss.[8]

But after the unhappy reception of *Mardi*, Melville forced himself to
turn away from the unpopular subject matter and the symbolic and
philosophical style of *Mardi* and, controlling the "something unmanageable" within him, concerning himself with writing popular novels. Driven by the need for money, "with duns all around him, &
looking over the back of his chair—& perching on his pen & diving
in his ink-stand,"[9] he produced a monetarily successful novel in
Redburn. But, resenting the necessity that drove him to write what he
considered to be a "beggarly" book, he lashed out at the circumstances in which the impecunious writer finds himself.[10] "And when
he attempts anything higher—God help him & save him! for it is not
with a hollow purse as with a hollow balloon—for a hollow purse
makes the poet *sink*—witness 'Mardi.'"[11] Despite the fact that *Redburn*
and *White-Jacket* put "money in an empty purse,"[12] Melville's opinion
of them was not only low, but tinged with bitter resentment:

> But no reputation that is gratifying to me, can possibly be
> achieved by with of these books. They are two jobs, which I have
> done for money—being forced to it, as other men are to sawing
> wood. . . . —Being books, then, written in this way, my only desire
> for their "success" (as it is called) springs from my pocket & not
> from my heart. So far as I am individually concerned, & inde-
> pendent of my pocket, it is my earnest desire to write those sort of
> books which are said to "fail."[13]

The aforementioned "something unmanageable"—this compulsion
to "fail"—began to assert itself again during the composition of *Moby-
Dick*, and by the time he began to write *Pierre*, the "unmanageable"
seemed to have completely gained the upper hand. In June of 1851,
while finishing *Moby-Dick*, Melville wrote to Hawthorne:

> What I feel most moved to write, that is banned,—it will not pay.
> Yet, altogether, write the *other* way I cannot. So the product is a
> final hash, and all my books are botches.[14]

Apparently when Melville wrote *Pierre* he had given up the struggle
to write "the other way." In *Pierre* he says of himself, "I write precisely as I please."[15] Thus we see in both *Mardi* and *Pierre* the unrestrained
Melville, writing of the things which seemed important to him
regardless of the opinions of the critics. Perhaps when he wrote *Mardi*

he did not realize that his views would be unpopular, but by the time he wrote *Pierre* he no longer cared about pleasing a popular audience.

While critical reaction to *Mardi*, *Moby-Dick*, and *Pierre* bear a close resemblance, it is important to note that, although these novels were labeled "Transcendental" by the critics, they were not *intended* as an espousal of Transcendentalism. It is true that *Mardi* was intentionally Transcendental in several ways. Not only do we find here a clear reflection of many Emersonian views, but also the whole motivating spirit behind the work was Transcendental, as well as the method of presentation. Melville was applying here the same sort of creative criticism that was used by Emerson in his "Divinity School Address," but Melville's work was received by a far more diverse public than Emerson's college oration was. Furthermore, Melville expressed himself in far different terms from those to be found in Emerson's high-flown oratory. While Emerson was also accused of "the dissemination of skeptical notions" when he delivered his "Divinity School Address," he did *not* commit a "grave offense" against "good taste" by employing a "flimsily-veiled irreverence." He took care *not* "to talk down the verities of the Christian faith by sophistry."[16]

Although both Emerson and Melville shared the same attitudes toward organized religion, and although both expressed their views and both were condemned for doing so, the extent of the condemnation and their reactions to it differed widely. Emerson, from his lofty, God-centered mountain peak, could accept such dissension from his views as a tribute to his higher mind and greater powers of intuition; but Melville, from his man-centered world, craving to be understood by his fellow men, suffered demonstrably from their lack of understanding. *Mardi* was a very special book to Melville. It not only represented what he thought was his best work, but it was also his attempt to share his newly gleaned insights and prove to the world-at-large that he was a "serious" author. Their "swinish" reaction to his efforts was a shock to his transcendentally oriented mind. Thus, the flickerings of darkness which had been seen but briefly in *Mardi* began to dominate his thinking.

It was while in this frame of mind that Melville discovered Hawthorne, who helped to crystallize his growing preoccupation with what he describes as "the power of blackness" in his famous review of Hawthorne's *Mosses From an Old Manse*. Melville saw in Hawthorne's sophisticated and ambiguous portraits of sin and its effects a positive affirmation of his own growing awareness of the dark side of morality. One English critic had stated that "nothing that Melville wrote after he encountered Hawthorne could resemble any-

thing that he had written before."[17] Hawthorne was but one year
younger than Emerson, while Melville was but two years younger
than Thoreau, and they were all persevering students of the mysteries of the soul. Just as Thoreau was, in a sense, a disciple of Emerson,
so Melville formed a similar relationship with Hawthorne. At this
time, both Hawthorne and Melville had undergone disillusioning
experiences with Transcendentalism—Hawthorne at Brook Farm and
Melville with *Mardi*—which provided a natural kinship between
them.

Hawthorne's wife, Sophia, had been active in Transcendental cir-
cles prior to her marriage. The Boston home of her sister, Elizabeth
Peabody, was the scene of the famous conversational classes of
Margaret Fuller (1839–1844), and her bookshop was a favorite meeting place of the Transcendental Club.[18] It was through Sophia that
Hawthorne had had his disenchanting experience with the
Transcendental movement at Brook Farm; he, in turn, became
Melville's main connection with the Transcendentalists—but it never
developed into a very deep union. According to Lewis Mumford, "it
was the blandness, the sunniness, the mildness, the absences of curses, shadows, shipwrecks" in Emerson's philosophy that set Melville
against it:

> Emerson was the perpetual passenger who stayed below in bad
> weather, trusting that the captain would take care of the ship:
> Melville was the sailor who climbed aloft, and knew that the cap-
> tain was sometimes drunk and that the best of ships might go
> down.[19]

It is no wonder, in the midst of this era of Emersonian sunshine,
which had come to seem artificial to Melville, that he should pounce
with such enthusiasm on the blackness in Hawthorne. This blackness
fascinated him because it was something he had seen in his own life,
and could therefore understand and appreciate. In writing of
Hawthorne he referred to it as "those occasional flashings-forth of the
intuitive truth in him; those short, quick probings at the very axis of
reality."[20]

There is little doubt that Hawthorne had a profound influence on
Melville's changing perspective during this transitional period in his
life. They spent much time deep in conversation about "Time and
Eternity and things that lie beyond human ken."[21] We have no way
of knowing exactly what views were exchanged during these intimate
moments, but we do know that during his association with
Hawthorne Melville's attitude toward Transcendentalism altered, as is

clearly evidenced in *Moby-Dick, Pierre,* "Benito Cereno," "Bartleby, the Scrivener," and *The Confidence-Man.* It is further worth noting that *Pierre* was published at the same time as Hawthorne's *Blithedale Romance* (1852), and that both novels deal with Transcendental idealists who are crushed in their attempts to pursue the ways of heaven on earth. One could fairly assume, then, that both men were preoccupied during this period with the limitations of Transcendental idealism, and it is probable that the subject was thoroughly discussed between them.

Although Hawthorne was a major force in setting Melville's feet on the path of blackness, there were other factors that caused him to pursue a course in the opposite direction from Transcendentalism. The wide gulf between Melville's and Emerson's later interpretations of truth can be partially accounted for by a brief assessment of their educational and religious differences.

There is a real contrast between the aesthetic and academic training Emerson received in the cloistered halls of Harvard and the brutal, disillusioning education Melville experienced within the wooden walls of a ship. The rugged, rough-and-tumble seamen with whom Melville was associated were a class of people not to be found in the polite society of Boston and Cambridge. It would be unfair, however, to assert that the hardships and the distress which Melville suffered were more difficult to bear than were those which came to Emerson in his quiet surroundings. Illness and loss of loved ones all caused Emerson sorrow, but did not lessen his basic optimism. Emerson, even in his later, darker works—such as "Experience" and "Fate"—continued to affirm man's inherent divinity.

William Braswell adheres to the theory that the difference in the religious training of the two men is probably one of the chief reasons why one's outlook on life was much brighter than the other's.[22] It is significant that Emerson was born and reared in a Unitarian world, whereas Melville spent his early years under the influence of Calvinism. Emerson was taught to believe that the Deity is benevolent and that man is good. Melville was instructed in the Calvinistic views that God is a jealous God and that man is innately corrupt. Moreover, because of the redemptory role it gave to Christ, Melville's religious training was on a more emotional level than was Emerson's. In both cases the teachings had an abiding influence.

Perhaps more important than religious training, however, is the natural spiritual inclination of each man. At the age of thirty Emerson wrote in his journal:

Men seem to be constitutionally believers and unbelievers. There
is no bridge that can cross from a mind in one state to a mind in
the other. All my opinions, affections, whimsies, are tinged with
belief,—incline that side. . . . But I cannot give reasons to a person of a different persuasion that are at all adequate to the force
of my conviction. Yet when I fail to find the reason, my faith is
not less.[23]

There is a dramatic contrast between this autobiographical passage
and the statement which Melville inserted as an editorial comment in
his novel *Pierre*:

For there is no faith, and no stoicism, and no philosophy, that a
mortal man can possibly evoke which will stand the final test of
a real impassioned onset of Life and Passion upon him. Then all
the fair philosophic or Faith-phantoms that he raised from the
mist, slide away and disappear as ghosts at cock-crow. For faith
and philosophy are air, but events are brass. Amidst his gray
philosophisings, Life breaks upon a man like a morning.[24]

Melville's inability to arrive at a satisfactory faith, or belief, did not
escape the notice of his friend Hawthorne. After a long talk with
Melville, with whom he had not conversed for some time,
Hawthorne wrote the following analytical comment in his journal in
1856:

Melville, as he always does, began to reason of Providence and
futurity, and of everything that lies beyond human ken, and he
informed me that he had "pretty much made up his mind to be
annihilated"; but still he does not seem to rest in that anticipa-
tion; and, I think, will never rest until he gets hold of a definite
belief. It is strange how he persists—and he has persisted ever
since I knew him, and probably long before—in wandering to
and fro over these deserts, as dismal and monotonous as the sand
hills amid which we were sitting. He can neither believe, nor be
comfortable in his unbelief; and he is too honest and too courageous not to try to do one or the other. If he were a religious man,
he would be one of the most truly religious and reverential; he
has a very high and noble nature, and is better worth immortality than most of us.[25]

While Emerson explored the bright side of the soul, Melville
explored the dark, stressing the soul's limitations more than its freedom. After his exposure to Hawthorne, Melville assumed an active

stance against Transcendentalism, although he was more than half a Transcendentalist himself. He was unlike Hawthorne, however, in his uncompromising rebellion against the limitations of the human condition. The problem of the individual, of God, and of being itself would not let him rest, although he could not find a solution for it. Thus he persisted, as Hawthorne noted, in wandering to and fro over the dismal and monotonous deserts of his soul. Writing to Hawthorne in March 1851, Melville said:

> But it is this Being of the matter; there lies the knot with which we choke ourselves. As soon as you say *Me*, a *God*, or a *Nature*, so soon you jump off from your stool and hang from the beam. Yes, that word is the hangman. Take God out of the dictionary, and you would have him in the street.[26]

Melville is saying that when a man builds a wall around a part of being, as he must do when he attempts to define it as *Me*, a separate self, he necessarily destroys the universality and immortality of being. God is obviously not a dictionary-defined and limited being, as here conceived, but Being itself. Melville's point is that so long as man looks out from his individuality to see God, God is necessarily seen as an individuality like himself. If it were possible to draw God into the self, then both the self and God might lose all limitation; thus man might dwell in Heaven and God would be found in the street.

It is important to recall, at this point, that Emerson's inquiry into the meaning and purpose of nature is, at bottom, an effort to assimilate nature into itself—to reduce the Not Me to Me. This effort took two directions: one, toward the conquest of nature intellectually, by achieving its idea of theory; the other, toward a practical conquest, a kingdom of man, achieved by learning lessons of power in the universe. Although Melville and Emerson started with the same problem, their end results were in direct contrast. Emerson attempted to achieve a complete monism through the Over-Soul; he eliminated dualism by regarding the physical world, or Nature, as the lower half of a circle which reflected, microcosmically, the upper half of the circle, or spiritual realm. There was no problem of dichotomy, ideally, in his theory, because the unity of the two halves of the circle was unquestionable; each half represented truth, but in a different form. Nature was merely a symbol on the lower level of a corresponding metaphysical truth on the upper level; man's function is that of interpreter or mediator between the two halves of the circle. Insofar as he is ignorant of the spiritual level, thus far is he ignorant of the physical level, and vice versa. Through an amalgamation of his understanding of the spiritual half of the circle (Intuition) and his comprehension of the physical half (Reason), he arrives at the whole truth.

Melville's view of man's problem in the universe, however, might be explained through the Christian symbol of the cross. He saw not only a clear-cut division between body and soul, but also a division that set one in opposition to the other, making life a battleground between the demands of the physical world and the god-aspiration of man's soul. The horizontal plane of the cross represents man's animal level of pure existence—the purely creature world of sensual pleasure and pain; his environmental orientation; the animal necessities that demand satisfaction. Here we find the *Typee* level of existence and the sensual lure of Hautia. The vertical line of the cross, on the other hand, represents man's undeniable and irrepressible spiritual desires—his god-aspiration and hunger; his quest for the absolute; those spiritual necessities which also demand satisfaction. Here we find the sources of the Yillahs of the world. The crossing place of these two lines is the crux of man's problem in the world. This X marks the spot where man must eternally struggle, caught between these two conflicting forces of his nature, forever incapable of making them compatible. As is pointed out in Plinlimmon's pamphlet in *Pierre*, spiritual truth and worldly truth are on two distinctly different levels and not interchangeable. It is at this point that the Ishmaels, Plinlimmons, and the Veres of the world solve their problems through rational compromise; but the Ahabs, Pierres, and Bartlebys must continue the struggle until they have destroyed themselves.

In making a comparative study of these two men, the reader becomes increasingly aware of a circuitous, spiraling effect in the thinking of each. The difference lies in the direction of the spiral. With Emerson there is always the effect of an upward direction, a scaling of the heights—or as Emerson himself puts it, a mounting "through all the spires of form."[27] Melville, on the other hand, sees the search for knowledge as a downward motion. Man seeks to solve his problems by going down in himself, searching the subcutaneous regions of his being—not by contacting some divinity outside himself. Perhaps a partial explanation for this difference in direction might be found in the fact that Emerson completely rejected the Calvinist doctrine of the Fall of Man which had played so large a part in Melville's early training.

Richard Chase has based his whole concept of Melville's works on what he calls Melville's "magnificent myth" about himself. As Chase sees it, the myth has two central themes: the Fall and the Search, the

Search for what was lost in the Fall or for the earthly and possible substitutes for what was lost. The idea of the Fall was Melville's instinctive image of his own fate and the fate of his family. The Melvilles and the Gansevoorts (the mother's family) had been proud, aristocratic, and successful Americans. They had been squires, soldiers, merchants, professional men, staunch patriots in the Revolution and builders of the New World. Chase says that an aspiring youth might think that to be born constituted a Fall in itself, a leaping down from a golden cloud and an irredeemable engrossment of oneself in earth—buried to the waist like Enceladus. But to see, as a young Melville did, his father go mad and die after having failed in business and having ruined the family fortune—was to be given fearfully tangible evidence that his instinctive sense of disaster and loss was well founded and was in fact the one "real" truth about life.[28] According to Chase, the brutal and immoral Western civilization of the nineteenth century is the adult level of the fallen world of Melville's myth. The pre-adult level is the fallen Eden, represented in *Pierre* by Saddle Meadows—a level of existence which wears the mask of childhood and innocence but is really guilty of terrible evils, committed in the name of "goodness." The plot of Melville's historical-cultural myth is that experience continuously presents itself to the young man as partaking of an innocent and unfallen nature. The hero is tested by encounters with masked experience; when he unmasks experience, he succeeds in taking one step further in self-education, in the discovery of reality. But sometimes he fails. The discovery of reality is the precondition, and the acceptance of reality is, perhaps, the whole condition of the atonement of the young man with the gods and the fathers from whose estate he has fallen.[29] The Emersonian theory, in contrast is a denial of the Fall theme—both in the Biblical context and as an actuality in life. Emerson did not acknowledge any separation of man and the divine; consequently, a Melvillean type of search, in Emerson's opinion, was unnecessary.

Chase's unfallen—or innocent—world parallels the Transcendentalist's view of reality, their insistence that no separation of God and man had occurred. A man such as Melville, struggling to accept such an ideal doctrine, and yet seeing it refuted daily in the realities of the world around him, would quite naturally develop a bitterness toward those who had originally perpetuated such a doctrine. Lawrance Thompson comments that "the turn which his [Melville's] life had taken translated him from a Transcendentalist and a mystic into an inverted Transcendentalist, and inverted mystic."[30] Such an interpretation, however, seems a little too neat. Much greater insight into Melville's actual position is seen in R. W. B. Lewis's comment that

"Melville . . . had penetrated beyond both innocence and despair to some glimmering of a moral order which might explain and order them both."[31] At the time Melville wrote *Pierre*, however, and his works immediately thereafter, he had not as yet achieved his "glimmering of a moral order." Although he felt that there was a great deal which was amiss in the Transcendental doctrine, he had not yet arrived at a solution of these problems.

Lewis says that Melville "took the loss of innocence and the world's betrayal of hope as the supreme challenge to understanding and to art."[32] Melville did not want to accept that betrayal, however, and for a while he kept going back over the ground of the betrayal, however, in an attempt to prove the betrayal untrue or avoidable. "That illusory effort . . . is most of the meaning of *Pierre*."[33] In order to understand Lewis's application of the word "innocence," one must know that he has stated earlier that "the key term in the moral vocabulary of Emerson, Thoreau, Whitman, and their followers and imitators . . . was 'innocence.'"[34] Thus, the betrayal that Melville wanted to prove untrue was that which the Transcendental belief in absolute virtue (or "innocence") could bring to its adherents.

Melville's major disagreement with the Transcendentalists, however, is based not upon an informing moral vision for physical existence, but upon the methods by which the vision is received. Melville could not understand the mystic experience by which the Transcendentalists believed themselves to have communication with God. In *Pierre* he says:

> That profound Silence, that only Voice of our God, which I before spoke of; from that divine thing without a name, those imposter philosophers pretend somehow to have got an answer; which is as absurd as though they should say they had got water out of a stone; for how can a man get a Voice out of Silence?[35]

One cannot hope, then, to understand God. Melville seems to have come to the conclusion that the same is true of the soul of man, for he writes: "He [Pierre] saw that human life doth truly come from that, which all men are agreed to call by the name of *God*, and that it partakes of the unravellable inscrutableness of God."[36] Let a man beware of rashly exploring the shoreless seas of his own being. "Appalling is the soul of a man! Better might one be pushed off into the material spaces beyond the uttermost orbit of our sun, than once feel himself fairly afloat in himself!"[37]

In all of this, Melville disagreed with the Transcendentalists on one major point. They believed that the soul, whether of God or man, can be known by intuition, and that this knowledge transcends human limitations. The evidence of this knowledge is present in the moral sense. Melville, on the other hand, denied that the soul can be known—and pointed out the danger of seeking knowledge of it—yet could not altogether resist the temptation himself. He scorned intuition, which could know spirit only in terms of spirit, caring only for that knowledge that can translate the soul's mysteries in terms of the intellect. In a letter to Hawthorne, Melville wrote:

> In reading some of Goethe's sayings. . . . I came across this, "Live in the all." That is to say, your separate identity is but a wretched one,—good; but get out of yourself, spread and expand yourself, and bring to yourself the tinglings of life that are felt in the flowers and the woods, that are felt in the planets Saturn and Venus, and the Fixed Stars. What nonsense! Here is a fellow with a raging toothache. "My dear boy," Goethe says to him, "you are sorely afflicted with that tooth; but you must *live in the all*, and then you will be happy!" . . . That "all" feeling, though, there is some truth in. You must have felt it, lying on the grass on a warm summer's day. Your legs seem to send out shoots into the earth. Your hair feels like leaves upon your head. This is the *all* feeling. But what plays the mischief with the truth is that men will insist upon a universal application of a temporary feeling or opinion.[38]

To Melville, application of the "all-feeling" was not a sufficient balm to sooth the "toothache" of existence. It is immediately apparent how appropriately Melville's criticism of Goethe could be applied to Whitman's "I loaf and invite my soul" doctrine. But this *all* feeling, as described by Melville, is also reminiscent of the mystic experiences Emerson describes as being the source of intuitive knowledge, the mystic experiences that Melville rejects as not being universally applicable. Upon a careful analysis, however, one becomes aware of the fact that Melville, himself, is a mystic—but, as Thompson has pointed out, an "inverted mystic." A consideration of this inverted mysticism is essential to an understanding of Melville's growing anti-Transcendentalism.

Chapter Four

Defying Nature: *Moby-Dick* and the Limits of Emersonian Individualism

REAT GENIUSES ARE PARTS OF THE TIMES," MELVILLE WROTE IN THE summer of 1850; "they themselves are the times, and possess a correspondent coloring."[1] This comment in the essay "Hawthorne and His Mosses," which Melville composed while working on *Moby-Dick*, indicates Melville's own relation to the predominantly Transcendental milieu of the 1840s and early 1850s as much as it does Hawthorne's. Melville's conception of genius suggests the underlying idea of Emerson's *Representative Men*, published early in 1850. Emerson had written that although a great man "inhabits a higher sphere of thought, into which other men rise with labor and difficulty," such a unique individual "must be related to us, and our life receive from him some promise of explanation." "All men," Emerson continued, "are at last of a size"; and "the key to the power of the greatest men" is that "their spirit diffuses itself."[2]

Even though thirteen years had elapsed since Emerson summed up the ideals of the period in "The American Scholar" address, Melville in praising Hawthorne restated its challenge for an independent national literature. "And we want no American Goldsmiths," Melville wrote; "nay, we want no American Miltons. . . . No American writer should write like an Englishman, or a Frenchman; let him write like a man, for then he will write like an American."[3] While other writers such as Irving and Longfellow were adapting European models to American subjects, Emerson had observed: "We have listened too long to the courtly muses of Europe. . . . We will walk on our own feet; we will work with our own hands; we will speak our own minds."[4] Like Emerson, who defined the poet or scholar as "Man Thinking," Melville would have the writer look into his own mind and heart and "write like a man."[5]

This Transcendentalist respect for personal integrity permeates Melville's self-revealing comments on Hawthorne. In a statement that suggests the thesis of Emerson's "Self-Reliance," Melville implies his own recovery of confidence after the failure of *Mardi*. "But it is better to fail in originality than to succeed in imitation," he wrote. "He who has never failed somewhere, that man cannot be great. Failure is the true test of greatness."[6] In a similar vein, Emerson said, "To be great is to be misunderstood"; and "Insist on yourself; never imitate. . . . Where is the master who could have taught Shakespeare? Where is the master who could have instructed Franklin, or Washington, or Bacon, or Newton? Every great man is unique."[7]

Although Melville in his essay praised Hawthorne for the Calvinistic blackness that sets off "the Indian-summer sunlight on the hither side of Hawthorne's soul," Melville's language reflects the polarity and reliance on intuition that characterize Emerson's perspective. "But this darkness," Melville wrote, "gives more effect to the evermoving dawn, that forever advances through it, and circumnavigates his world . . . in certain moods, no man can weigh this world, without throwing in something, somehow like Original Sin, to strike the uneven balance."[8] The idea is implicit in Emerson's essay on "Compensation," which opens with a poem on the polarities in nature:

> The wings of Time are black and white,
> Pied with morning and with night.
> Mountain tall and ocean deep
> Trembling balance duly keep.
> In changing moon, and tidal wave,
> Glows the feud of Want and Have.
> Gauge of more and less through space
> Electric star and pencil plays.
> The lonely Earth amid the balls
> That hurry through the eternal halls,
> A makeweight flying to the void,
> Supplemental asteroid,
> Or compensatory spark,
> Shoots across the neutral Dark.[9]

Both Melville and Emerson describe the balance of opposites in nature in terms of absolute black and white—Melville's reference to the darkness of Original Sin or human frailty corresponds to Emerson's "neutral dark" of skepticism; Melville's "ever-moving dawn" which he sees in Hawthorne's art parallels Emerson's "compensatory spark" of spiritual principle.[10] In other words, at the time

Melville admired Hawthorne's black thought and wrote about a white whale, his thinking reflected the Transcendental conception of the artist, whose task is to see nature whole from an independent point of view and to represent to the mortal senses this total vision with its paradoxes and contrasts.

At the beginning of *Moby-Dick*, Melville suggests this view of the artist as distinct from that of the Transcendental priest, who is concerned primarily with supersensual reality. In the brief section entitled "Etymology," which functions as an epic invocation to the Muse, Melville hints at both the Transcendental significance and the tragic tone of the novel:

> The pale Usher—threadbare in coat, heart, body, and brain; I see him now. He was ever dusting his old lexicons and grammars, with a queer handkerchief, mockingly embellished with all the gay flags of all the known nations of the world. He loved to dust his old grammars; it somehow mildly reminded him of his mortality. (xv)

Melville, it will be recalled, was himself a "pale Usher," or schoolmaster's assistant, in Pittsfield in the fall of 1837.[11] The reference to "grammars" as reminders of one's mortality parallels the moral and aesthetic link that Emerson described between words, nature, and the mind. "Every word which is used to express a moral or intellectual fact," Emerson wrote in *Nature*, "if traced to its root, is found to be borrowed from some material appearance."[12] In "The Poet," Emerson observed that "the etymologist finds the deadest word to have been once a brilliant picture. Language is fossil poetry."[13]

Any discussion of the Transcendental in *Moby-Dick*, however, must take into account Melville's close personal association with Hawthorne, which began shortly after Melville moved his family from New York City to Pittsfield in July 1850.[14] By a fortunate coincidence Hawthorne lived in nearby Lenox. The ensuing cordial relationship between the two authors undoubtedly is the primary reason that Melville delayed the completion of *Moby-Dick* for more than half a year. Melville had written in June to Richard Bentley, the London publisher of *Mardi*, *Redburn*, and *White-Jacket*, promising "a new work" in "the latter part of the coming autumn."[15] He did not complete the novel, however, until the following summer. During the interval, as Jay Leyda suggests, Hawthorne "compelled Melville to see his task newly, more deeply and daringly."[16] Melville inscribed *Moby-Dick* to Hawthorne as a "token" of "admiration for his genius" (vii).

In Hawthorne, Melville found an example of a self-reliant author who had overcome early failure to succeed. *The Scarlet Letter*, published in 1850, was a bestseller of the day. It had established Hawthorne's reputation as a novelist possessing a profound insight into what Hawthorne called in his famous preface to *The House of the Seven Gables* "the truth of the human heart."[17] If Melville needed a precept on art from a writer of fiction, rather than a lecturer-poet such as Emerson, it was available to him in the following passage from Hawthorne's short story "The Artist of the Beautiful" in *Mosses from an Old Manse*:

> It is requisite for the ideal artist to possess a force of character that seems hardly compatible with its delicacy; he must keep his faith in himself, while the incredulous world assails him with its utter disbelief; he must stand up against mankind and be his own sole disciple, both as respects his genius, and the objects to which it is directed.[18]

Melville triple-scored this sentence in his copy of Hawthorne's *Mosses*, which he received from his Aunt Mary Melville on July 18, 1850, one month before the first installment of his review of the book was published in Evert Duyckinck's *The Literary World*.[19]

Had Melville desired, however, he could easily have found a parallel passage in Emerson's "The Poet," which appeared in *Essays, Second Series* in 1844, the same year Hawthorne wrote "The Artist of the Beautiful."[20] In "The Poet," Emerson also stressed the artist's need to keep faith with himself in the face of public indifference:

> O poet! a new nobility is conferred in groves and pastures, and not in castles or by sword-blade any longer. The conditions are hard, but equal. . . . The world is full of renunciations and apprenticeships, and this is thine; thou must pass for a fool and a churl for a long season. . . . And this is the reward; that the ideal shall be real to thee, and the impressions of the actual world shall fall like summer rain, copious, but not troublesome to thy invulnerable essence.[21]

The conclusion of Hawthorne's story, in which Owen Warland spiritually triumphs even though he sees the destruction of his mechanical butterfly, so impressed Melville that he alluded to it in the opening lines of "Hawthorne and His Mosses":

> Would that all excellent books were foundlings without father or mother, that so it might be, we could glorify them, without

including their ostensible authors! Nor would any true man take exception to this—least of all, he who writes: 'When the Artist rises high enough to achieve the Beautiful, the symbol by which he makes it perceptible to mortal senses becomes of little value in his eyes, while his spirit possesses itself in the enjoyment of the reality.'[22]

These passages linking both Hawthorne and Melville to Emerson's thought suggest that the friendship which developed between the novelists when Melville was writing *Moby-Dick* was based at least in part on their tacit awareness and appropriation of Transcendental tropes and forms. Although Melville particularly admired Hawthorne's Calvinistic strain, which is appropriate for tragedy, the evidence indicates that through Hawthorne, Melville had his most important personal access to American Transcendentalism. Hawthorne, who was fifteen years older than Melville, was married to a younger sister of Elizabeth Peabody, a prominent member of the Transcendental Club.[23] Furthermore, despite Hawthorne's satirical treatment of Transcendentalism in "The Celestial Railroad," he and his wife Sophia had a long-standing business and personal relationship with Emerson, as well as with Alcott and other Transcendentalists. In addition to residing briefly at Brook Farm in 1841 and even serving in the offices of Trustee and Chairman of the Committee on Finance, Hawthorne had rented the "Old Manse" in Concord from Emerson for three years.

In the fall of 1850, when Hawthorne and Melville were exchanging neighborly visits, Sophia Hawthorne reported in a letter to her mother not only that Melville "shut himself into the boudoir" one morning "and read Mr. Emerson's essays," but also that Melville described her husband's features in a manner suggesting Emerson's characterization of the Transcendental poet. Sophia wrote:

> [Melville] said Mr. Hawthorne was the first person whose physical being appeared to him wholly in harmony with the intellectual and spiritual . . . "the gleam—the shadow—and the peace supreme" all were in exact response to the high calm intellect, the glowing, deep heart—the purity of actual and spiritual life.[24]

Similarly, in "The Poet," Emerson referred to the poet as one who "stands among partial men for the complete man." He is "the person in whom these powers are in balance, the man without impediment, who sees and handles that which others dream of, traverses the whole scale of experience, and is representative of man, in virtue of being the largest power to receive and to impart."[25]

Though Emerson did not visit the Hawthornes at Lenox, he wrote in December of 1850, inviting Hawthorne to join with Theodore Parker, Thoreau, Holmes, Lowell, and others in contributing to a projected New England magazine. "So I hope," Emerson concluded,

> since they proceed so gently, you will not be taught to deny them, but will let them lay siege to your heart with their soft approaches. A good magazine we have not in America, and we are all its friends beforehand. If they win you, I shall think a great point gained.[26]

Nothing resulted from this proposal; but in 1852, Hawthorne moved back to Concord, the center of American Transcendentalism. He purchased Bronson Alcott's former residence, "The Hillside," and renamed it "The Wayside." Emerson, who was part owner, lived less than a mile away. Though Hawthorne served as American consul in Liverpool from 1854 to 1857, he returned to The Wayside in 1860, where he lived until his death in 1864. Emerson was an honorary pallbearer at his funeral.[27]

Like Melville, Hawthorne expressed a qualified admiration for Emerson in a passage which Melville must have read in *Mosses from an Old Manse*. "For myself," Hawthorne wrote in "The Old Manse,"

> there had been epochs of my life when I too might have asked of this prophet the master word that should solve the riddle of the universe; but now, being happy, I felt as if there were no questions to be put, and therefore admired Emerson as poet of deep beauty and austere tenderness, but sought nothing from him as a philosopher. It was good, nevertheless, to meet him in the wood-paths, or sometimes in our avenue, with that pure intellectual gleam diffused about his presence like the garment of a shining one; and he so quiet, so simple, so without pretension, encountering each man alive as if expecting to receive more than he could impart. And, in truth, the heart of many an ordinary man had, perchance, inscriptions which he could not read. But it was impossible to dwell in his vicinity without inhaling more or less the mountain atmosphere of his lofty thought, which, in the brains of some people, wrought a singular giddiness,—new truth being as heady as new wine.[28]

Hawthorne's quiet appraisal clearly elevates Emerson the artist and individualist over Emerson the philosopher and separates him from other Transcendentalists with their "singular giddiness." Similarly, Melville refused to "oscillate in Emerson's rainbow" after hearing him lecture in 1849. Melville nevertheless noted that Emerson was not like other Transcendentalists with their "oracular gibberish," and praised him in a curious reference to whaling: "I love all men who *dive*," Melville wrote to Evert Duyckinck. "Any fish can swim near the surface, but it takes a great whale to go down stairs five miles or more; and if he dont [sic] attain bottom, why, all the lead in Galena can't fashion the plummet that will."[29] Implicit in the comments of both Hawthorne and Melville is a sense of the limitation of human comprehension, a concept foreign to the Emersonian philosophy. For though Hawthorne and Melville clearly admired Emerson's poetic voice, they found his sense of "truth" somewhat hollow.

In the Preface to the 1851 edition of *Twice-Told Tales*, which he composed at the time Melville was working nearby on *Moby-Dick*, Hawthorne commented that his stories "have the pale tint of flowers that blossomed in too retired a shade—the coolness of a meditative habit, which diffuses itself through the feeling and observation of every sketch."[30]

On June 1, 1851, Melville echoed Hawthorne's Preface to *Twice-Told Tales* in commenting that "the calm, the coolness, the silent grass-growing mood in which a man ought always to compose,— that, I fear can seldom be mine." He followed this Transcendental reference to the organic conception of a work of art with a vigorous criticism of his own work: "Dollars damn me. . . . What I feel most moved to write, that is banned,—it will not pay. Yet, altogether, write the other way I cannot. So the product is a final hash, and all my books are botches."[31] In November, after Hawthorne had read *Moby-Dick*, Melville wrote to him about imperfections in the design of his new book: "You were archangel enough to despise the imperfect body, and embrace the soul," he said. "Once you hugged the ugly Socrates because you saw the flame in the mouth, and heard the rushing of the demon,—the familiar,—and recognized the sound; for you have heard it in your own solitudes."[32]

Melville's new self-consciousness over form in the letters to Hawthorne is in striking opposition to his earlier apparent indifference to planning in *Mardi*. In what is probably an autobiographical passage from that book, Melville speaks through the philosopher Babbalanja in describing the writing methods of the great Mardian poet Lombardo:

> When Lombardo set about his work, he knew not what it would
> become. He did not build himself in with plans; he wrote right on;
> and so doing got deeper and deeper into himself; and like a res-
> olute traveler, plunging through baffling woods, at last was
> rewarded for his toils.[33]

Replacing this oversimplified conception of a Transcendental artist
who writes solely by instinct, Melville found in Hawthorne a more
complex living model, who could balance poetic intuition with critical judgment and employ techniques of fiction to gain preconceived
effects.

Partly as a result of Melville's fortunate association with
Hawthorne, *Moby-Dick* is Melville's most carefully constructed novel.
Hawthorne's influence on the form of this novel not only served to
intensify Transcendental elements already inherent in Melville's work
but also infused it with a profoundly anti-Transcendental metaphysical darkness.[34]

In the central dramatic conflict between Ahab and the white
whale, Melville sums up the total relationship between mortal man
and the primal powers of creation. By comparison, even Hawthorne's
masterpiece, *The Scarlet Letter*, though more symmetrical in structure
than any of Melville's novels, is far more restricted in scope than the
all-encompassing panorama of experience portrayed in *Moby-Dick*. In
this novel—or, more properly, prose epic—Melville retained a breadth
of vision that has its closest parallels in the expansive concepts of
nature and the human mind in the writings of Emerson and
Whitman while infusing this work with Hawthorne's characteristic
blackness. Thus the novel emerged as a pivotal work, one that incor-
porates some of the Emersonian ideas that initially enchanted
Melville, yet at the same time reveals their inadequacies in certain
contexts—inadequacies that Hawthorne's blackness helped enable
Melville to perceive.

In conception, the well-plotted voyage of *Moby-Dick* is in some
respects an inversion of the chartless voyage of *Mardi*, which until
1850 was Melville's most ambitious book and his only failure.
Melville had described *Mardi* as a "Romance of Polynesian
Adventure" with "a story wild enough, I assure you, and with a meaning too."[35] Similarly, he characterized *Moby-Dick* to Richard Bentley as
"a romance of adventure founded upon certain wild legends in the
Southern Whale Fisheries, and illustrated by the author's own personal experiences of two years and more, as a harpooneer."[36] The
terms "romance," "adventure," and particularly "wild" suggest not
only a link between the two novels, but also a further association

with a Transcendental conception of the poet's frenzy, which Emerson expressed in "The Poet":

> The poet knows that he speaks adequately then only when he speaks somewhat wildly, or 'with the flower of the mind'; not with the intellect used as an organ, but with the intellect released from all service and suffered to take its direction from its celestial life; or as the ancients were wont to express themselves, not with intellect alone but with the intellect inebriated by nectar.[37]

Like *Mardi*, *Moby-Dick* begins with a straightforward narrative of seafaring adventure that satirizes the Transcendental religion. In contrast to Taji's naive reliance on intuition which motivates him to jump ship in mid-ocean, Ishmael's more plausible desire for spiritual renewal impels him to go to sea. "It is a way I have of driving off the spleen," Ishmael confides:

> Whenever I find myself growing grim about the mouth; whenever it is damp, drizzly November in my soul; whenever I find myself involuntarily pausing before coffin warehouses, and bringing up the rear of every funeral I meet . . . then, I account it high time to get to sea as soon as I can. (3)

Ishmael, whose Biblical name links sailors to outcasts, is more direct than Taji in criticizing the basis for the Transcendental faith in a benevolent nature. Though a Platonist, like Taji, in associating the sea with thought, Ishmael nevertheless respects the validity of sensory experience and warns "pantheists" against the dangers of excessive meditation, especially if they are in "the tops" one hundred fifty feet above the deck:

> "Why, thou monkey," said a harpooner to one of these lads, "we've been cruising now hard upon three years, and thou hast not raised a whale yet. Whales are scarce as hen's teeth whenever thou art up here." Perhaps they were; . . . but lulled into such an opium-like listlessness of vacant, unconscious reverie is this absent-minded youth by the blending cadence of waves with thoughts, that at last he loses his identity; takes the mystic ocean at his feet for the visible image of that deep, blue, bottomless soul, pervading mankind and nature; and every strange, half-seen, gliding, beautiful thing that eludes him; every dimly-discovered, uprising fin of some undiscernible form, seems to him the embodiment of those elusive thoughts that only people the soul by continually flitting through it. . . . But while this sleep, this dream is

on ye, move your foot or hand an inch; slip your hold at all; and
your identity comes back in horror. Over Descartian vortices you
hover. And perhaps, at midday, in the fairest weather, with one
half-throttled shriek you drop through the transparent air into
the summer sea, no more to rise for ever. Heed it well, ye
Pantheists! (159)

Despite Ishmael's realistic warning, the narrator recedes into the
background midway in the narrative, like Taji in *Mardi*, as Melville in
the guise of the omniscient author portrays the world of the mind. In
Mardi, the shift in focus occurs when Taji and his companions, representing the faculties of the mind, set out on a tour of the Mardian
Isles, a microcosm of the world, in search of the blonde Yillah, whom
Taji regards as a symbol of Transcendental beauty. By comparison, in
Moby-Dick the shift occurs with the introduction of Captain Ahab,
who directs his world-ship, the *Pequod*, in a single-minded pursuit of
the white whale—whose whiteness containing all colors of the spec-
trum—epitomizes the totality of nature. Ishmael's philosophical
meditation on the evil of whiteness in the chapter "The Whiteness of
the Whale" should be read in relation to the larger context of the
novel, in which white is the predominant color. It is represented in
the whalebone fittings on the *Pequod*, a dark, melancholy, cannibal of
a craft; in Ahab's livid scar and artificial whalebone leg setting off his
bronzed complexion; in dark Fedallah's turban of white braided hair
resembling a second moon when he is aloft at night searching for the
whale;[38] in the waves shining in the calm moonlit sea like silver
scrolls; in the mysterious lightness of the squid and in the St. Elmo's
fire, balls of electricity that illuminate the masts of the Pequod with
a pallid glow; in the sun that brightens the sea during the climactic
days of struggle with the whale, and finally in the creamy pool of
foam that marks the spot where the *Pequod* sinks.

   While *Moby-Dick* is, among other things, about the search for an
albino whale, it is more certainly about the incredible dangers of
myth-making. The whale symbolizes nothing. He is there, an occasion for others to create myths. Melville states as much in a chapter
entitled "Moby Dick." Generations of critics have busied themselves
with worrying about what the whale symbolizes. They should have
been concerned with the creator of meanings, Captain Ahab, for it is
he, not Melville, who has created the Transcendental "meaning" of
the white whale. He fashions the myth of Moby Dick to give substance, form, and value to his own unhappy life, and he is aided in
his efforts by other mariners who in turn project their own meanings
onto the animal. His entire crew begins to share his vision, until the

men are nothing more than instruments of their captain. When they agree to impose Ahab's arbitrary categories on the world, they give up their own free will—whatever that may be—and join him in a mass suicide. Narcissus saw his reflection in the pool and drowned trying to merge with it. In the first chapter Ishmael tells us that the meaning of Narcissus is "the key to it all" (5). And he further admits that going out to sea and committing himself to the watery world is his "substitute for pistol and ball" (3).

From Ahab's extreme Transcendental perspective, the white whale of *Moby-Dick* represents nature in its totality. Although the characters in the novel conjure their own self-revealing phantoms of the whale, the creature Melville describes in the climax of the narrative is a synthesis of their varied associations of the beauty, savagery, and final mystery of nature. When the *Pequod* finally encounters Moby Dick at the end of a long, circuitous voyage, the whale first appears as a Transcendental symbol suggesting the apparent—from a Transcendental perspective—unity of the spiritual and mythical with the visible world:

> A gentle joyousness—a mighty mildness of repose in swiftness, invested the gliding whale. Not the white bull of Jupiter swimming away with ravished Europa clinging to his graceful horns; his lovely, leering eyes sideways intent upon the maid; with smooth bewitching fleetness, rippling straight for the nuptial bower in Crete; not Jove, not that great majesty Supreme! did surpass the glorified White Whale as he so divinely swam. (548)

In contrast to this impression of a "glorified White Whale," gliding with "a mighty mildness of repose in swiftness," Melville next describes Moby Dick as an embodiment of the primal animal forces in nature:

> And thus, through the serene tranquilities of the tropical sea, among waves whose hand-clappings were suspended by exceeding rapture, Moby Dick moved on, still withholding from sight the full terrors of his submerged trunk, entirely hiding the wrenched hideousness of his jaw. But soon the fore part of him slowly rose from the water; for an instant his whole marbleized body formed a high arch, like Virginia's Natural Bridge, and warningly waving his bannered flukes in the air, the grand god revealed himself, sounded, and went out of sight. (548–549)

The two passages are complementary in suggesting the polarity of the natural with the supernatural, the real with the ideal. "An inevitable dualism bisects nature," Emerson wrote in "Compensation," "so that each thing is a half, and suggests another thing to make it whole . . ."[39]

Yet in "Moby Dick" Melville warns us at length that the so-called symbolism of the white whale has been manufactured by ignorant sailors and a mad captain. The chapter begins shortly after Ahab, on the quarter deck, has enlisted the aid of the crew in his search. Ishmael admits that "a wild, mystical, sympathetical feeling was in me; Ahab's quenchless feud seemed mine" (179). He admits to sharing his captain's vision. The he begins to recount the growth of the Moby Dick legend.

Moby Dick had been widely known among whalers, although mainly through rumor; few sailors had actually seen him in the flesh. There had, however, been a number of recent incidents in the sperm-whale fishery "marked by various and not unfrequent instances of great ferocity, cunning, and malice in the monster attacked" (180). Ishmael emphasizes the superstitiousness of sailors and stresses that in their work whalemen come across "whatever is appallingly astonishing in the sea" (180).

> No wonder, then, that ever gathering volume from the mere transit over the widest watery spaces, the outblown rumors of the White Whale did in the end incorporate with themselves all manner of morbid hints, and half-formed foetal suggestions of supernatural agencies, which eventually invested Moby Dick with new terrors unborrowed from anything that visibly appears. (181)

Coupled with Moby Dick's "supernatural" aspect is the general range of myths surrounding sperm whales. Ishmael notes that even such great naturalists as Cuvier have believed these fantastic legends. Sailors who fish for right whales feel that "to chase and point lance at such an apparition as the Sperm Whale was not for mortal man" (182). When these myths are married to the prodigiousness of Moby Dick, the following is the result:

> One of the wild suggestions referred to, as at last coming to be linked with the White Whale in the minds of the superstitiously inclined, was the unearthly conceit that Moby Dick was ubiquitous; that he had actually been encountered in opposite latitudes at one and the same instant of time. (182)

If this sense of ubiquity is coupled with the seeming indestructibility that Moby Dick has displayed in his many encounters with whaling vessels,

> it cannot be much matter of surprise that some whalemen should go still further in their superstitions; declaring Moby Dick not only ubiquitous, but immortal (for immortality is but ubiquity in time). (183)

In the eyes of superstitious sailors Moby Dick has become a god, capable of ubiquity and immortality. Ishmael thus gives a lesson in how myths and gods are created; the other half of the lesson shows that an individual can respond to such a myth and use it as a projection of his disturbed mind.

Pitted against the whale in a death struggle is Captain Ahab, who more than any previous character in Melville's fiction is a composite portrait of mortal man, a representation of Emerson's "god in ruins." Ahab's cracked nature corresponds to his physical disfigurement. The first mention of the skipper in the novel suggests the Transcendental symbolism of his character: "He's a grand, ungodly, god-like man, Captain Ahab," says Captain Peleg, part owner of the *Pequod*, to Ishmael. "Ahab's above the common; Ahab's been in colleges, as well as 'mong the cannibals; been used to deeper wonders than the waves; fixed his fiery lance in mightier, stranger foes than whales" (79). Ishmael's first glimpse of Ahab, once the *Pequod* is at sea, reveals Ahab's white scar that divides his body like "a perpendicular seam":

> He looked like a man cut away from the stake, when the fire has overrunningly wasted all the limbs without consuming them, or taking away one particle from their compacted aged robustness. His whole high, broad form seemed made of solid bronze, and shaped in an unalterable mould, like Cellini's cast Perseus. Threading its way out from among his gray hairs, and continuing right down one side of his tawny scorched face and neck, till it disappeared in his clothing, you saw a slender rod-like mark, lividly whitish. It resembled that perpendicular seam sometimes made in the straight, lofty trunk of a great tree, when the upper lightning tearingly darts down it, and without wrenching a single twig, peels and grooves out the bark from top to bottom, ere running off into the soil, leaving the tree still greenly alive, but branded. (123)

Ahab's wound represents the mark of moral imperfection in man, which Emerson described in "Compensation" as inherent in the character of great epic heroes:

> Achilles is not quite invulnerable; the sacred waters did not wash the heel by which Thetis held him. Siegfried, in the Nibelungen, is not quite immortal, for a leaf fell on his back whilst he was bathing in the dragon's blood, and that spot which it covered is mortal. And so it must be. There is a crack in everything God has made.[40]

With such a crack extending from Ahab's head to the white whalebone leg, the skipper resembles a living figurehead for the doomed *Pequod*, as he stands on his quarter-deck steadying his bone leg in an auger hole and "looking straight out beyond the ship's ever-pitching prow" (124).

On his previous voyage Captain Ahab had lost a limb to Moby Dick, who "reaped away Ahab's leg, as a mower a blade of grass in the field. No turbaned Turk, no hired Venetian or Malay, could have smote him with more *seeming* malice" (184; italics mine). "Seeming" is the key word. To Ahab the whale "seems" malicious; but Moby Dick is no more malicious than he is godlike. His reaping of Ahab's leg is an animal's dumb, instinctive response to danger. In order to give himself significance, Ahab must imagine malice on the part of the whale. He feels chosen as the victim of fate, and his only response— given his nature—is to rebel outwardly and strike back at the universe, which he sees incarnate in Moby Dick.

> Small reason was there to doubt, then, that ever since that almost fatal encounter, Ahab had cherished a wild vindictiveness against the whale, all the more fell for that in his frantic morbidness he at last came to identify with him, not only all his bodily woes, but all his intellectual and spiritual exasperations. The White Whale swam before him as the monomaniac incarnation of all those malicious agencies which some deep men feel eating in them, till they are left living on with half a heart and half a lung. That intangible malignity which has been from the beginning. . . . All that most maddens and torments; all that stirs up the lees of things; all truth with malice in it; all that cracks the sinews and cakes the brain; all the subtle demonisms of life and thought; all evil, to crazy Ahab, were visibly personified, and made practically assailable in Moby Dick. He piled upon the whale's white hump the sum of all the general rage and hate felt by his whole

race from Adam down; and then, as if his chest had been a mortar, he burst his heart's hot shell upon it. (184)

Ahab's monomania demands that Moby Dick be more than a whale. He is "intent on an audacious, immitigable, and supernatural revenge" (186). For him the White Whale "might have seemed the gliding great demon of the seas of life" (187). And the success with which Ahab is able to get the crew to share his projections of value onto a mute albino whale is stated by Ishmael in the last lines of the chapter:

> For one, I gave myself up to the abandonment of the time and the place; but while yet all a-rush to encounter the whale, could see naught in that brute but the deadliest ill. (187)

Ishmael, like the rest of the crew, comes to see the whale as Ahab wishes.

In the most famous lines of his April letter to Hawthorne Melville writes:

> There is the grand truth about Nathaniel Hawthorne. He says NO! in thunder; but the Devil himself cannot make him say yes. For all men who say yes, lie; and all men who say no,—why they are in the happy condition of judicious, unencumbered travelers in Europe; they cross the frontiers into Eternity with nothing but a carpet-bag,—that is to say, the Ego. Whereas those yes-gentry, they travel with heaps of baggage, and, damn them! they will never get through the Custom House. What's the reason, Mr. Hawthorne, that in the last stages of metaphysics a fellow always falls to swearing so? I could rip an hour.[41]

Ishmael—not Ahab the extreme Transcendentalist—stands, not on the side of those who would project value onto the world or would tell how things are or should be made, but with the skeptic who takes an ironic stance and carries nothing with him but his ego, or sense of self. For he has now taken an even stronger post-Transcendentalist position. The individual must bring nothing to confront the world but his unfettered self. In order to "get through" the Custom House, or the universe, it is necessary to travel light, as Ishmael does. But if a man comes, as does Ahab, to impose a vision, the customs inspector will never let him through.

Melville puts it more gently in the letter than in his novel. There the yes-sayer or projector of value, Ahab, not only fails to make it past the metaphorical Custom House, he even leads an entire crew through the doors of eternity. Ahab expresses figuratively the ideas stated in Melville's letters, and it is through his example that Melville most effectively discredits Transcendentalism and Emerson.

Emerson postulated a universe whose ultimate reality is a spirit from which all of nature derives. All natural creations are therefore equally endowed with divinity. If each person is potentially divine, then the godlike in the individual man can be explored, exploited, and developed, with no limitation other than the size of the universe, which is infinite. There is no definable limitation or sanction on the will of an individual who develops his potential divinity. The "great man" has charisma. This quality was recognized and positively encouraged by Emerson and Whitman. Other men follow the "great man" because he is the model for their own quest for greatness or, at least, meaning. They are potentially he. This works well if he is a good man as well as a great one. But with no sanctions, the man of infinite will can do whatever he wants.

Ahab is the embodiment of Emerson's "great man," limited by nothing, privileged to do anything. His boundless hatred for the whale and sense of emancipation from conventional morality cause him to stand apart in the manner of the Transcendentalist hero.

> That inscrutable thing is chiefly what I hate; and be the white whale agent, or be the white whale principal, I will wreak that hate upon him. Talk not to me of blasphemy, man; I'd strike the sun if it insulted me . . . Who's over me? Truth hath no confines. (164)

Ahab's charisma is apparent in the very way the crew follows him many times in dangerous situations with a veneration bordering on worship and cosmic fear. A single word or gesture from their captain turns them from any thought of dissatisfaction or glimmer of mutiny.

But Ahab is not a "good" man. He has shut himself off from the most basic Romantic virtue—empathy. Even when his instincts lead him toward affection for and identification with another character— as in several confrontations with Starbuck and Pip near the end—he deliberately stiffens himself against his feelings. He tries to be all mind, all calculation. Ahab best characterizes himself during his conversation with the carpenter:

> Hold; while Prometheus [the blacksmith] is about it, I'll order a complete man after a desirable pattern. Imprimis, fifty feet high in his socks; then, with his chest modelled after the Thames Tunnel; then, legs with roots to 'em, to stay in one place; then,

arms three feet through the wrist; no *heart* at all, brass forehead, and about a quarter of an acre of fine brains; and let me see—shall I order eyes to see outwards? No, but put a sky-light on top of his head to illuminate inwards. (470; italics mine)

On June 1, 1851 Melville wrote to Hawthorne, "I stand for the heart. To the dogs with the head!"[42] Melville is on the side of heart and emotion; this statement to Hawthorne underscores the same attitude in the book. All of Ahab's *passion* is connected to his monomania; it is utterly one-directional and has nothing to do with compassion.

Ahab is a figure of genuine magnificence, but in his delusion of a malign universe, embodied in Moby Dick, that has done him in; he uses his unchecked will to lead an entire crew to its death. In the nature of human relationships lesser men will follow a greater if he can supply their unconscious with the proper image. Emerson was right in this. But Melville contends that Emerson did not take sufficiently seriously the possibility that spirit could be anything other than "good." Although Emerson admitted the existence of evil, it was more than counterbalanced cosmically by a prevailing tendency to goodness in the collective actions of the world. He thus gave the impression to his contemporaries and to following generations that evil was of no great consequence in human events. By making Ahab the symbol of Transcendental magnificence, but by giving him a flaw he felt that Emerson had not foreseen, Melville dramatizes this fallacy of the Transcendentalist position. Ironically, he accepts Emerson's prime image, while rejecting the value Emerson placed upon it.[43]

Melville's naysayer is Ishmael, who comes to the whaling ports in a state of deep depression and disorientation, lacking a sense of values to project upon the world. Indeed, his sense of identity is so stunted at this point that he must gain it from contacts with stronger men such as Queequeg and Ahab. Ishmael's stance is a peculiar blend of alienation and empathy. Because he lacks a strong sense of self (the cardinal sin for Emerson), Ishmael can understand the positions of all the characters in *Moby-Dick* and yet become permanently infected by none. To realize intuitively that man's greatest weakness is his need for illusion and to realize as well that any projection of meaning onto the world will result in illusion necessitates a withdrawal from the traditional affairs of men to a kind of personal confrontation between the individual, naked self and the world as naked object. Ishmael is the new post-Transcendentalist man, whose ultimate ironic detachment will become a commonplace pose for the new "hero" of the "realistic" novel.

Even the concepts of fate and free will that Ishmael proposes are consistent with Melville's total position. These ideas, illustrated most clearly in the chapter entitled "The Mat-Maker," are an attempt to avoid a fixed abstract stance. Neither fate nor free will as philosophical poles governs human events, nor can one compromise a position by blending the two according to some formula and arriving at a set of regulations for running a life. The warp of necessity and the woof of free will still need "Queequeg's impulsive, indifferent sword" of chance to complete the pattern. Chance "has the last featuring blow at events" (215). An unknown factor in the play of reality makes it impossible ever to describe or control it. Melville attempts to take a position that is in reality no position at all. No metaphysic is sufficient to account for the way things are; to this stage of Romanticism more than any other, all metaphysical systems are ultimately illusory. Ishmael therefore adds the final irony of chance, and Melville then exemplifies this position by having Ishmael's survival depend on an incredible series of coincidences.

For instance, Queequeg decides he is going to die, and he requests that a coffin be built for him and it is, but he then decides to live. A sailor falls from the mast and the original life buoy is thrown in after him, and both sink to the bottom. Queequeg's coffin is then caulked and used as a replacement for the life buoy. On the second day of the chase Fedallah is dragged from Ahab's boat and killed; Ahab thus becomes harpooneer, the lead oarsman is put into Fedallah's place, and everyone moves up a notch. Because Ishmael is in Starbuck's crew, he is on the *Pequod* rather than in another boat on the sea, and on the final day of the chase he is picked to replace the oarsman on Ahab's boat. Because he has the seat near the block, he is knocked overboard. Because the chase goes away from him, he can float free of the battle, and when the *Pequod* sinks, he is just far enough away not to be sucked down in the whirlpool. And here is the pièce de résistance: to help Ishmael float an entire day and night on the ocean is Queequeg's coffin, which, because it has been caulked to make a life buoy, has not sunk to the bottom along with everything else.

None of these incidents is inevitable. They are all a matter of the most intricate and yet random kind of coincidence. Chance certainly "has the last featuring blow" at Ishmael. And that is the point. There is no figuring out why things happen—they just do. But the most seductive danger of the Transcendentalist point of view is described best in Melville's June 1 letter to Hawthorne. It is the feeling that man is at one with the world, as expressed in a passage I previously quoted in chapter three:

> In reading some of Goethe's sayings, so worshiped by his votaries,
> I came across this, 'Live in the all.' That is to say, your separate
> identity is but a wretched one,—good; but get out of yourself,
> spread and expand yourself, and bring to yourself the tinglings of
> life that are felt in the flowers and the woods, that are felt in the
> planets Saturn and Venus, and the Fixed Stars. What nonsense!
> Here is a fellow with a raging toothache. 'My dear boy,' Goethe
> says to him, 'you are sorely afflicted with that tooth; but you
> must *live in the all*, and then you will be happy!' As with all great
> genius, there is an immense deal of flummery in Goethe, and in
> proportion to my own contact with him, a monstrous deal of it in
> me.[44]

The "all" feeling corresponds to the Freudian "oceanic" feeling. The
danger Melville felt in it, apart from its sentimentality, was that it
deluded one into thinking life is comfortable and without danger.
Throughout the book the readers are warned that to become unwary
brings with it the danger of death. At the end of "The Mast-Head,"
Melville sounds a cautionary note regarding the situation of the pre-
cariously poised dreaming Ishmael: "While this sleep, this dream is
on ye, move your foot or hand an inch; slip your hold at all; and your
identity comes back in horror," and that "perhaps, at midday, in the
fairest weather, with one half-throttled shriek you drop through that
transparent air into the summer sea, no more to rise for ever. Heed it
well, ye Pantheists!" (159). It is possible without distortion to translate "pantheist" to mean Transcendentalist. Later on, in "The Try-
Works," Ishmael is lulled into dropping his guard by the speeding
motion of the ship and by the brightness of the fire that melts the
blubber. He almost overturns the ship while he stands at the tiller,
immobilized. After finally recovering, he gives us this warning:

> Look not too long in the face of the fire, O man! Never dream
> with thy hand on the helm! Turn not thy back to the compass;
> accept the first hint of the hitching tiller; believe not the artificial
> fire, when its redness makes all things look ghastly. To-morrow, in
> the natural sun, the skies will be bright; those who glared like
> devils in the forking flames, the morn will show in far other, at
> least gentler, relief; the glorious, golden, glad sun, the only true
> lamp—all others are but liars! (424)

Feelings of calm should alert men to the dangers of living that lie
around the corner. But instead, for the early Romantic visionaries
these "all" experiences were meaningful, "mystical" moments—
meaningful in themselves and leading to no positive action other

than sitting back and feeling "the tinglings of life that are felt in the flowers and the woods." Melville is quite aware of the attractiveness of the "all" feeling, for he writes in his second postscript of the June 1 letter:

> N.D. This "all" feeling, though, there is some truth in. You must often have felt it, lying on the grass on a warm summer's day. Your legs seem to send out shoots into the earth. Your hair feels like leaves upon your head. This is the all feeling. But what plays the mischief with the truth is that men will insist upon the universal application of a temporary feeling or opinion.[45]

And yet, characteristically, Melville is quick to counter the attractiveness with a caution against overemphasizing its significance.

In *Moby-Dick* calm is always a mask for dark and mysterious terrors. Melville emphasizes the contrasts at the heart of existence, the calms at the heart of storms. On the day before Moby Dick's arrival, the sea and air seem quieter than ever. Melville does not claim that this is in the design of things, that there is a plan that makes these contrasts a part of the essential fabric of the world's structure. To the contrary, there is no design at all. The problem is that this mystical sense of oneness makes man relax just a bit too much. For Melville, man's prime virtue is his ability to perceive the world as object and to survive in it on the basis of his clear perceptions. If one feels so comfortable that he ignores the possibilities of danger inherent in just living in the world, he is in trouble.

After realizing that there is no profit in imposing value on a world without value, one must accept things as they are and retreat from the field of battle. In the ecstasy of sperm-squeezing Ishmael realizes the transience of his Transcendent emotion:

> Would that I could keep squeezing that sperm for ever! For now, since by many prolonged, repeated experiences, I have perceived that in, all cases man must eventually lower, or at least shift, his conceit of attainable felicity; not placing it anywhere in the intellect or the fancy; but in the wife, the heart, the bed, the table, the saddle, the fire-side, the country. (416)

This hope has at least some possibility of attainment, for it is tied to the physically tangible. The kind of quest undertaken by Ahab has none. Yet Ahab's quest is magnificent nonetheless.

Perhaps it is the imagination that must ultimately be condemned. Imagination must lead to illusion, as it does with Ahab. For that matter, so must art. And yet it is the use of imagination and will that led the earliest Romantics out of their sloughs of despond to seek value in the world. That has been the continuous paradox of all Romantic "solutions" until now. Imagination redeems, but it also destroys. For someone like Melville there is no choice left but lowering his gaze. That is why Ishmael concludes, years after his experience on the *Pequod*, that retreat is the only possibility left for him; and that is why Melville retreated during the latter half of his own life. Retreat and acceptance, but no struggle. In Melville's final and most awful irony, Billy Budd goes to the yardarm blessing the name of his executioner.

In the imperfect world of mortal mind that Melville portrays in *Moby-Dick*, Ahab represents the defective human will, defying nature rather than submitting to its power. Having lost a leg in a previous encounter with Moby Dick, Ahab is motivated to seek physical revenge against the white whale. His underlying hostility, however, is directed against the primal cause of his imperfection. Although he stands before the crew "with a crucifixion in his face, in all the nameless regal overbearing dignity of some mighty woe," his defiance is absolute (124). Addressing the spiritual power of nature, he says:

> I now know thee, thou clear spirit, and I now know that thy right worship is defiance. To neither love nor reverence wilt thou be kind; and e'en for hate thou canst but kill; and all are killed. No fearless fool now fronts thee. I own thy speechless, placeless power; but to the last gasp of my earthquake life will dispute its unconditional, unintegral mastery in me. (507)

Ahab first discloses his basic intention in "The Quarter Deck."[46] After telling the crew that they are to search for "a white-headed whale with a wrinkled brow and a crooked jaw," he says:

> Hark ye yet again,—the little lower layer. All visible objects, man, are but as pasteboard masks. But in each event—in the living act, the undoubted deed—there, some unknown but still reasoning thing puts forth the mouldings of its features from behind the unreasoning mask. If man will strike, strike through the mask! How can the prisoner reach outside except by thrusting through the wall? To me, the white whale is that wall, shoved near to me. Sometimes I think there's naught beyond. But 'tis enough. He tasks me; he heaps me; I see in him outrageous strength, with an inscrutable malice sinewing it. That inscrutable thing is chiefly what I hate; and be the white whale agent, or be the white whale principal, I will wreak that hate upon him. Talk not to me of blasphemy, man; I'd strike the sun if it insulted me. (164)

The speech sets forth the basic Emersonian conception that "the Universe is the externisation of the soul."[47] The soul one perceives behind external appearances, however, ultimately proves to be one's own self. Nature, as Emerson said in "The American Scholar," provides "the keys which unlock my thoughts and make me acquainted with myself."[48] Ahab's tirade, therefore, is the inciting force for a tragic drama of the human will. Out of harmony with nature, the skipper passes judgment on himself in a manner that applies the Emersonian doctrine of compensation. "A man cannot speak but he judges himself," Emerson said in "Compensation": "With his will or against his will he draws his portrait to the eye of his companions by every word."[49] Because Ahab rebels against nature, which to him seems governed by an inscrutable malice, he condemns himself to inevitable destruction. The sun that Ahab in his egotism would strike if it insulted him is more than a pagan deity to be worshipped or defied; it is an Emersonian and Platonic symbol of moral truth, which most men are unable to face.[50]

Melville depicts the deterioration of Ahab's character in two broad stages, which suggest the identification of the self with nature. In chapter 41, "Moby Dick," Ahab sees the whale no longer as a pasteboard mask or wall shoved near, but as "the monomaniac incarnation of all those malicious agencies which some deep men feel eating in them, till they are left living on with half a heart and half a lung" (184). The whale, to Ahab, becomes a personification of "all that cracks the sinews and cakes the brain; all the subtle demonisms of life and thought; all evil . . ." (184). Consumed by his monomania, Ahab ultimately projects his own uncontrolled ego on the universe. In chapter 99, "The Doubloon," he looks at the gold coin he had nailed to the mast as a reward for the sailor who first sees Moby Dick and meditates on its cryptic design:

> There's something ever egotistical in mountain-tops and towers, and all other grand and lofty things; look here,—three peaks as proud as Lucifer. The firm tower, that is Ahab; the volcano, that is Ahab; the courageous, the undaunted, and victorious fowl, that, too, is Ahab; all are Ahab; and this round gold is but the image of the rounder globe, which, like a magician's glass, to each and every man in turn but mirrors back his own mysterious self. (431)

Ahab's reference to the circle of nature recalls Emerson's aphorism in "Circles" that "the eye is the first circle," which represents "the Unattainable, the flying Perfect, around which the hands of man can never meet."⁵¹ At this point in Ahab's quest, however, the skipper's conception is exactly antithetical to the extreme position of the Transcendental priest, who rejects the orthodox forms of religion and views nature as a window through which one can see God. Emerson had stated this belief in *Nature* in the often-quoted lines:

> Standing on the bare ground,—my head bathed by the blithe air and uplifted into infinite space,—all mean egotism vanishes. I become a transparent eyeball; I am nothing; I see all; the currents of the Universal Being circulate through me; I am part and parcel of God.⁵²

If Melville through Ahab rejects this Neoplatonic idea on the grounds that it exceeds the limits of mortal comprehension, he nevertheless portrays in Ahab's relation to nature the Emersonian perspective that "the whole of nature is a metaphor of the human mind. The laws of moral nature answer to those of matter as face to face in a glass."⁵³

Seeing in nature nothing more than an image of himself, Ahab resembles Narcissus, whose story Melville mentions early in the narrative as "the key to it all":

> And still deeper the meaning of that story of Narcissus, who because he could not grasp the tormenting, mild image he saw in the fountain, plunged into it and was drowned. But that same image, we ourselves see in all rivers and oceans. It is the image of the ungraspable phantom of life; and this is the key to it all. (5)

When Ahab finally encounters the whale, he has his private vision of Moby Dick as he peers over the side of his whaleboat, in the attitude of Narcissus looking at his image in the water:

> But suddenly as he peered down and down into its depths, he profoundly saw a white living spot no bigger than a white weasel, with wonderful celerity uprising, and magnifying as it rose, till it turned, and then there were plainly revealed two long crooked rows of white, glistening teeth, floating up from the undiscoverable bottom. It was Moby Dick's open mouth and scrolled jaw; his vast, shadowed bulk still half-blending with the blue of the sea. The glittering mouth yawned beneath the boat like an open-doored marble tomb; and giving one sidelong sweep with his steering oar, Ahab whirled the craft aside from this tremendous apparition. (549)

In this moment of encounter between Ahab and the whale, Melville dramatizes the meeting of the human mind and its metaphor in nature. Ahab, however, is destroyed not so much by the whale's intent as by his own actions in a manner Emerson describes in "Compensation":

> Every opinion reacts on him who utters it. It is a thread-ball thrown at a mark, but the other end remains in the thrower's bag. Or rather it is a harpoon hurled at the whale, unwinding, as it flies, a coil of cord in the boat, and, if the harpoon is not good, or not well thrown, it will go nigh to cut the steersman in twain or to sink the boat.[54]

Similarly, Melville portrays Ahab's death as punishment for a curse. In his last speech Ahab cries:

> "I turn my body from the sun . . . from hell's heart I stab at thee; for hate's sake I spit my last breath at thee. Sink all coffins and all hearses to one common pool: and since neither can be mine, let me then tow to pieces, while still chasing thee, though tied to thee, thou damned whale: Thus, I give up the spear!" (571–572)

Retribution is instant and complete:

> The harpoon was darted; the stricken whale flew forward; with igniting velocity the line ran through the groove;—ran foul. Ahab stooped to clear it; he did clear it; but the flying turn caught him round the neck, and voicelessly as Turkish mutes bowstring their victim, he was shot out of the boat, ere the crew knew he was gone. Next instant, the heavy eye-splice in the rope's final end flew out of the stark empty tub, knocked down an oarsman, and smiting the sea, disappeared in its depths. (565)

This climactic struggle with its Transcendental implications is the crucial action in *Moby-Dick*. Considered as a tragic reversal of fortune, it has little resemblance to the melodramatic death scene in Hawthorne's *The Scarlet Letter*, in which the Rev. Dimmesdale makes a public confession of his sins on the scaffold before he dies in the arms of Hester Prynne. Despite Melville's indebtedness to Shakespearean tragedy, especially *King Lear*, in the employment of theatrical devices in parts of the novel and also in the obvious parallel of Ahab and his cabin boy Pip to Lear and his fool, Ahab's death is clearly related to the pattern of retribution in Emerson's "Compensation," in which words have the significance of deeds.

Unlike Lear and other tragic heroes, who repent or achieve a measure of painful insight before they die, Ahab dies as the unredeemed victim of his own thought and language.

In describing the moral law that governs the universe, Emerson chose to emphasize in his essays the absolute rewards of living in harmony with nature. The punishment, however, for such a mind as Ahab's at war with the scheme of things, is inevitable. "The beautiful laws and substances of the world," Emerson said in "Compensation," "persecute and whip the traitor. . . . You cannot recall the spoken word, you cannot wipe out the foot-track, you cannot draw up the ladder, so as to leave no inlet or clew. Some damning circumstance always transpires."[55] Ahab, who symbolically turns his back on the sun before he curses and hurls his harpoon, fits Emerson's concept of human frailty.[56]

Melville magnifies the central conflict between Ahab and the whale in two important ways, each of which applies Transcendental ethical and aesthetic principles to the pattern of tragic fiction. In the first place, the exhaustive exposition of the whaling industry, which Melville derived largely from his reading, presents a microcosm of experience, a part of man's work that epitomizes the whole of life. The expansiveness of Melville's treatment suggests itself in the preliminary section entitled "Extracts," which begins with the Biblical reference, "And God created great whales," and concludes with the whaler's song:

> "Oh, the rare old Whale, mid storm and gale
>   In his ocean home will be
> A giant in might, where might is right,
>   And King of the boundless sea." (xxviii)

Within the narrative, the chapters on various aspects of whaling lore serve to separate stages of the action and to give the impression of the passage of time in the long sea voyage of the *Pequod*. Unlike the digressive essays in Melville's earlier plotless novels, these chapters serve in part to relieve dramatic tension and at the same time to add to the texture of the novel as a whole. Melville indicates this functional purpose in the opening lines of the chapter entitled "Cetology," which follows the introduction of Ahab and his officers, once the *Pequod* is at sea:

> Already we are boldly launched upon the deep; but soon we shall be lost in its unshored, harborless immensities. Ere that come to pass; ere the *Pequod's* weedy hull rolls side by side with the bar-

nacled hulls of the leviathan; at the outset it is but well to attend
to a matter almost indispensable to a thorough appreciative
understanding of the more special leviathanic revelations and
allusions of all sorts which are to follow. (134)

Secondly, as in all great tragedies, the fall of the tragic "hero," here
Ahab, has as an inevitable consequence the destruction of his world,
or more particularly, the unnatural order he has imposed on men.
Ahab's world is the *Pequod*, named after an extinct tribe of
Massachusetts Indians and representing in the novel the perils of
conformity.[57] Although the mates and harpooneers—"knights and
squires" in Ahab's floating realm—display competence and even
heroism in the performance of the hazardous routines of whaling,
they are so caught up in their traditional beliefs, customs, and super-
stitions that they are either unable or unwilling to oppose Ahab's
unbending will. As a result of their lack of self-reliance, they become
in effect his accomplices and share his punishment in the sinking of
the *Pequod*. Only Ishmael, an orphan in this degenerate society, is
saved.

Yet, earlier in *Moby-Dick*, Melville offers a radically different
assessment of the concept of Emersonian self-reliance. In "Self-
Reliance," Emerson argues that existence is based on the soul's affinity with God, and, although it does not require withdrawal from society, friends, and family, it does involve a spiritual solitariness. He
writes: "Society everywhere is in conspiracy against the manhood of
every one of its members."

> Society is a joint-stock company in which the members agree for
> the better securing of his bread to each shareholder, to surrender
> the liberty and culture of the eater. The virtue in most request is
> conformity. Self-reliance is its aversion. It loves not realities and
> creators, but names and customs.[58]

Emerson argues that society—the "joint-stock company" of
mankind—necessitates an ethics of self-trust because it has made us
afraid of "truth," "fortune," "death," and "each other."[59] We are "par-
lor soldiers," he says, and "shun the rugged battle of fate, where
strength is born."[60] Life demands a certain stoicism, so that men may
realize "they are not leaning willows, but can and must detach themselves." Emerson suggests that a person inform his friends of the
necessity that he must be himself and that they must love him for
who he is. He admits that this may give pain to one's closest com-
rades: "Yes, but I cannot sell my liberty and my power, to save their

sensibility. Besides, all persons have their moments of reason, when they look out into the region of absolute truth; then will they justify me and do the same thing."[61] For Emerson, there are two ways of satisfying duties: one is reflexive, absolving debts toward family or friends; the other is direct, wherein a man absolves himself to himself, which Emerson regards as the strictest responsibility of all, for he finds divinity in man's setting himself as his own taskmaster.

Although Melville did not annotate "Self-Reliance" in his copy of Emerson's *Essays*,[62] Merton Sealts has established that he read sections of the book not long before, and possibly during, his composition of *Moby-Dick*.[63] Without the discovery of new evidence it is impossible to determine if Melville had Emerson's essay specifically in mind when he wrote "The Monkey-rope," chapter 72 of his most famous novel, but it is nevertheless clear he was at least responding to the kind of contemporaneous philosophical position most frequently associated with Emerson.

This chapter begins with Ishmael relating the hazards of fastening blubber hooks to the "scarfs" of a recently harpooned whale—a task to which he and Queequeg are assigned. He explains that fastening the hooks is a dangerous job, even within the context of the whaling industry, for the harpooneer must walk the slippery back of the whale, which is submerged most of the time. To add to Queequeg's peril, circumstances require that he stay upon the whale during the entire "flensing" (stripping) operation. Aboard the *Pequod*, the practice is to attach the harpooneer who does this work to the man who pulls the oar immediately behind him—so Ishmael is linked to Queequeg by means of a line, called a monkey-rope. Ishmael contemplates his precarious position:

> So strongly and metaphysically did I conceive of my situation then, that while earnestly watching his [Queequeg's] motions, I seemed distinctly to perceive that my own individuality was now merged in a joint stock company of two: that my free will had received a mortal wound; and that another's mistake or misfortune might plunge me into unmerited disaster and death. Therefore, I saw that here was a sort of interregnum in Providence; for its even-handed equity never could have sanctioned so gross an injustice. And yet still further pondering— while I jerked him now and then from between the whale and the ship, which would threaten to jam him—still further pondering, I say, I saw that this situation of mine was the precise situation of every mortal that breathes; only, in most cases, he, one way or other, has this Siamese connection with a plurality of other mortals. If your banker breaks, you snap; if your apothecary by mis-

take sends you poison in your pill, you die. True, you may say
that, by exceeding caution, you may possibly escape these and
the multitudinous other evil chances of life. But handle
Queequeg's monkey-rope heedfully as I would, sometimes he
jerked it so, that I came very near to sliding overboard. Nor could
I possibly forget that, do what I would, I had only the management of one end of it. (320)

Ishmael finds that his bond with Queequeg reflects the interdepend-
ence of all men, drawing the conclusion that no man can survive
without the aid of others—a far cry from the concept of "the joint-
stock company" in "Self-Reliance," where Emerson suggests that such
a relationship is optional, with men at liberty to "detach themselves"
whenever their individuality becomes threatened by the proximity of
others. Ishmael conceives of his situation "strongly and metaphysi-
cally"—as well he might, for several times he is almost pulled over the
side. To add to Queequeg's difficulties, the sharks persist in attacking
the whale while Daggoo and Tashtego continue to butcher them with
whaling-spades. Ishmael muses that Queequeg's situation is every
man's: "those sharks, your foes; those spades, your friends; and what
between sharks and spades you are in a sad pickle and peril, poor lad"
(321).

While Emerson emphasizes man's free will in forging his own
destiny, Melville underscores the close bond that exists between
Ishmael and Queequeg, even going so far as to say that they "were
wedded" (320).[64] As usual, however, Ishmael conceives of his personal experience as analogous to a larger truth: the "hempen bond" that
brings "dangerous liabilities" with it implies exactly what Ishmael has
suggested earlier, in chapter 60: "All men live enveloped in whale
lines" (281).

Encapsulating its theme, Emerson's epigram to "Self-Reliance"
comes from Persius: "Ne te quaesiveris extra."[65] This phrase can be
interpreted several ways: do not seek yourself outside yourself; do not
ask any opinion but your own; and, when read in the context of the
essay as a whole, do not yield your sense of personal identity to the
"conspiracy" of human society. In "The Monkey-rope" we see two
loving "brothers," Ishmael and Queequeg, bound together by a cord
that means life and death to them. Ishmael, the orphan, outcast, and
wanderer, goes to sea to discover something of the meaning and mystery of life. Instead, he finds himself alone in the middle of a vast,
pitiless ocean. Has he learned from his explorations? Perhaps not.
Perhaps the novel suggests that the brotherly love of Queequeg beto-
kened by the coffin that saves Ishmael's life—and the parental love

represented by the *Rachel*—make sense of an existence that persist-ently seems bereft of meaning. But another interpretation might lead Ishmael, and, by extension, the reader, to consider another metaphorical monkey-rope in the novel that unites two other men— Starbuck and Ahab—inferring a completely different, and far more tragic meaning.

Yet Melville prepares for his climax with episodes that radiate out-ward in significance as Transcendental symbols suggesting the whole of the novel in the part. This tendency accounts for the variety of conflicting interpretations in the past forty years based on the close analysis of individual episodes interpreted as microcosms of the novel, such as Father Mapple's sermon, which Ishmael alone hears; "The Town Ho's Story," which Ahab and his officers do not hear; the varied reactions of Ahab and the crew to the cryptic doubloon; and the Parsee's prophecy, which the climax fulfills.

Melville, however, has artfully worked into the structure of his episodes limitations in point of view and inversions of details that serve as much to disguise as to reveal his climax and the Transcendental and anti-Transcendental themes. For example, the symbolic picture that Ishmael alone sees upon entering the Spouter Inn near the beginning of the novel is a reversal of the final scene, in which the white whale rams and sinks the *Pequod* in daylight on a calm sea. Ishmael's description of the painting stresses instead the darkness of the whale and the violent action of a storm:

> But what most puzzled and confounded you was a long, limber, portentous, black mass of something hovering in the center of the picture over three blue, dim, perpendicular lines floating in a nameless yeast. . . . It's the Black Sea in a midnight gale.—It's the unnatural combat of the four primal elements.—It's a blasted heath.—It's a Hyperborean winter scene.—It's the breaking-up of the ice-bound stream of Time. But at last all these fancies yielded to that one portentous something in the picture's midst. That once found out, and all the rest were plain. . . .
>
> In fact, the artist's design seemed this: a final theory of my own, partly based upon the aggregated opinions of many aged persons with whom I conversed upon the subject. The picture rep-resents a Cape-Horner in a great hurricane; the half-foundered ship weltering there with its three dismantled masts alone visible; and an exasperated whale, purposing to spring clean over the craft, is in the enormous act of impaling himself upon the three mast-heads. (12–13)

The alternative explanations leading to the image of a whale in the masts comprise a fictional technique that Melville probably learned from Hawthorne, who also uses inversions with more than one possible meaning. Midway in *The Scarlet Letter*, Hawthorne foreshadows his climax by having his guilt-ridden minister stand at midnight with Hester and Pearl on the scaffold in a symbolic tableau, repeated at the end in broad daylight before an astonished public. The essential difference in the inversions of the two writers lies in the greater flexibility of Melville's symbols. Where the dominant images in *The Scarlet Letter* are the scaffold and Hester's "A," static reminders of human frailty, in *Moby-Dick* the central image is the white whale, whose varied qualities serve to reflect in the course of the narrative each character to himself.

Even when Melville's narrative appears to be clear and uncomplicated, separate incidents nearly always take on cryptic significance when considered in relation to the larger context of the novel. Melville's analogies between nature and the mind are linked; they lose significance when considered individually. As an illustration, Father Mapple's sermon on Jonah and the whale is a vigorous retelling of the familiar story of God's divine interference in nature. The character of the preacher, modeled after Father Edward Taylor, an acquaintance of Emerson and occasional visitor to the Transcendental Club, displays a dramatic fervor and spiritual detachment, especially in his conclusion, which can be described as a mariner's version of Emerson's doctrine of self-reliance.[66] "Delight is to him," Father Mapple says, "a far, far upward, inward delight—who against the proud gods and commodores of this earth, ever stands forth his own inexorable self" (48). This defiance of worldly authority parallels Emerson's rejection of conformity in "Self-Reliance": "Nothing is at last sacred but the integrity of your own mind."[67] Father Mapple's assertion of the spiritual primacy of the self also is in harmony with Emerson's attack on religious orthodoxy in "The Divinity School Address" (1838), which led conservative Unitarians such as the Rev. Andrews W. Norton to accuse Emerson of heresy.[68]

Like Emerson, Father Mapple declares his independence of the ways of men while retaining his allegiance to God:

> Delight is to him, whom all the waves of the billows of the seas of the boisterous mob can never shake from his sure Keel of the Ages. And eternal delight and deliciousness will be his, who coming to lay him down, can say with his final breath—O Father!— chiefly known to me by Thy rod—mortal or immortal, here I die. I have striven to be Thine, more than to be this world's or my

own. Yet this is nothing; I leave eternity to Thee; for what is man
that he should live out the lifetime of his God? (48)

Father Mapple's submission to the divine will contrasts with Ahab's
rejection of all authority—man's law as well as nature's—in his mad
pursuit of the white whale.[69] Ishmael, however, in the chapter following the sermon worships the wooden idol Yojo with his cannibal
friend Queequeg and says, "'I'll try a pagan friend, since Christian
kindness has proved but hollow courtesy" (51). Furthermore, the last
vessel the *Pequod* meets before encountering Moby Dick is the tragic
whaler *Delight*, five of whose crewmen lost their lives in a struggle
with a different kind of whale from the one described by Father
Mapple.

Considered in the context of the novel, Father Mapple's sermon
is part of the larger argument on the limitation of human comprehension. Father Mapple's spiritual detachment, however, is also part
of Ishmael's worldview, which contrasts sharply with Ahab's egotisti-
cal vision, and contributes to Ishmael's spiritual rebirth.

By contrast, the moral and spiritual limitations of Ahab's world
aboard the doomed *Pequod* are perhaps brought into sharpest focus
preceding the climax in the enigmatic chapter, "The Doubloon," in
which the leading characters meditate on the meaning of Ahab's gold
coin. As the central figure in his realm, Ahab sees his unbounded ego.
The other characters, however, reflect conventional attitudes of civilized and savage man, which illustrate their readiness to conform.
Starbuck, the competent though cautious first mate, reveals the lack
of conviction underlying his orthodox religious point of view in his
remarks on the coin:

> A dark valley between three mighty, heaven-abiding peaks, that
> almost seem the Trinity, in some faint earthly symbol. So in this
> vale of Death, God girds us round; and over all our gloom, the
> sun of Righteousness still shines a beacon and a hope. If we bend
> down our eyes, the dark vale shows her mouldy soil; but if we lift
> them, the bright sun meets our glance half way to cheer. Yet, oh,
> the great sun is no fixture; and if, at midnight, we would fain
> snatch some sweet solace from him, we gaze for him in vain! This
> coin speaks wisely, mildly, truly, but still sadly to me. I will quit it,
> lest Truth shake me falsely. (432)

Concerned with spiritual values, but insecure in his faith, Starbuck
lacks the will to turn Ahab aside from his revengeful pursuit of Moby
Dick.

In contrast to Starbuck, whose underlying skepticism suggests the Transcendentalist criticism of Unitarianism, the two other mates reflect amoral civilized attitudes. Stubb, the second mate, is a pipe-smoking hedonist, who makes himself and his men comfortable and takes perils as they come with a journeyman's indifference. Looking at the design on the doubloon, he concludes: "There's a sermon now, writ in high heaven, and the sun goes through it every year, and yet comes out of it all alive and hearty. Jollily he, aloft there, wheels through toil and trouble; and so, allow here, does jolly Stubb. Oh, jolly's the word for aye: Adieu, Doubloon" (433). On the other hand, Flask, the third mate, is an unimaginative materialist who regards the doubloon as merely "a round thing made of gold, and whoever rais-es a certain whale, this round thing belongs to him. . . . It is worth sixteen dollars, that's true; and at two cents the cigar, that's nine hundred and sixty cigars."[70]

The two pagan harpooneers who next examine the coin do not use words but reveal in their gestures corresponding limitations in their attitudes. Queequeg suggests the animal nature of man as he tries to compare figures on the coin with those tattooed on parts of his body. "What says the Cannibal? As I live he's comparing notes," Flask observes with a civilized man's air of superiority (434). Fedallah, the white-turbaned Parsee, represents primitive superstition with its intuition of evil. He "makes a sign to the sign and bows himself" (434). Again Flask remarks, "There is a sun on the coin—fire wor-shipper, depend on it" (434). Actually, in worshiping fire and the sun, Zoroastrian symbols for Ahura Mazda, the god of light and morality, Fedallah is opposed to Ahab, who would strike the sun. The Parsee as a man of primitive faith contrasts with his master, who defies God. In the conclusion of the chapter, the wisely mad Pip sums up the scene with a cryptic reference to the variety of human perception: "I look, you look, he looks; we look, ye look, they look" (434). "Upon my soul," Flask tells himself, "he's been studying Murray's Grammar: Improving his mind, poor fellow" (434). Flask's ironic comment recalls Melville's reference to the Muse as a pale usher who likes to dust his old grammars as a reminder of man's mortality.

In a broad sense, the entire novel is a series of self-revealing looks at nature and the whale. Even Ahab in his meditation on the secret knowledge of the "black and hooded head" of a whale in the chapter entitled "The Sphynx" can perceive the Transcendental dimensions and the worldly limitations of his search.[71] "O Nature, and O soul of man!" he says, "how far beyond all utterance are your linked analo-gies! not the smallest atom stirs or lives on matter, but has its cunning duplicate in mind" (312). The linked analogies lead Ahab to self-

destruction, since the nature he perceives wears the colors of his egotism. For Emerson, however, the "shadow of the soul, or *other me*" is
the basis for positive action, in which what he called "mean egotism"
vanishes. "I run eagerly into this resounding tumult," he said in "The
American Scholar." "I grasp the hands of those next me, and take my
place in the ring to suffer and to work, taught by an instinct that so
shall the dumb abyss be vocal with speech. I pierce its order; I dissi-
pate its fear, I dispose of it within the circuit of my expanding life."[72]

Interspersed among events presenting the interactions of the
Pequod's crew is a separate series of episodes that dramatize the pro-
gressive isolation of Ahab and his world from the broader society of
mankind. During the voyage, the *Pequod* has visits or "gams" with
nine other whaling ships for the primary purpose of obtaining information about Moby Dick. Like the islands Taji visits in *Mardi*, the
gams present separate points of view toward nature, all of which are
unacceptable to Ahab. These contribute to the composite impression
of the whale in the climax and to the total worldview of the novel.

The *Pequod*'s first gam is with the appropriately named *Albatross*,
a mysterious bleached craft whose skipper accidentally drops his
speaking trumpet as his ship passes by in silence. The action suggests
both the difficulty of communication between the self and the outer
world and the essential enigma of nature. Denied the information he
seeks, Ahab cries "in his old lion voice,—'Up helm! Keep her off
round the world.'"[73] In the next two gams, however, Melville presents
sharply contrasted religious views, each dramatizing the whale as an
instrument of divine power. "The Town Ho's Story," which Ishmael
tells to friends in Lima after the sinking of the *Pequod*, portrays Moby
Dick as an agent of God's justice in destroying the mate Radney and
ending his tyranny over Steelkilt, a rebellious, self-reliant seaman.
Ahab's ignorance of this exemplum of a reasonable God's interference
in the affairs of men provides an instance of dramatic irony that sets
off Ishmael's view of nature from Ahab's decidedly *unnatural* monomania. Ahab, however, obtains his first lead on Moby Dick in the
next gam with the *Jeroboam*, a ship quarantined with an epidemic
and tyrannized by a religious fanatic, who calls himself Gabriel. To
the mad seaman, whose zeal is as intense and irrational as Ahab's
hatred, the white whale is "the Shaker God incarnated" (316). After
hearing of a wrathful God who destroys a blasphemer, Ahab
exchanges curses with Gabriel and continues his search.

In contrast to these mystical and religious views, the next three
gams offer to Ahab and his crew three wordly attitudes towards
nature represented by whalers from Germany, France, and England.
Instead of repeating the thinly disguised references to European civi-

lization in *Mardi*, in which islands represent national attitudes, Melville employs inversions in this second series of gams as instruments of satire. He represents German culture with its emphasis on metaphysical learning in terms of its opposite: Derek De Deer (or "die Deern" in low German for "girl"), skipper of the ship *Jungfrau* expresses to Ahab "complete ignorance of the White Whale."[74] He is interested, however, in oil for his lamp, which Ahab provides; but he later tauntingly pitches it overboard as the *Pequod's* whaleboats race his crew to harpoon a whale. In describing the climax of this episode, Melville contrasts the awkwardness of Derick's crew with the superior skill and instinctive knowledge of the *Pequod's* men:

> But so decided an original start had Derick had, that spite of all their gallantry, he would have proved the victor in this race, had not a righteous judgement descended upon him in a crab which caught the blade of his midship oarsman. While this clumsy lubber was striving to free his white-ash, and while, in consequence, Derick's boat was nigh to capsizing, and he thundering away at his men in a mighty rage;—that was a good time for Starbuck, Stubb and Flask. With a shout, they took a mortal start forwards, and slantingly ranged up on the German's quarter. (354)

An instant later, Derick chooses to hazard "what to him must have seemed a most unusually long dart" (355):

> But no sooner did his harpooner [sic] stand up for the stroke, than all three tigers—Queequeg, Tashtego, Dagoo—instinctively sprang to their feet, and standing in a diagonal row, simultaneously pointed their barbs; and darted over the head of the German harpooner, their three Nantucket irons entered the whale. (355)

In the "blinding vapors of foam and white-fire" of the stricken whale's headlong rush, Derick and his harpooneer fall overboard. "Don't be afraid, my butter-boxes," Stubb cries, as his craft shoots by the floundering Germans; ye'll be picked up presently—all right—I saw some sharks astern—St. Bernard's dogs, you know—relieve distressed travellers" (355).

Similarly, Melville satirizes French culture with its reputation for political finesse, refinement, and worldly experience by means of irony. The whaler *Bouton de Rose*, or Rosebud, whose skipper is a former cologne manufacturer out on his first voyage, has alongside two whale corpses. Their unsavory odor, "worse than an Assyrian city in the plague," is a subject of humor to Stubb; but of the French sailors,

Melville writes: "All their noses upwardly projected from their faces like so many jib-booms" (405). Although their spokesman, a Guernseyman with a knowledge of English, can find a name for the white whale, "Cachalot Blanche," this particular whale is beyond his experience. "Never heard of such a whale," he tells Stubb (404). Taking advantage of the inexperience of the French, Stubb through clever negotiation obtains the shriveled second whale, which he knows despite its odor, contains precious ambergris used in making perfume.

With his single-minded desire for complete knowledge of the white whale, Ahab—an Emersonian Faust—understandably remains in his cabin during the gams with the *Jungfrau* and *Bouton de Rose*; but he makes his first visit aboard another whaler in the gam with the *Samuel B. Enderby* of London. Its skipper, having lost an arm in an encounter with Moby Dick, has the knowledge born of practical experience, which Ahab also has. In describing this gam, Melville is direct in his portrayal of British common sense, which contrasts with Ahab's monomania. Captain Boomer's description of his encounter with Moby Dick anticipates Ahab's final struggle with the whale. Both episodes occur in broad daylight, although Boomer does not turn his back on the pervading Platonic sun; both characters receive injuries from their harpoons, but the English captain shows no malice and lives to relate his experience. "As I was groping at midday," Boomer says,

> with a blinding sun, all crown-jewels; as I was groping, I say, after the second iron, to toss it overboard—down comes the tail like a Lima tower, cutting my boat in two, leaving each half in splinters; and, flukes first, the white hump backed through the wreck, as though it were all chips. We all struck out. To escape his terrible flailings, I seized hold of my harpoon-pole sticking in him, and for a moment clung to that like a sucking fish. But a combing sea dashed me off, and at the same instant, the fish, taking one good dart forwards, went down like a flash; and the barb of that cursed second iron towing along near me caught me here (clapping his hand just below his shoulder). (439)

Unlike Captain Ahab, who resents his mortal imperfection, Captain Boomer replaces his amputated arm with a club-hammer fashioned on the end of a whalebone and engages in jovial banter with the ship's doctor, a rationalist.

In the portrait of the ship's doctor, however, Melville satirizes the pretension of scientific learning. Like Surgeon Cuticle in *White-Jacket*,

Dr. Bunger is sure of himself even though his logic extends beyond the boundaries of his own experience. Possessing limited data on whales and having no firsthand knowledge of Moby Dick, he nevertheless urges Captain Boomer to have a second try. "Do you know, gentlemen," Dr. Bunger reasons, "that the digestive organs of the whale are so inscrutably constructed by Divine Providence, that it is quite impossible for him to completely digest even a man's arm. And he knows it too. So that what you take for the White Whale's malice is only his awkwardness. For he never means to swallow a single limb."[75] Unimpressed by this logical speculation about a whale's motives, Captain Boomer prudently declines. "No thank ye, [Dr.] Bunger, he's welcome to the arm he has, since I can't help it, and didn't know him then; but not to another one" (441). Together the captain and the doctor represent an empirical approach to nature, with experience supplemented by logic but restrained by prudence.

Rejecting this practical accommodation of man to nature, with its tolerance of human imperfection, Ahab comments that the white whale is "all a magnet" to him and angrily breaks off the interview. "Is your captain crazy?" Boomer whispers to Fedallah, who is the sailor least capable aboard the *Pequod* of answering objectively (441–442). The Parsee merely puts a finger to his lips and follows Ahab into the whaleboat. Melville concludes this episode with a description of Ahab's proud indifference to a sane acceptance of man's mortal state: "In vain the English captain hailed him," Melville writes. "With back to the stranger ship, and face set like a flint to his own, Ahab stood upright till alongside of the Pequod" (442). Ishmael, however, in a later gam with the *Samuel Enderby* after the sinking of the *Pequod* finds the English ship "a noble craft in every way. . . . It was a fine gam we had, and they were all trumps—every soul on board" (444).

The last three gams dramatize the alternative results of man's relation to nature, none of which is acceptable to Ahab. In the seventh gam, the *Bachelor's* captain indicates his disbelief in Moby Dick and reports his amazing good luck. The ship's hold is full, its decks lined with extra casks of sperm oil, and its crew engaged in revelry:

> On the quarter-deck, the mates and harpooners were dancing with olive-hued girls who had eloped with them from the Polynesian isles; while suspended in an ornamented boat, firmly secured aloft between the foremast and mainmast, three Long Island negroes, with glittering fiddlebows of whale ivory, were presiding over the hilarious jig. Meanwhile, others of the ship's company were tumultuously busy at the masonry of the try-

works, from which the huge pots had been removed. You would
have almost thought they were pulling down the cursed Bastille,
such wild cries they raised, as the now useless brick and mortar
were being hurled into the sea. (494)

In rejecting the hospitality of the *Bachelor*, Ahab suggests the sterility
of his single-minded quest: "Thou art a full ship and homeward
bound, thou sayest; well, then, call me an empty ship and outward-
bound. So go thy ways, and I will mine. Forward there: Set all sail and
keep her to the wind!" (495).

Following his refusal to be distracted by the fellowship of the fortunate, Ahab meets in the *Rachel* a ship which has encountered the
white whale and is involved in a search for a missing whaleboat with
the captain's son aboard. Captain Gardiner, whom Ahab knows,
comes aboard the *Pequod* to request help in his search for the lost
crewmen. Though Ahab refuses, the *Rachel* later picks up Ishmael,
lone survivor of the *Pequod*. In contrast to the crewmen of the *Rachel*,
with their partial knowledge of Moby Dick and primary concern for
human welfare, the men aboard the *Delight*, the last whaler the
Pequod meets, possess the sorrow and wisdom of tragic insight.
Having recovered the body of one of five crewmen lost in an
encounter with the white whale, the stunned skipper warns, "God
keep thee, old man," when Ahab arrogantly waves his harpoon (541).
The episode is an ironic reversal of the conclusion of Father Mapple's
sermon with its celebration of the delight of the faithful.

In the nine gams, Ahab's world of the *Pequod* dominated by the
skipper's perverse will is set off against the prevalent attitudes and
alternative reactions to nature that characterize the normal human
condition. The chapter immediately following the meeting with the
Delight and preceding the climactic encounter with Moby Dick brings
into focus the central paradox of Ahab's total isolation from the outer
world. "Is Ahab, Ahab?" the skipper meditates:

> Is it I, God, or who, that lifts this arm? But if the great sun move
> not of himself; but is as an errand-boy in heaven; nor one single
> star can revolve, but by some invisible power; how then can this
> one small heart beat; this one small brain think thoughts; unless
> God does that beating, does that thinking, does that living, and
> not I. By heaven, man, we are turned round and round in this
> world, like yonder windlass, and Fate is the handspike. (545)

In this passage, the most willful of skippers suddenly reverses his
position and denies his own power of self-determination. Whether

willful or merely a victim of fate, Ahab considers himself to be one or the other and is therefore out of harmony with the delicate balance of opposites or polarities in man and nature. His singleness of view contrasts with Ishmael's reconciliation of the determiners of action in his meditation on mat making. Free will, Ishmael says, plies "her shuttle between given threads" from "the straight warp of necessity," while "chance, though restrained in its play" by necessity and free will "by turns rules either, and has the last featuring blow at events" (215).

With an integrated vision, Ishmael comes closer to reality than does Ahab, whose irreconcilable contradictions dramatize the crack in Ahab's nature. Inevitably, Ahab and his world-ship meet in the white whale the nemesis that Emerson describes in "Compensation":

> It would seem there is always this vindictive circumstance steal-
> ing in at unawares even into the wild poesy in which the human
> fancy attempted to make bold holiday and to shake itself free of
> the old laws, this backstroke, this kick of the gun, certifying that
> the law is fatal; that in nature nothing can be given, all things
> are sold.[76]

Melville's factual basis for the sinking of the *Pequod* is Owen Chase's account of the actual destruction of the whaler *Essex* by an eighty-five foot sperm whale which rammed it twice on the same day, November 20, 1820.[77] Melville first heard of this remarkable incident in 1841, while he was serving on the whaler *Acushnet*.[78] In April 1851, when he had nearly completed *Moby-Dick*, his father-in-law, Judge Lemuel Shaw, gave him a copy of Chase's narrative to refresh his memory.[79] Melville, however, portrays a symbolic three-day struggle between the men of the *Pequod* and Moby Dick, who flails apart their pursuing whaleboats, and after snapping Ahab's line destroys the *Pequod* in a single headlong attack. At the moment Moby Dick rams the *Pequod*, the crew display a noticeable inability to act. Caught in the middle of their routines, they look up immobilized:

> From the ship's bows, nearly all the seamen now hung inactive;
> hammers, bits of plank, lances, and harpoons, mechanically
> retained in their hands, just as they had darted from their vari-
> ous employments; all their enchanted eyes intent upon the
> whale, which from side to side strangely vibrating his predesti-
> nating head, sent a broad band of overspreading semicircular
> foam before him as he rushed. Retribution, swift vengeance, eter-
> nal malice were in his whole aspect, and spite of all that mortal
> man could do, the solid white buttress of his forehead smote the

ship's starboard bow, till men and timbers reeled. Some fell flat
upon their faces. Like dislodged trucks, the heads of the harpooners aloft shook on their bull-like necks. Through the breach,
they heard the waters pour, as mountain torrents down a flume.
(571)

Though Melville employed details from Chase's narrative, such as
the apparent malice of the whale which plunged under the sinking
ship, the crew of the Essex recovered from their shock and reacted
with far more presence of mind than the transfixed characters aboard
the *Pequod.* "I ordered the men to cease pumping," Chase wrote, "and
every one to provide for himself; seizing a hatchet at the same time,
I cut away the lashings of the spare boat, which lay bottom up across
two spars directly over the quarter deck, and cried out to those near
me to take her as she came down."[80] As a result of such vigorous
emergency measures, all hands aboard the *Essex* escaped into the
boats.[81]

By contrast, the officers of the *Pequod* talk largely to themselves in
the moment of disaster, revealing the inadequacy of their civilized
attitudes. First Mate Starbuck is beset by self-doubt:

"The whale, the whale! Up helm, up helm! Oh, all ye sweet powers of air, now hug me close! Let not Starbuck die, if die he must,
in a woman's fainting fit. Up helm, I say—ye fools, the jaw! the
jaw! Is this the end of all my bursting prayers? all my life-long
fidelities?" (570)

On the other hand, Stubb, the second mate, is imprisoned by his conventional hedonistic attitude. With a foolish consistency, he forces
himself to grin at death:

"I grin at thee, thou grinning whale! Who ever helped Stubb, or
kept Stubb awake, but Stubb's own unwinking eye? And now
poor Stubb goes to bed upon a mattress that is all too soft; would
it were stuffed with brushwood! I grin at thee, thou grinning
whale!" (570–571)

The third mate, Flask, is resigned to his fate and says, "Oh, Stubb, I
hope my poor mother's drawn my part-pay ere this; if not, few cop-
pers will now come to her, for the voyage is up" (571). Like Ahab, the
officers are condemned by their language.

Even after Moby Dick strikes the *Pequod,* no one acts to save himself. The ship goes down with the pagan harpooners still at their

lookout posts, unable to comprehend their own imminent destruction:

> For an instant, the tranced boat's crew stood still; then turned. "The ship? Great God, where is the ship?" Soon they through dim, bewildering mediums saw her sidelong fading phantom, as in the gaseous Fata Morgana; only the uppermost masts out of water; while fixed by infatuation, or fidelity, or fate, to their once lofty perches, the pagan harpooners still maintained their sinking look-outs on the sea. And now, concentric circles seized the lone boat itself, with all its crew, and each floating oar, and every lance-pole, and spinning, animate and inanimate, all round and round in one vortex, carried the smallest chip of the *Pequod* out of sight. (572)

The total inaction of the *Pequod's* crew dramatizes the defect Emerson perceived in traditions, customs, and conventions which degrade the individual. In "The American Scholar," Emerson presents action as one of three important influences on "Man Thinking"; it enables him to live with the polarities of nature.

As the *Pequod* disappears beneath the sea, the harpooneer Tashtego, still at his post, pins a white sky-hawk to the mast in a dramatic final gesture. "And so," Melville writes, "the bird of heaven, with archangelic shrieks, and his imperial beak thrust upwards, and his whole captive form folded in the flag of Ahab, went down with his ship, which, like Satan, would not sink to hell till she had dragged a living part of heaven along with her, and helmeted herself with it" (572). The irony of Tashtego's symbolic gesture is that the crew of the *Pequod*, like the bird, were captives shrouded in Ahab's flag.

Ishmael's rescue provides the final polarity in this drama concerning the earthly limitations of Transcendental aspirations. Though saved in the end by chance, he floats on a coffin–life buoy made by his cannibal friend Queequeg and is picked up by the humanitarian crew of the *Rachel*. He survives, however, with a balanced worldview, and he lives in harmony with nature:

> Now small fowls flew screaming over the yet yawning gulf; a sullen white surf beat against its steep sides; then all collapsed, and the great shroud of the sea rolled on as it rolled five thousand years ago. (572)

For Melville the vast universe is indifferent. The universe he creates, whose king and whose inhabitants are taken so seriously for so many pages, is swallowed up quietly and quickly at the end, and nothing is left of the drama that has been enacted. To claim indifference for the universe is not to say that it is hostile; it is just to say that men should not conduct their battles against it. For these battles have no business being fought; they can never be won, since men are the only ones fighting. And yet, if pushed hard enough, the universe may, in recoil, destroy, or at least swallow. But if men wait long enough, it will swallow them anyway.

Melville's achievement in balancing the Transcendental perspective and Hawthorne's "power of blackness"—the inherent limitations of the human condition—mark a major development in the history of the American novel. With its tragic form and symbolism reflecting the Emersonian doctrine of compensation, Melville's greatest novel provides an insight into the farthest reaches of the mortal mind, dramatizing its quest for an integrated moral vision. Because Melville chose to focus on the absolute conditions of the present moment, his novel illuminates the essential polarities of the age.

Chapter Five

A Hell-Fired Rural Bowl of Milk: Melville's *Pierre* and Transcendental Rebellion

H ERMAN MELVILLE PROBABLY WOULD HAVE LIKED TO SOLVE THE problems of the world as optimistically as Emerson did, but his experiences and his recognition of the limitations of the human condition seem to have made the Transcendental doctrine appear shallow and superficial to him at times. The doctrine did not offer any solace for the situation as he saw it:

> Watch yon little toddler, how long it is learning to stand by itself! First it shrieks and implores, and will not try to stand at all, unless both father and mother uphold it; then a little more bold, it must, at least, feel one parental hand, else again the cry and the tremble; long time is it ere by degrees this child comes to stand without any support. But, by and by, grown up to man's estate, it shall leave the very mother that bore it, and the father that begot it, and cross the seas. . . . There now, do you see the soul. In its germ on all sides it is closely folded by the world, as the husk folds the tenderest fruit; then it is born from the world-husk, but still now outwardly clings to it;—still clamors for the support of its mother the world, and its father the Deity. But it shall yet learn to stand independent, though not without many a bitter wail, and many a miserable fall.[1]

Melville has here established that man is the offspring of Deity and the world, or that he is partly natural and partly spiritual. This duality, only vaguely intimated in Emerson's doctrine, assumed the proportions of a real dilemma to Melville. Melville's discovery that man is alone in the universe, unaided by either God or the world, produced a growing bitterness and resentment in him that was reaching its culmination at the time he wrote *Pierre*. His acceptance of this bitter discovery was not calm or philosophical, but was accompanied with a heavy sense of the tragic:

> That hour of the life of a man when first the help of humanity fails him, and he learns that in his obscurity and indigence humanity hold him a dog and no man; that hour is a hard one, but not the hardest. There is still another hour which follows, when he learns that in his infinite comparative minuteness and abjectness, the gods are equally willing that he should starve in the street for all that either will do for him. Now cruel father and mother have both let go his hand, the little soul-toddler, now you shall hear his shriek and his wail, and often his fall. (296)

Melville believed that man must "learn to stand independent." In many respects, then, Melville would seem to be an adherent to Emersonian individuality. But where Emerson sees man as supported by both natural and spiritual worlds, Melville sees man as being left to his own self-sufficiency—forced to be a God unto himself, without being allowed to partake of the attributes of God: "Our God is a jealous God; he wills not that any man should permanently possess the least shadow of his own self-sufficient attributes" (261). For Melville, the real tragedy lies in the fact that man, forced to search within himself for the ultimate answer to his problems, can find no answer there:

> Deep, deep, and still deep and deeper must we go, if we would find out the heart of a man; descending into which is as descending a spiral stair in a shaft, without any end, and where that endlessness is only concealed by the spiralness of the stair, and the blackness of the shaft. (289)

No matter how much man may dive into himself in search of the elusive answer, Melville believed, he finds nothing short of inconclusiveness. Emerson described the same sort of soul-searching, but with the opposite result: "The deeper he dives into his privatest, secretest presentiment, to his wonder he finds this is the most acceptable, most public, and universally true."[2] Melville not only finds no universal truths at the end of the search, but he is also overcome by a sense of desolation and bereavement at the utter nothingness that confronts him:

> But, far as any geologist has yet gone down into the world, it is found to consist of nothing but surface stratified on surface. To its axis, the world being nothing but superinduced superficies. By

> vast pains we mine into the pyramid; by horrible gropings we
> come to the central room; with joy we espy the sarcophagus; but
> we lift the lid—and no body is there;—appallingly vacant as vast
> is the soul of a man! (285)

This vacancy and vastness of the soul would not have been so appalling to Melville if he had not been so attracted to Transcendentalism in the earlier years of his life. Lewis observes that it is the illusion or vision of innocence which stimulates a positive and original sense of tragedy.[3] If Melville had not at one time sought to believe in this vision himself, he would not have experienced such tragedy at its loss. There must be an original Eden if one is to experience a "fall" from it. Pessimism, therefore, is thus connected to optimism. If one expects little of the world, it is not difficult to find numerous things for which to be grateful. Perhaps in this respect, then, Melville and Emerson should be considered from a different perspective from that usually taken. Emerson compared the American world with the European world, and with the long panorama of history back to ancient times. Melville, on the other hand, with his minimum of classical education and with his middle-class American heritage, was prone to accept the ideals of American democracy as accomplished fact rather that as projected ideal. Thus, what he saw as reality fell far short of that which he had expected reality to be, and gave rise to the problem of appearances versus realities that serves as a theme for many of his works.[4] Emerson, on the other hand, cherished few real ideas about the "unintelligent brute force that lies at the bottom of society."[5] He expected little from reality, and consequently found much to exceed those expectations.[6] The end result is that Emerson appears to be an optimist, while Melville, the supreme idealist, is labeled the great pessimist based on his works following his transitional epic, *Moby-Dick*.

It was the Emersonian optimism, hope, and belief in innocence that produced the paradise that Melville had lost. Emerson asserts in *Nature* that "the advantage of the ideal theory over the popular faith is this, that it presents the world in precisely that view which is most desirable to the mind."[7] The ideal theory of Emerson *did* present the world in "precisely that view" which was "most desirable" to Melville, the idealist. But this theory proved to be disadvantageous to Melville, the realist, because theory and fact did not coincide. He indicated his disillusion when he said, "Faith and philosophy are air, but events are brass" (289). Emerson's belief in the mystical revelation of divine truth to men through intuition became a stumbling block for Melville. Emerson believed that man has access to all knowledge of the universal laws through the Over-Soul. Melville, however, saw the human mind not as an answerer of riddles, but as a riddle in itself:

> . . . the profounder emanations of the human mind, intended to illustrate all that can be humanly know of human life; these never unravel their own intricacies, and have no proper endings, but in imperfect, unanticipated, and disappointing sequels (as mutilated stumps), hurry to abrupt intermergings with the eternal tides of time and fate. (141)

"Fate" working through circumstance is unacceptable to the Transcendentalists, but it is an ever-recurring word in the text of Melville. Emerson minimized the influence of circumstance in the life of man almost to the point of complete negation: "The laws of the soul . . . execute themselves. They are out of time, out of space, and not subject to circumstance."[8] He sees history as being "an impertinence and an injury if it be any thing more than a cheerful apologue or parable of my being and becoming."[9] Melville, in contrast, was extremely conscious of the effects of history and circumstance on the individual. Much of what Melville refers to as "Fate" is actually the accumulated burden of a man's heritage:

> Sucked within the Maelstrom, man must go round. Strike at one end the longest conceivable row of billiard balls in close contact, and the furthermost ball will start forth, while all the rest stand still; and yet that last ball was not struck at all. So, through long previous generations, whether of birth or thoughts, Fate strikes the present man. Idly he disowns the blow's effect, because he felt no blow, and indeed, received no blow. (182)

Melville could not believe, as Emerson did, that "the man is all," and that nothing could damage him "but himself."[10] Even though a man's emotional reactions to a situation might harm him, he could not necessarily, according to Melville, control his responses. He saw many elements as being involved in a final result—elements of which a man was not only unaware, but over which, even if he were aware, he would have little control:

> In their precise tracings-out and subtile causations, the strongest and fieriest emotions of life defy all analytical insight . . . these are things not wholly imputable to the immediate apparent cause, which is only one link in the chain; but to a long line of dependencies whose further part is lost in the mid-regions of the impalpable air. (67)

Emerson maintained that "there is no need of struggles, convulsions, and despairs, of the wringing of the hands and the gnashing of the teeth." It was his belief that man miscreates his own evils by interfering with the "optimism of nature."[11] Such a theory would obviously be unacceptable to Melville, a man who believed that

> . . . in tremendous extremities human souls are like drowning men; well enough they know they are in peril; well enough they know the causes of that peril; nevertheless the sea is the sea, and those drowning men do drown. (303)

Although Melville did indicate that he believed man could occasionally see a flash of intuitive truth, the way in which man received this perception was quite opposite to the Emersonian type of revelation. In Emerson there is always the upward motion—the rising of man's soul to commune with the Divine:

> As a plant upon the earth, so a man rests upon the bosom of God; he is nourished by unfailing fountains, and draws at his need inexhaustible power. . . . Once inhale the upper air, being admitted to behold the absolute natures of justice and truth, and we learn that man has access to the entire mind of the Creator.[12]

And in another essay, Emerson states that "a more secret, sweet, and overpowering beauty appears to man when his heart and mind open to the sentiment of virtue. Then he is instructed in what is above him."[13] Not only is there an emphasis on man's ascension to revelation, but there is also a definite intimation of the light, or brightness, which accompanies there revelations: "The soul is light: where it is, is day; where it was, is night."[14] Compare Emerson's preceding descriptions, both as to directions and color, with those of Melville:

> The intensest light of reason and revelation combined, cannot shed such blazonings upon the deeper truths in man as will sometimes proceed from his own profoundest gloom. Utter darkness is then his light, and cat-like he distinctly sees all objects through a medium which is mere blindness to common vision. (169)

Melville intimates here that the deeper truths are not always fully revealed in man's radiant revelations; at times, in man's deepest despair, he finally perceives the true nature of things. Paradoxically, it is only when man reaches the bottom of the "depths" that he can perceive the "heights":

> It is the not impartially bestowed privilege of the more final
> insights, that at the same moment they reveal the depths, they
> do, sometimes, also reveal—though by no means so distinctly—
> some answering heights. But when only midway down the gulf,
> its crags wholly conceal the upper vaults, and the wanderer
> thinks it all one gulf of downward dark. (170)

Besides these differences in direction and color of intuitive
knowledge, Melville and Emerson also appear to disagree on the
effect that these revelations have on the receiver. Emerson sees this
intuitive revelation as a pleasant, even thrilling, event:

> We distinguish the announcements of the soul, its manifestations
> of its own nature, by the term *Revelation*. These are always attend-
> ed by the emotion of the sublime. . . . Every distinct apprehension
> of this central commandment agitates men with awe and delight.
> A thrill passes through all men at the reception of new truth. . . .
> Every moment when the individual feels himself invaded by it is
> memorable . . . a certain enthusiasm attends the individual's con-
> sciousness of that divine presence. The character and duration of
> this enthusiasm vary with the state of the individual, from an
> ecstasy and trance and prophetic inspiration . . . to the faintest
> glow of virtuous emotion.[15]

In contrast with the glowing description that Emerson offers of man's
joy, consider what Melville has to say:

> When suddenly encountering the shock of new and unanswer-
> able revelations, which he feels must revolutionize all the cir-
> cumstances of his life, man, at first, ever seeks to shun all con-
> scious definitiveness in his thoughts and purposes; as assured
> that the lines that shall precisely define his present misery, and
> thereby lay out his future path; these can only be defined by
> sharp stakes that cut into his heart. (92)

Melville sees man as a creature of habit, safe within the fortress of his
convictions. Even though a person may begin to realize, dimly, that
his most cherished beliefs are no longer valid, he still tries to defend
them both to others and to himself. Thus, realizations become
painful ordeals to be shunned rather than sought after.

The whole idea of a mystic type of revelation seems to have
appeared slightly ridiculous to Melville. He left little doubt about his
opinion on the subject when he said:

> For he who is most practically and deeply conversant with mysticism and mysteries; he who professionally deals with mysticisms and mysteries himself . . . is often inclined at the bottom of his soul to be uncompromisingly skeptical on all novel visionary hypotheses of any kind. It is only the no-mystics, or the half-mystics, who, properly speaking, are credulous. (354)

Melville found the Transcendental emphasis on revelations and the sovereignty of the soul, to the exclusion of such worldly and material items as experience, myopic. Though he seemed willing to admit that the soul contains some potentiality of assisting the intellect, he did not consider the soul as being as all-encompassing as Emerson believed it to be. In contrast, Melville declared:

> For though the naked soul of man doth assuredly contain one latent element of intellectual productiveness; yet never was there a child born solely from one parent; the visible world of experience being that procreative thing which impregnates the muses; self-reciprocally efficient hermaphrodites being but a fable. (259)

Apparently Melville did not share the opinion with Emerson that the history of genius and of religion in the nineteenth century would be a history of the Transcendental perspective.[16]

Emerson's belief that absolute virtue and absolute truth were obtainable through intuition, provided another stumbling block for Melville. Melville not only believed that absolute virtue and truth were unobtainable, but he also questioned the desirability of obtaining them even if it were possible to do so. Emerson's doctrine of self-reliance was based on the importance of man's acting upon his intuitive knowledge of truth: "if we follow the truth it will bring us out safe at last."[17] Melville doubted the validity of this statement, as the following passage from *Pierre* reveals:

> IN THOSE HYPERBOREAN REGIONS, to which enthusiastic Truth, and Earnestness, and Independence, will invariably lead a mind fitted by nature for profound and fearless thought, all objects are seen in a dubious, uncertain, and refracting light. Viewed through that rarefied atmosphere the most immemorially admitted maxims of men begin to slide and fluctuate, and finally become wholly inverted; the very heavens themselves being not innocent of producing this confounding effect, since it is mostly in the heavens that these wonderful mirages are exhibited.
>
> But the example of many minds forever lost, like undiscoverable Arctic explorers, amid those treacherous regions, warns us

> entirely away from them; and we learn that it is not for man to
> follow the train of truth too far, since by so doing he entirely loses
> the directing compass of his mind; for arrived at the pole, to
> whose barrenness only it points, there, the needle indifferently
> respects all points alike. (165)

That Melville refers to the regions of "absolute truth" as being in the
cold, barren, sterile region of the Arctic indicates that he considers
that its relentless pursuit can only end in cold sterility. In contrast to
the Transcendental belief that the heavens are the source of truth,
Melville accuses the heavens themselves of being the major perpetra-
tors of these "confounding effects." In contrast to Emerson's advice
that following truth leads to safety, Melville warns that following
truth "too far" leads to a loss of sanity. Though Emerson admitted
that in following the truth a man places himself in a position to be
misunderstood by others, he believed that eventually a man would be
vindicated and admired for his efforts: "All persons have their
moments of reason, when they look out into the region of absolute
truth, then they will justify me and do the same thing." He maintains
also that if a man will exercise "self-truth," and act on his own, "toss-
ing the laws, the books, idolatries and customs out of the window,"
man will pity him no more, but will "thank and revere him."[18]
Melville provided another dissenting opinion in *Pierre*:

> . . . almost every thinking man must have been some time or
> other struck with the idea, that in certain respects, a tremendous
> mistake may be lurking here, since all the world does never gre-
> gariously advance to Truth, but only here and there some of its in
> individuals do; and by advancing, leave the rest behind; cutting
> themselves forever adrift from their sympathy, and making them-
> selves always liable to be regarded with distrust, dislike, and
> often, downright—though, ofttimes, concealed—fear and hate.
> (166)

Emerson saw Truth as the shining emancipator of man. He had
little to say about Falsehood, however, except to negate it as he did
evil: "Falsehood, may indeed stand as the great Night or shade on
which as a background the living universe paints itself forth, but no
fact is begotten by it; it cannot work, for it is not."[19] Melville saw
Truth as the ambiguity; to him, Truth was the elusive essence that
could never be defined or contained—the "ungraspable phantom of
life."[20] Not only did he see Truth itself as being ambiguous and elusive, but also he thought that the pursuit of Truth could result in
making the soul of man ambiguous as well:

> As a statue, planted on a revolving pedestal, shows now this limb, now that; now front, now back, now side; continually changing, too, its general profile; so does the pivoted, statued soul of man, when turned by the hand of Truth. Lies only never vary. . . . (337)

Emerson believed that "the soul active sees absolute truth and utters truth, or creates" and that this is "not the privilege of here and there a favorite, but the sound estate of every man."[21] He deplored man's lack of faith in himself and his tendency to accept public opinion as correct—those people who "think society wiser than their own soul, and know not that one soul, and their soul, is wiser than the whole world."[22] His advice to man was to trust himself and then act upon that trust; to believe in his own thought that what is true for him in his "private heart is true for all men."[23]

Melville saw Emerson's advice as noble in sentiment, but lacking in judgment. His reaction to this opinion concerning man's complete independence and self-reliance is reflected in this statement: "Surely no mere mortal who has at all gone down into himself will ever pretend that his slightest thought or act solely originates in his own defined identity" (176). As for Emerson's directive for man to break free from the confines of conformity to society, Melville warned:

> Such, oh thou son of man! are the perils and the miseries thou callest down on thee, when, even in a virtuous cause, thou steppest aside from those arbitrary lines of conduct, by which the common world, however base and dastardly, surrounds thee for thy worldly good. (176)

There can be little doubt that Melville was satirizing the Transcendental man when he wrote:

> A proud man likes to feel himself in himself, and not by reflection in others. He likes to be not only his own Alpha and Omega, but to be distinctly all the intermediate gradations, and then to slope off on his spine either way, into the endless, impalpable ether. (261)

If there is any doubt as to Melville's intentional disavowing of the Transcendental doctrine in the novel *Pierre*, this doubt is dispelled by the chapter entitled "The Flower-Curtain Lifted From Before a Tropical Author, With Some Remarks on the Transcendental Flesh-Brush Philosophy." Not only did Melville specifically name a chapter after this group of thinkers, but he also made some direct remarks that could be interpreted only as criticism of the Transcendentalists:

> If the grown man of taste, possess not only some eye to detect the picturesque in the natural landscape, so also, has he as keen a perception of what may not unfitly be here styled, the *povertiresque* in the social landscape. To such an one, no more picturesquely conspicuous is the dismantled thatch in a painted cottage of Gainsborough, than the time-tangled and want-thinned locks of a beggar, *povertiresque* diversifying those snug little cabinet-pictures of the world, which, exquisitely varnished and framed, are hung up in the drawing room minds of humane men of taste, and amiable philosophers of either the "Compensation," or "Optimist" school. They deny that any misery is in the world, except for the purpose of throwing the fine *poverterisque* element into its general picture. Go to! God hath deposited cash in the Bank subject to our gentlemanly order; he hath bounteously blessed the world with a summer carpet of green . . . . The lamentations of the rain are but to make us our rainbows! (277)

A brief survey of a few of Emerson's remarks quickly establishes a source for Melville's commentaries. Not only are the sentiments of the above passages paralleled in Emerson, but the choice of analogy as well. As Emerson phrases it, "behind us, as we go, all things assume pleasing forms, as clouds do far off. Not only things familiar and stale, but even the tragic and terrible are comely as they take their place in the pictures of memory."[24] Elsewhere he states that as fast as one conforms his life to the pure idea in his mind, "so fast will disagreeable appearances, swine, spiders, snakes, pests, mad-houses, prisons, enemies, vanish; they are temporary and shall be no more seen."[25] Idealism, he tells us, sees the world "as one vast picture which God paints on the instant eternity for the contemplation of the soul."[26]

Emerson was undeniably categorized by Melville as a member of the "Compensation" and "Optimist" school. In his essay, "Compensation," Emerson wrote: "The soul refuses limits, and always affirms an Optimism, never a Pessimism."[27] Perhaps Melville had the preceding comment in mind when he wrote:

> it is often to be observed of the shallower men, that they are the very last to despond. It is the glory of the bladder that nothing can sink it; it is the reproach of a box of treasure, that once overboard it must down. (280)

It would appear from this remark that Melville believed the pessimist to be more astute than the optimist. He seemed irritated by smug men who appear too secure in their beliefs and convictions. Perhaps Melville envied them their self-satisfaction; if he had been able to share the complacency of their beliefs, perhaps he would not have said: "It holds true, in every case, that the wiser a man is the more misgivings he has on certain points" (258). One of the qualities Melville found unforgivable in the Transcendentalists was their cheerful lack of misgivings—he had many misgivings himself, especially concerning Emerson's theory of "Compensation."

The principle of compensation represents Emerson's first and most explicit attempt to cite objective evidence of a truth he could not live without: that "all things are moral."[28] Emerson was not satisfied with the Christian doctrine of inevitable retribution in another world. He felt compelled to establish a theory whereby justice could be done in *this* world. He confronted simultaneously two classic human problems—the relations of virtue to happiness, and the problem of evil—and seemingly proceeded to deny that they *are* problems. Melville could not accept such theories as "the world looks like a multiplication-table, or a mathematical equation, which turn it how you will, balances itself";[29] or such an optimistic view as "the good man has, absolute good . . . so that you cannot do him any harm."[30]

Although Melville approached Transcendentalism with serious reservations at this time of his life, he had even less use for some of the other attitudes evidenced in the world. He decried a system that will provide a superfluity of the world's goods to a man who already has a sufficiency while, at the same time, "he who is deplorably destitute of the same, he shall have taken away from him even that which he hath" (261). He saw this policy of the world as "ridiculous and subversive of all practical sense" and as indicative of the practice of "absurd and all-displacing transcendentals" (262). Melville realized that in actuality, the utilitarian world was a greater danger than the Transcendentalists, because the utilitarians practice what the Transcendentalists only preach:

> Wherefore we see that the so-called Transcendentalists are not the only people who deal in transcendentals. On the contrary, we seem to see that the Utilitarians,—the everyday world's people themselves, far transcend those inferior Transcendentalists by their own incomprehensible worldly maxims. And—what is vastly more—with the one party, their transcendentals are but theo-

retic and inactive, and therefore harmless; whereas with the other, they are actually-clothed in living deeds. (262)

Melville's personal idea of compensation seemed to apply neither to this world nor to another; he subscribed neither to the Christian nor to the Transcendental views of retribution, but had a view of his own: "I joy that Death is this Democrat; . . . that though in life some heads are crowned with gold, and some bound round with thorns, yet chisel them how they will, head-stones are all alike" (278).

Emerson and Melville also disagreed about eminent philosophers. Emerson thought highly of Immanuel Kant, judging from his essay "The Transcendentalist," in which he credits Kant with having provided the nomenclature for the class of intuitive thought known as Transcendentalism. He describes Kant's thought as having "extraordinary profoundness and precision."[31] Melville had some dissenting opinions concerning not only Kant, but also the whole school of German philosophers. He saw them as so ridiculous that he resorted to puns to convey his thoughts:

> Their mental tendencies, however heterodox at times, are still very fine and spiritual upon the whole; since the vacuity of their exchequers leads them to reject the coarse materialism of Hobbes, and incline to the airy exaltations of the Berkelyan philosophy . . . while the abundance of leisure in their attics (physical and figurative), unite with the leisure in their stomachs, to fit them in an eminent degree for that undivided attention indispensable to the proper digesting of the sublimated Categories of Kant; especially as Kant (can't) is the one great palpable fact in their pervadingly impalpable lives. These are the glorious paupers, from whom I learn the profoundest mysteries of things; since their very existence in the midst of such a terrible precariousness of the commonest means of support, affords a problem on which many speculative nut-crackers have been vainly employed. (267)

While one German critic, perhaps in defense of German idealism, interprets this passage as Melville's admission of his admiration for the basic tenets of Transcendentalism, it seems rather apparent, in view of the context in which his words appear, that Melville intended his comments as a satirical gibe at the movement in general.[32]

Melville states his attitude toward the Transcendental emphasis on simple living in his annotated copy of the *Essays* by Emerson, but he carries his comments still further in *Pierre.* In answer to the Emersonian theory that the "great calm presence of the Creator, comes not forth to the sorceries of opium or of wine," but that the "sublime vision comes to the pure and simple soul in a clean and chaste body"; that the "epic poet, he who shall sing of the gods and their descent unto men, must drink water out of a wooden bowl"; that the "poet's habit of living should be set on a key so low that the common infiuences should delight him"; and that "air should suffice for his inspiration, and he should be tipsy with water,"[33] Melville responds with some advice of his own:

> Ah! ye poor lean ones! ye wretched Soakites and Vapourites: have not your niggardly fortunes enough rinsed ye out, and wizened ye, but ye must still be dragging the hose-pipe, and throwing still more cold Croton on yourselves and the world? Ah! attach the screw of your hose-pipe to some fine old butt of Madeira! pump us some sparkling wine into the world! see, see, already, from all eternity, two-thirds of it have lain helplessly soaking! (300)

Melville's sense of the distinct duality in man, the immutable division of body and soul, prompts him further to advise the would-be poet:

> Feed all things with food convenient for them,—that is, if the food be procurable. The food of thy soul is light and space; feed it then on light and space. But the food of thy body is champagne and oysters; feed it then on champagne and oysters, and so shall it merit a joyful resurrection, if there is any to be. (299)

A consideration of Melville's marginal notations in his copies of Emerson's *Essays* evidences once more the strong attraction that the idealism of Transcendentalism held for Melville. He frequently underscored Emerson's lines, with the word "noble" added in the margin— yet at the same time his untrained but keen mind was attempting to free itself from many of Emerson's implications. These annotations were not made until Melville was past forty because he did not buy these particular volumes of the *Essays* until the first year of the Civil War. The same mixture of attraction and repulsion is expressed in this marginalia, however, that he had communicated to Duyckinck upon his first contact with Emerson at a lecture several years before. He had found himself "very agreeably disappointed." He had heard of him as "full of transcendentalism, myths and oracular gibberish," but "say what they will, he's a great man. . . . I love all men who dive."[34] But as he followed Emerson into his soaring ideas, he quickly felt himself being suffocated. Emerson's intellectual atmosphere was too rarefied for an elemental man like Melville.

The annotations on passages concerning men of letters show that Melville, like Emerson, was more concerned with thought in literature than with craftsmanship. The two men were in agreement on the timeless, universal qualities in the works of great men. In "Spiritual Laws" Emerson wrote:

> We are always reasoning from the seen to the unseen. Hence the perfect intelligence that subsists between wise men of remote ages. A man cannot bury his meaning so deep in his book but time and like-minded men will find them. Plato had a secret doctrine, had he? What secret can be concealed from the eyes of Bacon? of Montaigne? of Kant? Therefore Aristotle said of his works, "They are published and not published."[35]

Melville drew a line beside this passage and annotated, "Bully for Emerson!—Good."[36] Although Melville agreed with many of Emerson's ideas in "The Poet," he did not agree with all of Emerson's statements concerning creative artists. He opposed the view that a man's ambitions and powers are necessarily commensurate. In "Spiritual Laws" he marked the following sentences as "True":

> He [each man] inclines to do something which is easy to him and good when it is done, but which no other man can do. He has no rival. For the more truly he consults his own powers, the more difference will his work exhibit from the work of any other.[37]

But the sentences immediately succeeding these he marked as "False":

> His ambition is exactly proportioned to his powers. The height of the pinnacle is determined by the breadth of the base. Every man has this call of the power to do somewhat unique, and no man has any other call.[38]

Melville's opinion of this passage is reflected in a letter he wrote to Duyckinck in 1850, in which he "inquired if he could be supplied with about fifty fast-writing youths." He explains that "since I have been here I have planned about that number of future works & cant [sic] find enough time to think about them separately."[39]

Another point upon which the two men's views conflict, as *Pierre* reveals, concerns the effect upon the artist of the stimulants that are sometimes used to produce what Emerson called "animal exhilaration."[40] In the paragraph on the harm of intoxicants to poets in which Emerson suggests that the poet should become tipsy on water,

Melville annotated, "This makes the Wordsworthian poet—not the Shakespearean."[41] As for the intoxicating powers of water, as opposed to stronger beverages, Melville had already stated his opinion of that subject in a letter written in reply to Duyckinck's complaint concerning Emerson's sobriety: "Ah, my dear Sir, that's his misfortune, not his fault. His belly, sir, is in his chest, & his brains descend down into his neck, and offer an obstacle to a draughtful of ale or a mouthful of cake."[42] During the composition of *Moby-Dick* Melville wrote a letter to Hawthorne that left little doubt as to his views on the subject of temperance:

> If ever, my dear Hawthorne, in then eternal times that are to come, you and I shall sit down in Paradise, in some little shady corner by ourselves; and if we shall by any means be able to smuggle a basket of champagne there (I won't believe in a Temperance Heaven), and if we shall then cross our celestial legs in the celestial grass that is forever tropical, and strike our glasses and our heads together, till both musically ring in concert,— then, O my dear fellow-mortal, how shall we pleasantly discourse of all the things manifold which now so distress us,—when all the earth shall be but a reminiscence, yea, its final dissolution an antiquity.[43]

The conflicting views of the two authors concerning indulgence of the senses coincide with the differences in temperament evidenced by the austerity of Emerson's essays and poems and by the spirit of revelry in parts of Melville's novels.

As Melville took exception to the puritanical standards of living prescribed in "The Poet," so he objected to statements made there regarding the poet's understanding and interpretation of life. Emerson maintained that it is the "dislocation arid detachment from the life of God that makes things ugly," but he believed that the poet, by reattaching things to nature and the Whole—"re-attaching even artificial things and violations of nature, to nature,—by a deeper insight—disposes very easily of the most disagreeable facts."[44] Melville underlined "disposes very easily of the most disagreeable facts" and commented, "So it would seem. In this sense, Mr. E. is a great poet."[45] Further on in the essay, Emerson asserted that the poet alone knows astronomy, chemistry, vegetation and animation, but he does not stop at the mere factual level; he employs the facts as signs and interprets the real truth behind them. "He knows why the plain or meadow of space was strown with these flowers we call suns and moons and stars; why the great deep is adorned with animals, with men, and gods."[46] Melville marked the last sentence, underscoring "He knows," and wrote, "Would some poet be pleased to tell us 'why.' Will Mr. E?"[47] The unhappy result of Melville's search for some purpose in the universe explains his attitude toward Emerson's faith in the poet's vision. Melville agreed with Emerson that poets are "liberating gods"[48] in that they present intellectually compelling views on certain aspects of life, but he did not share Emerson's enthusiasm over the poet's ability to reconcile man to the deepest mysteries.

Although in several instances Melville recorded a favorable opinion of Emerson's ideas about particular aspects of the individual and of society, he found a great deal to criticize in Emerson's views upon the problem of "evil." Melville objected to what he considered an insinuation by Emerson that man himself is responsible for the origin of his own ills. In "Heroism" Emerson said:

> The disease and deformity around us certify the infraction of natural, intellectual and moral laws, and often violation on violation to breed such compound misery. A lock-jaw that bends a man's head back to his heels; hydrophobia that makes him bark at his wife and babes; insanity that makes him eat grass; war, plague, cholera, famine, indicate a certain ferocity in nature, which, as it had its inlet by human crime, must have its outlet by human suffering.[49]

Melville marked the last part of this passage and commented: "Look squarely at this, and what is it but mere theology—Calvinism?—The brook shows the stain of the banks it has passed thro. Still, these essays are noble."[50] Melville's use of the word "Calvinism" indicated that he perceived in the passage evidence of Emerson's belief in the fall of man through his own agency. This dissenting comment came naturally enough from one who, brought up to believe in the doctrine of the Fall, had in maturity come to the conclusion that God is responsible for the presence of evil as well as for the presence of good. Melville's elaborates on his remark that "the brook shows the stain of the banks it has passed thro" in *Pierre*:

> Ah, if man were wholly made in heaven, why catch we hell-glimpses? Why in the noblest marble pillar that stands beneath the all-comprising vault, ever should we descry the sinister vein? We lie in nature very close to God; and though, further on, the stream may be corrupted by the banks it flows through; yet at the fountain's rim, where mankind stand, there the stream infallibly bespeaks the fountain. (108)

Melville here states his belief that, if man is evil, God must also be evil. As the "stream infallibly bespeaks the fountain," just so does man, created in God's image, stand as testimony of a duality in God.

Similarly, Melville was disturbed by Emerson's belief that by obeying the immutable natural laws, which Emerson thought to be at one with a Beneficent Tendency of the universe, man attains goodness, whereas by disobeying them he becomes depraved. Emerson wrote: "It is the undisciplined will that is whipped with bad thoughts and bad fortunes."[51] This statement caused Melville to accuse Emerson again of being theological: "Jumps into the pulpit from off the tripod here," Melville annotated.[52] Another passage concerning the punishment that a man suffers for his sins evoked a humorous comment. In "Spiritual Laws" Emerson wrote: "Our dreams are the sequel of our waking knowledge. The visions of the night bear some proportion to the vision of the day. Hideous dreams are exaggerations of the sins of the day."[53] Melville annotated the last sentence thus: "Meaning, of course, the sins of indigestion."[54]

Like Emerson, Melville believed that man can improve his condition if he lives by the best that is in him, but Melville was not as sanguine as Emerson concerning man's ability to overcome evil. He stressed more than Emerson that there are differences between men and also seemed to possess a greater awareness of the undesirable elements in human nature.

Melville's criticism of Emerson on these matters is merely a component of his criticism of Emerson's optimism in regard to the problem of evil. Emerson believed that evil is temporary. "Good is positive," he asserted, "Evil is merely privative, not absolute: it is like cold, which is the privation of heat."[55] Believing in a universal scheme that tends toward absolute good, Emerson made some statements that Melville disagreed with. Emerson's remark that "we use defects and deformities to a sacred purpose, so expressing our sense that the evils of the world are such only to the evil eye,"[56] caused Melville to inquire:

> What does the man mean? If Mr. Emerson traveling in Egypt should find the plague-spot come out on him—would he consider that an evil sight or not? And if evil, would the eye be evil because it seemed evil to his eye, or rather to his sense using the eye for instrument?[57]

It was against the metaphysical assumptions of "Spiritual Laws" that Melville made his most determined attack. When Emerson tried to establish the merely negative nature of evil by stating, "The good, compared to the evil which he [a man] sees, is as his own good to his own evil," Melville replied:[58]

> A perfectly good being, therefore, would see no evil.—But what did Christ see?—He saw what made him weep— . . . To annihilate all this nonsense read the Sermon on the Mount, and consider what it implies.[59]

Melville also found fault with the statement in *The Conduct of Life*: "The first lesson of history is the good of evil."[60] To that Melville retorted: "He still bethinks himself of his optimism—he must make that good somehow against the eternal hell itself."[61]

The annotations upon the subject of evil help to explain the most important critical remark that Melville made concerning Emerson. In "The Poet," Melville marked the passage that declared that the poet "names the thing because he sees it, or comes one step nearer to it than any other. This expression or naming is not art, but a second nature, grown out of the first, as a leaf out of a tree."[62] At the end of that passage Melville wrote his most comprehensive comment. By expressing admiration for much of Emerson, and by censuring at the same time what appeared to Melville to be intellectual smugness and an imperfect recognition of human suffering, this comment summarizes Melville's criticism of Emerson:

> This is admirable as many other thoughts of Mr. Emerson's thoughts are. His gross and astonishing errors and illusions spring from a self-conceit so intensely intellectual and calm that at first one hesitates to call it by its right name. Another species of Mr. Emerson's errors, or rather blindness, proceeds from a defect in the region of the heart.[63]

Once more we see evidence of the controversy between head and heart in Melville, his distrust of the intellectual approach to understanding when it threatens to overshadow the emotional approach.

In addition to Melville's comments in *Pierre* and his annotations of Emerson's *Essays*, there is one other source that gives an insight into Melville's opinions—the passages he underlined in the *Essays* but did not annotate. Especially pertinent to a discussion of *Pierre* is this proverb, found in the essay "Illusions," which was heavily marked by Melville:

> Fooled thou must be, though wisest of the wise:
> Then be the fool of virtue, not of vice.[64]

Emerson praised this proverb, and at first glance, one would be led to believe, as William Braswell suggests, that Melville underlined this passage because it was "obviously in accord with what he believed."[65] However, consider Melville's discussion of the virtue-vice idea in *Pierre*. In a scene between Pierre and Isabel, Pierre exclaims:

> Ye heavens, that have hidden yourselves in the black hood of the night, I call to ye! If to follow Virtue to her uttermost vista, where common souls never go; if by that I take hold on hell, and the uttermost virtue, after all, prove but a betraying pander to the monstrousest vice,—then close in and crush me, ye stony walls, and into one gulf let all things tumble together! . . . Ah! now I catch glimpses, and seem to half see, somehow, that the uttermost ideal of moral perfection in man is wide of the mark. The demigods trample on trash, and Virtue and Vice are trash! (273)

Isabel asks Pierre to define Virtue and Vice for her, and he replies: "Look! a nothing is the substance, it casts one shadow one way, and another the other way; and these two shadows cast from one nothing; these, seems to me, are Virtue and Vice" (274). Obviously, Emerson and Melville did not interpret the Persian proverb in the same light. Here Melville has set forth his belief that the universal power is both good and evil, in contrast with the Emersonian belief in the sheer benevolence of the Divine Power. It almost seems as though Melville purposely set out to create a character in the image of the proverb. Here Pierre calls himself "the fool of Truth, the fool of Virtue, the fool of Fate." In view of the fact that Melville had penciled in the margin of his copy of Emerson—opposite a statement on the malleability and goodness of man—"God help the poor fellow who squares his life according to this"[66]—it would appear that Melville intentionally created, in the character of Pierre, just such a fellow.

In the character of Pierre, Melville created an embodiment of the Transcendental man. The flowery, ornate language employed by Melville in the passages concerning nature, young love, and extreme idealism serve to heighten the implicit satire of the subject matter. Some of the early critics condemned this novel partially on the basis of Melville's style. They believed that Melville employed this style in all seriousness, and concluded that he had flouted all the traditions of good literary taste. More recent critics, however, have recognized that Melville assumed the flamboyant style to achieve a sort of satiric lyricism.

In addition to the satiric tone, which implies more than surface meaning to many of Melville's words, another aspect of his technique must be pointed out. Melville employed an interesting technique resembling the musical use of a thematic melody with a counterpoint accompaniment. On the surface, Pierre's idealistic nobility dominates, accompanied by the low rumble of Melville's ominous comments forming a counterpoint of foreboding. It is through his running commentary that Melville clarifies the meaning of his lyrical, and superficially innocent passages. The following discussion is formulated on the basis of (1) establishment of the Emersonian ideal; (2) Pierre's adherence to the ideal; and (3) Melville's clarifying commentary.

A brief summary of the plot of the novel follows. Pierre Glendinning, a gifted and noble young man, has had the advantages of culture and wealth during his early boyhood on the rural family estate near Albany, New York. Although his father has died shortly before the story begins, his mother is competent to supervise the considerable estate. She is a domineering woman and extremely possessive in her relationship with her only child; nevertheless, she approves his engagement to an ethereal young lady named Lucy Tartan. In his courtship, Pierre conducts himself with the gallantry and high-mindedness of a storybook knight.

The first important complication in the narrative occurs when Pierre makes the disillusioning discovery that his late father, whom he has idealized and worshiped as a model of virtue, once seduced a beautiful young French girl, and that the illegitimate daughter of that affair, Isabel, is now a forlorn social outcast, reduced to servitude. Motivated by genuinely high idealism, Pierre resolves that he must find some way to protect her from the world and to share with her his position and honorable name. His mother is ignorant of the early scandal involving his father, and Pierre realizes that the shock of discovering such an affair would probably ruin her life; furthermore, her temperament is such that she would never accept Isabel into the family. He decides to confide the facts to no one; instead he will secretly sacrifice his love for Lucy, his honorable reputation, and his future life for the sake of Isabel. He breaks his engagement to Lucy, leaving her grief-stricken, and devises a quixotic scheme of pretending that he has secretly married a stranger named Isabel and that he is moving to New York.

A further complication occurs when Pierre is prompted to assume an additional burden. In the dreary farmhouse where Isabel has been working, there is another young lady in distress: Delly Ulver has recently given birth to an illegitimate child, now dead, and is being driven from the community by the town's leading benefactress— Pierre's mother—assisted by the local "man of God," the Reverend

Mr. Falsgrave. Prompted by his higher social conscience, Pierre plays protector to both girls, taking them to New York City, where the three of them set up housekeeping behind the deception that Pierre and Isabel are man and wife. Pierre's mother, enraged by his unorthodox behavior, disowns him, leaving him to earn a living through his literary talents.

Glendinning Stanley, Pierre's cousin and very close childhood friend, refuses to stand by Pierre as he has promised to do. Because Pierre has depended on his cousin's assistance in New York, he now finds himself penniless and friendless in a strange city. To make matters worse, Stanley subsequently inherits Pierre's estate after the death of Mrs. Glendinning; Stanley even courts Pierre's former fiancée, Lucy. But the spiritual Lucy perceives intuitively that Pierre is acting out an idealistic role, and she decides to join his household in New York, determined to assist him in whatever way she can. She is still unaware of the true relationship between Pierre and Isabel. Now Pierre has three women for whom he is responsible.

Beset on all sides by the unsympathetic cruelties of society, tortured by his fraudulent position in the eyes of the world, torn between aesthetic Lucy and earthy Isabel, the idealistic Pierre sinks deeper and deeper into disillusionment. His cousin Stanley harasses and insults him. His publishers, who have been paying advances on a novel, reject the finished manuscript and start legal action against him. Bewildered by the tragic results of his virtuous idealism and convinced that his Prometheanism is opposed by God and by society, Pierre resorts to one final self-annihilating gesture of defiance—he kills his cousin Stanley. That night in jail, Isabel and Lucy join him to share his fate, which, tragically, they do: in the final scene all lie dead in Pierre's prison cell.

Throughout this novel, Pierre attempts to put into action the ethical standards and the code of conduct recommended by Emerson and his fellow Transcendentalists. Pierre is a nonconformist; he searches deeply into his heart and soul before he decides upon his course of action; the action he takes is motivated by the highest virtue; once he has reached a decision, nothing can deter him from what he sees as Truth; he does not flinch in the face of cruel circumstance, but struggles to transcend all external situations, confident in his Transcendental belief that Virtue will eventually win out over all obstacles; he does not hesitate to sacrifice himself on the altar of Principle because he knows intuitively that this is the thing he must do.

Specific Emersonian ideals, as evidenced in specific actions of Pierre, will be analyzed in the following pages.

Emerson regarded Nature as the "universal tablet" from which man could read the divine, universal laws that would guide him correctly.[67] He saw man as nestling against the maternal, beneficent bosom of Nature, drawing divine inspiration from this intimate association. Only by withdrawing from other men and retiring into the solitude of Nature could man reorient himself and reattune himself with the Over-Soul. Emerson saw Nature as "the circumstance which dwarfs every other circumstance, and judges like a god all men that come to her."[68] He idealized the country man as the one "who knows the most . . . the rich and royal man."[69]

Pierre begins his life on a country estate, which furnishes him with the Transcendental background of solitude, simplicity, and the opportunity to have close communion with nature. His childhood surroundings are idyllic, almost Eden-like. Melville establishes the virtues of country life by saying: "It had been his choice fate to have been born and nurtured in the country, surrounded by scenery whose uncommon loveliness was the perfect mould of a delicate and poetic mind" (5). To insure that the reader understands the supreme importance of this "choice fate," Melville goes on to say: "In the country then Nature planted our Pierre; because Nature intended a rare and original development in Pierre" (13). It is at this point that Melville interjects a few notes of his ominous counterpoint: "Never mind if hereby she proved ambiguous to him in the end; nevertheless, in the beginning she did bravely" (13). Having established this foreboding note, Melville goes on to describe—in language that echoes Emerson's—the powerful, intuitive influence of Nature. In reading this passage personifying Nature, one cannot miss the satirical tone:

> She blew her wind-clarion from the blue hills, and Pierre neighed out lyrical thoughts, as at the trumpet-blast, a war-horse paws himself into a lyric of foam. She whispered through her deep groves at eve, and gentle whispers of humanness, and sweet whispers of love, ran through Pierre's thought-veins, musical as water over pebbles. She lifted her spangled crest of a thickly starred night, and forth at that glimpse of their divine Captain and Lord, ten thousand mailed thoughts of heroicness started up in Pierre's soul, and glared round for some insulted good cause to defend. (14)

The last part of this passage calls to mind Emerson's remark that "whoso is heroic will always find crises to try his edge."[70] As the story progresses, Pierre succeeds in fulfilling Emerson's prediction.

By the time Emerson wrote his essay "Culture," he had arrived at the opinion that a truly rounded gentleman should possess a few attributes beyond the essential goodness he acquired through communion with Nature. Although he still believed that a man should develop his character and moral perceptions in the solitary and natural surroundings of the country, Emerson was ready to grant that the city also played a part in a man's development by offering him access to the necessary social graces and academic education. Melville is careful not to neglect this cultural side of his Transcendental hero. He makes an issue of advising the reader that Pierre was not lacking in any of the essential ingredients of an Emersonian ideal man:

> . . . the breeding of Pierre would have been unwisely contracted, had his youth been unintermittingly passed in those rural scenes. At a very early period he had begun to accompany his father and mother . . . in their annual visits to the city; where naturally mingling in a large and polished society, Pierre had insensibly formed himself in the earlier graces of life, without enfeebling the vigour derived from a martial race, and fostered in the country's clarion air. (6)

The training of Pierre's mind in the proper classical channels was accomplished in the "deep recesses of his father's fastidiously picked and decorous library." Here Pierre was introduced to the "Spenserian nymphs," who "led him into many a maze of all-bewildering beauty" (6). Again Melville is not content to impart a mere statement of fact about his hero—he follows up with a hint to the reader of what is to come, a cynical comment about the real, basic value of this "all-bewildering beauty":

> Thus, with a graceful glow on his limbs, and soft, imaginative flames in his heart, did this Pierre glide toward maturity, thoughtless of that period of remorseless, insight, when all these delicate warmths should seem frigid to him, and he should madly demand more ardent fires. (6)

Throughout this novel, Melville carefully establishes his intentions. To prevent the reader from passing over the preceding descriptions of Pierre's early years, considering such facts mere background material, Melville somewhat heavy-handedly explains: "Nor will any man dream that the last chapter was merely intended for a foolish bravado, and not with a solid purpose in view" (12). Immediately following this statement, Melville further clarifies his intentions by stating his "solid purpose":

> Now Pierre stands on this noble pedestal; we shall see if he keeps
> that fine footing; we shall see if Fate hath not just a little bit of a
> small word or two to say in this world. (12)

Thus Melville directly states that he is developing this ideally virtuous young man for the explicit purpose of showing the reader that all
Pierre's nobility cannot prevent Fate's toppling him from his pedestal.
According to Emerson, a man who possesses the noble virtues propounded by the Transcendentalists is beyond the power of circumstance and Fate—he is his own fate. Thus, Melville appears to have
explicitly set out to disprove this Transcendental belief.

Emerson felt strongly about his precepts of simple living. He
could not accept the idea that a man could be aesthetic and poetic
and at the same time concern himself with such earthly considerations as good food. In addition to his comments in "The Poet,"
Emerson stated in "Heroism" that "a great man scarcely knows how
he dines, how he dresses."[71] He was even more specific in "Prudence":
"Genius is always ascetic; and piety, and love. Appetite shown to the
finer souls as a disease, and they find beauty in rites and bounds that
resist it."[72] With heavy satire, Melville states that

> there was one little uncelestial trait, which in the opinion of
> some, may mar the romantic merits of the gentlemanly Pierre
> Glendinning. He always had an excellent appetite, and especial-
> ly for his breakfast. (16)

In view of the many derogatory comments Melville makes throughout the novel concerning the Transcendental emphasis on simple living, there is little doubt as to whom he means when he says "the
opinion of some." He continues in this passage with a long, derisive
defense of the "uncelestial trait" that mars his hero. He itemizes the
many manly pursuits of Pierre, emphasizing his athletic inclinations,
and ends the passage by humorously vindicating him on the grounds
that

> to have a bountiful appetite, was not only no vulgar reproach,
> but a right royal grace and honour to Pierre; attesting him a man
> and a gentleman; for a thoroughly developed gentleman is
> always robust and healthy. . . . (17)

On the subject of love, Emerson evidenced a Platonic perspective.
He saw earthly love as a foreshadowing of the infinitely higher spiritual love of divinity. As beauty of Nature is but a physical manifesta-

tion of the Over-Soul, so natural love is but a manifestation of the Divine love toward which man must always strive. In his essay "Friendship," he defines his concept of true love as that which "transcends the unworthy object and dwells and broods on the eternal, and when the poor interposed mask crumbles, it is not sad, but feels rid of so much earth and feels its independency the surer."[73] This same Platonic note emerges in Melville's description of a beautiful woman's effect on a man. In this passage Melville has been describing, with almost delirious lyricism, the charm of Lucy Tartan:

> if that man shall haply view some fair and gracious daughter of the gods, who, from unknown climes of loveliness and affluence, comes floating into sight, all symmetry and radiance; how shall he be transported, that in a world so full of vice and misery as ours, there should yet shine forth this visible semblance of the heavens. For a lovely woman is not entirely of this earth. (24)

Thus Lucy becomes symbolic of the infinitely greater beauties of the heavens, in keeping with Emerson's creed. Pierre's entire relationship with Lucy partakes of the Emersonian tradition; an ethereal quality pervades all of their scenes together. There is a consistent denial of any earthy quality in their love. In the opening pages of the novel, Pierre gazes at Lucy and thinks: "Truly the skies do ope, and this invoking angel looks down." He tells her that he cannot wish her a good morning, because that would seem to presume that she had "lived through a night; and by Heaven, thou belong'st to the regions of an infinite day!" Lucy coyly inquires as to why it is that youths always swear when they love. Pierre's answer establishes the quality of their relationship: "Because in us love is profane, since it mortally reaches toward the heaven in ye!" (4).

Melville's passages of mock-rhapsody, describing Pierre's and Lucy's love, are the major sources for criticism of his style in this novel. Viewed, however, as a burlesque parody of the lofty attitudes held by the Transcendentalists, these passages are less assailable. Compare the following passages, for example. First, Emerson's description of a young lover in his essay "Love":

> Behold there in the wood the fine madman! He is a palace of sweet sounds and sights; he dilates; he is twice a man; he walks with arms akimbo; he soliloquizes; he accosts the grass and the trees; he feels the blood of the violet, the clover and the lily in his veins; and he talks with the brook that wets his foot.[74]

Melville makes use of many of Emerson's romantic symbols, and adds a few of his own:

> Love is both Creator's and Saviour's gospel to mankind; a volume bound in rose-leaves, clasped with violets, and by the beaks of humming-birds printed with peach-juice on the leaves of lilies. (34)

Melville continues at great length, waxing more lyrical with every line, until he climaxes this passage by proclaiming: "Oh, Love is busy everywhere. Everywhere Love hath Moravian missionaries. No Propagandist likes to Love" (34).

Emerson proclaims that all Nature takes part in a young man's love. He says that "every bird on the boughs of the tree sings now to this [the lover's] heart and soul. The notes are articulate."[75] Melville also employs an articulate bird, but his bird sings a rapturous parody of biblical psalms extolling the beauties of the earth. Keeping in mind Melville's professed disenchantment with religion at this period of his life, the double-edged satiric undertone becomes apparent:

> Oh, praised be the beauty of this earth; the beauty, and the bloom, and the mirthfulness thereof! We lived before, and shall live again; and as we hope for a fairer world than this to come; so we came from one less fine. From each successive world, the demon Principle is more and more dislodged; he is the accursed clog from chaos, and thither, by every new translation, we drive him further and further back again. Hosannahs to this world! (33)

Melville expresses in this passage the same sort of evolutionary sentiment found in Emerson's predictions at the end of his essay "Culture":

> The age of the quadruped is to go out, the age of the brain and the heart is to come in . . . . And if one shall read the future of the race hinted in the organic effort of nature to mount and meliorate, and the corresponding impulse to the Better in the human being, we shall dare affirm that there is nothing he will not overcome and convert, until at last culture shall absorb the chaos and gehenna. He will convert the Furies into Muses, and the hells into benefits.[76]

The resemblance between Melville's rapturous passages and the equally rapturous Transcendental expressions of Emerson is probably one of the reasons why the early critics referred to *Pierre* as being "incomprehensibly transcendental." They mistakenly took Melville's words at face value, disregarding his accompanying commentary; thus, they did not recognize his hyperbolic mock-heroics as being something other than a serious statement of his beliefs. It is true that Melville emphasizes the Platonic elements in his discussions of love—even to the point of referring to Pierre and Lucy as "two Platonic particles . . . roaming in quest of each other" (27). These remarks of Melville's, however, must be considered in the total context, where the primary object of his satire—Emersonian Transcendentalism—becomes apparent.

As the story progresses, dark premonitions persistently haunt Pierre. He receives intuitive perceptions of some evil that seems to surround him. Nature speaks to him, but it speaks of sadness, which leads Pierre to question God's own emotional state:

> Hark, now I hear the pyramidical and numberless, flame-like complainings of this Eolean pine;—the wind breathes now upon it:—the wind,—that is God's breath! Is He so sad? Oh tree! so mighty thou, so lofty, yet so mournful! This is most strange! (41)

Pierre refuses to let himself dwell on such thoughts, however, and declares, with cheerfulness and optimism, that he feels joy again: "Joy, which I also feel to be my right as man . . . . Now, then, I'll up with my own joyful will; and with my joy's face scare away all phantoms:—so, they go, and Pierre is Joy's, and Life's again" (42). In these lines, Pierre evidences his determination to believe in such Transcendental principles as Emerson espouses in his theory that "what a man does, that he has. What has he to do with hope or fear? In himself is his might . . . . A man's genius . . . determines for him the character of the universe."[77]

Pierre continues valiantly attempting to determine the character of the universe as he feels it should be, but the dark, brooding face of Isabel returns repeatedly to haunt him. Melville comments that "such faces, compounded so of hell and heaven, overthrow in us all foregone persuasions, and make us wondering children in the world again" (43). Pierre's recurring doubt of the all-benevolent quality of the Deity, which "foregone persuasions" have taught him to accept, distresses him. In the Emersonian tradition, the good, as compared to the evil a man sees, "is as his own good to his own evil."[78] Thus, a man who sensed an evil principle in the universe would necessarily feel guilty of a strain of evil in himself, and, because the Transcendental doctrine makes no allowances for Original Sin in man, he would become increasingly bewildered as to the source of his evil. Emerson stated that if a man does and says "what strictly belongs to him . . . his nature shall not yield him any intellectual obstructions and doubts." He further asserted that "theological problems of original sin, origin of evil, predestination and the like are the soul's mumps and measles and whooping-coughs."[79] Pierre, striving to retain his belief in the ideal principle of a beneficent universe, struggles to subordinate the sadness and evil to his "joyful will." Melville does not leave the reader in doubt as to his personal opinion concerning the necessity of such a struggle: "Here, in imperfect inklings, tinglings, presentiments, Pierre began to feel—what all mature men . . . sooner or later know, and more or less assuredly— that not always in our actions, are we our factors" (51). Melville apparently believes that the Emersonian concept of "the man is all" is a sign of immaturity. Thus Pierre, faced with the unhappy possibility of finding that his cherished belief in his own invincibility is, perhaps, not solidly grounded, finds himself suffering from what Melville might consider "growing pains." Pierre, however, lacks the maturity to accept this unhappy reality and so "he shrank abhorringly from the infernal catacombs of thought, down into which this foetal fancy beckoned him" (51). Pierre fears that if he once allowed the serpent of doubt into his Eden-like world, it might insidiously "poison and embitter his whole life—that choice, delicious life which he had vowed to Lucy for his one pure and comprehensive offering" (53).

Pierre is dealt a tragic blow when Isabel makes herself known to him as his illegitimate half-sister. His idyllic Eden is suddenly swept from beneath his feet, and his faith in his childhood idols is shaken. Melville says:

> For thee, the before undistrusted moral beauty of the world is forever fled; for thee, thy sacred father is no more a saint; all brightness hath gone from thy hills, and all peace from thy plains; and now, now for the first time, Pierre, Truth rolls a black billow through thy soul! (65)

Truth is expressed here as a Hawthornian blackness, contrary to the luminous Truth of Emerson. In this way Melville depicts Truth as the facts of reality—which bear little resemblance to Emerson's ideal Truth. Pierre, however, still thinks of Truth from the Transcendental viewpoint. He exalts and idolizes Truth, almost to the point of deification; consequently, he exhibits the appropriate mindset of a Transcendentalist when he leaps to his feet and shouts:

> Myself am left, at least . . . . With myself I front thee! Unhand me
> all fears, and unlock me all spells! Henceforth I will know noth-
> ing but Truth; glad Truth, or sad Truth; I will know what is, and
> do what my deepest angel dictates. (65)

Pierre here behaves in exactly the manner Emerson recommended
when he wrote:

> When in innocency, or, when by intellectual perception he
> attains to say—'I love the Right; Truth is beautiful within and
> without for evermore. Virtue, I am thine; save me; use me; thee
> will I serve, day and night, in great, in small, that I may be not
> virtuous, but virtue'; then is the end of the creation answered,
> and God is well pleased.80

The irony of Pierre's situation, however, is that he behaves in accordance with Emerson's concepts based on *ideal* Truth, but he is motivated by the *real* Truth of the external world, rather than the spiritual world; thus he finds himself trying to apply Transcendental creeds,
which belie circumstance, to a situation created entirely by circumstance.

Faced with the need to make some decision in this seemingly
impossible situation, Pierre emerges as a true hero in the Transcendental tradition as set forth by Emerson:

> Heroism feels and never reasons, and therefore is always right;
> and although a different breeding, different religion and greater
> intellectual activity would have modified or even reversed the
> particular action, yet for the hero that thing he does is the high-
> est deed, and is not open to the censure of philosophers or
> divines.81

The decision Pierre reaches—to pretend that his half-sister was his
wife, in order to share with her his position in the world—was not
reached on the basis of sheer, hard-headed logic. It was an emotional and intuitive decision that brought tragedy into the lives of everyone involved. If Pierre had had "different breeding"—if he had not
been reared to believe that protection of the family name and honor
was of the greatest importance—he would not have been driven to
act as he did. Had his "intellectual activity" been greater, he might
have been capable of arriving at a more satisfactory solution to his
problem, thereby avoiding much of the resulting misery. If he had
been more strongly under the influence of orthodox religion, he
would, perhaps, have been more likely to let himself be swayed by

the reasoning of the Reverend Mr. Falsgrave, and thus his action would most certainly have been "modified or even reversed." Emerson says that "there is somewhat not philosophical in heroism."[82] Melville apparently agreed with this statement, explaining Pierre's actions by saying:

> Surprising, and past all ordinary belief, are those strange oversights and inconsistencies, into which the enthusiastic meditation upon unique or extreme resolves will sometimes beget in young and over-ardent souls. That all-comprehending oneness, that calm representativeness, by which a steady philosophic mind reaches forth and draws to itself, in their collective entirety, the objects of its contemplations; that pertains not to the young enthusiast. (175)

Emerson goes on to state that "heroism is an obedience to a secret impulse of an individual's character."[83] In the case of Pierre, the very necessity for the secretiveness with which he had to cloak his true motives was one of the major reasons why his actions could be called heroic. The false position in which he placed himself in the eyes of others brought about much of his suffering. As Melville expresses it:

> to the world all his heroicness, standing equally unexplained and unsuspected, therefore the world would denounce him as infamously false to his betrothed; reckless of the most binding human vows; a secret wooer and wedder of an unknown and enigmatic girl; a spurner of all a loving mother's wisest counsellings; a bringer down of lasting reproach upon an honourable name; a besotted self-exile from a most prosperous house and bounteous fortune; and lastly, that now his whole life would, in the eyes of the wide humanity, be covered with an all-pervading haze of incurable sinisterness, possibly not to be removed even in the concluding hour of death. (176)

Emerson said that "every heroic act measures itself by its contempt of some external good."[84] On the basis of this measurement, Pierre's act is one of heroic proportions. In the eyes of the world he is guilty of contempt of many "external goods." He feels justified, however, in his secrecy. Although he will be held responsible for numerous wrongs in the opinions of others, and although these wrongs will reflect negatively on the family name, he believes that the real truth would be far more injurious to both the family honor and to the people involved.

Another characteristic of heroism, according to Emerson, is its persistency: "When you have chosen your part, abide by it, and do not weakly try to reconcile yourself with the world."[85] Pierre persists in his deceptive role, right to the tragic end. He does not swerve in his resolve, nor does he attempt in any way to explain himself, even to those most dear to him. He lets Lucy suffer the anguish of believing that he has rejected her for another; he lets his mother die in ignorance of the truth and makes no effort to effect a reconciliation with her; he almost starves himself and Isabel in New York—all rather than swerve from his chosen path. He believes, with Emerson, that "what your heart thinks great, is great. The soul's emphasis is always right."[86] Acting upon this belief, he persists in his chosen role, regardless of the cost to himself and to others. As Emerson said:

> Truly it demands something godlike in him who has cast off the common motives of humanity and has ventured to trust himself for a taskmaster. High be his heart, faithful his will, clear his sight, that he may in good earnest be doctrine, society, law, to himself, that a simple purpose may be to him as strong as iron necessity is to others![87]

Committed to what he sees as his obligation and duty to Isabel, Pierre completely cuts himself off from all familial ties. Melville comments: "Thus, in the Enthusiast to Duty, the heaven-begotten Christ is born; and will not own a mortal parent, and spurns and rends all mortal bonds" (106). Emerson asserts that heroism is "scornful of being scorned."[88] Pierre, as he "rends all mortal bonds," reaches the point where he becomes so completely his own "doctrine, society and law" that he concerns himself not at all with the opinions of others. "His was the scorn which thinks it not worth the while to be scornful. Those he most scorned, never knew it" (339).

Melville, having accompanied Pierre through his agonizing ordeal of soul-searching and decision-making, cannot resist adding his own little note of foreboding—this time undeniably aimed at the Transcendental belief in the beneficent universe. Melville says: "Ah, thou rash boy! are there no couriers in the air to warn thee away from these emperilings? [sic] . . . Where now are the high beneficences? Whither fled the sweet angels that are alleged guardians to man?" (176). At this point in the novel, Pierre is at the height of his Transcendental pinnacle. He is strong in his resolves, firm in his convictions that Virtue will be its own reward, fearless in his search for absolute Truth. From this point on Melville concentrates on proving that Fate *does* have "just a little bit of a small word or two to say in this world" (12).

Many critics of Melville have occupied themselves with interpreting the symbolic nature of the characters in *Pierre*. Elaborate theories have been expounded concerning their significance—theories based on everything from etymology to theology. The following interpretation represents an attempt to take cognizance of the major opinions of various scholars while, at the same time, presenting an interpretation of those aspects of the symbolism that bear on Transcendentalism.

The ambiguous characters of Lucy and Isabel have received considerable critical attention. On one point, critics generally agree—Lucy and Isabel represent, respectively, the light and dark aspects prevalent in Melville's work. The terms *good* and *evil* applied to Isabel and Lucy would, however, be entirely too reductive and oversimplified. Their positions in this respect are often interchangeable, and neither could be said to be either good or evil, *per se.* They might be considered symbolic of the bright and dark sides of humanity's nature, which were reconciled in the Transcendental doctrine—but this reconciliation was one that Melville never accepted. They could be considered the conscious and unconscious parts of the psyche, or optimism and pessimism.

Lucy is fair and ethereal, described repeatedly by such words as "angelic," "heavenly," and "unearthly." Her very name, Lucy, suggests light, and she appears to be symbolic of the bright idealism that the Transcendentalists sought to perpetuate at all times. She is the conscious mind's determination to view, with an optimistic emphasis on the ultimate good of all things, the whole of life. Just as such an attitude is sometimes productive of good, so Lucy sometimes appears as Pierre's "bright angel," and sometimes as something entirely different—because such an attitude can sometimes cause tragic results.

Isabel, on the other hand, represents the moody, dark, pessimistic, subconscious mind which, in moments of despondency, compels one to reevaluate his own idealistic standards, motivations, and beliefs, even though consciously he would prefer to refrain from such explorations. Isabel is mysterious, brooding, simultaneously natural and supernatural; she is enchanting and bewitching to Pierre, and when he is with her he feels "caught and fast, bound in some necromancer's garden" (128). Isabel does not crave what the world considers happiness; rather, she says that her "spirit seeks different food from happiness" (119). She prays for peace and motionlessness instead of happiness; she is obsessed by a sense of isolation and rejection. She has an overwhelming desire to be accepted as a part of the universal scheme of things: "I feel that there can be no perfect peace in individualness. Therefore I hope one day to feel myself drank [sic] up into the pervading spirit animating all things. I feel I am an exile here" (119). She is uninhibited and unrestrained by the conventional mores of the world. "All my thoughts well up in me," she says, "and I cannot alter them, for I had nothing to do with putting them in my mind, and I never affect any thoughts, and I never adulterate any thoughts." Her speech is like a stream of consciousness: "When I speak, think forth from the tongue, speech being sometimes before the thought; so, often, my own tongue teaches me new things" (123). Like Lucy, she is neither good nor evil in herself, but is sometimes productive of both.

Pierre is caught between these two sides of his own nature, which is just one more of the ambiguities which Melville heaps upon this novel. To follow either side of his nature to the exclusion of the other can only result in tragedy, and yet Pierre can neither completely accept nor completely reject either—nor can he succeed in reconciling them. Alone in his room, he finds himself haunted by an interchangeable Isabel and Lucy:

> For an instant, he almost could have prayed Isabel back into the wonder-world from which she had so slidingly emerged. For an instant, the fond, all-understood blue eyes of Lucy displaced the as tender, but mournful and inscrutable dark glance of Isabel. He seemed placed between them, to choose one or the other; then both seemed his; but into Lucy's eyes there stole half of the mournfulness of Isabel's, without diminishing hers. (129)

As a Transcendentalist, Pierre constantly fights against an admission of a duality within either himself or the world. For him there is no midpoint; he is stranded at the crossroads of the physical and spiritual sides of his nature and, in his inability to compromise what-should-be with what-is, he can only conclude that if *all* cannot be good; then *all* must be evil. In his refusal to admit his human condition and limitations, in his quixotic effort to transcend the bonds of his historical and social setting, Pierre eventually brings about his own destruction.

Lucy is the acceptable—to the family, to the community, to the world at large—alternative to Isabel. She represents the secret, passionate, undiscovered side of Pierre's father's life, as well as of Pierre's own life. Since she is the offspring of Pierre's father, Isabel comes to represent the inexplicable—the subconscious—side of Pierre's nature. As Pierre's physical father becomes symbolic in his mind of the heavonly Father, so Isabel comes to symbolize to Pierre the dark, mysterious, elusive quality of human nature which, although also created by the Father, is denied by mankind. Pierre's sense of obligation to Isabel, his belief that she is entitled to all the rights, privileges, and recognition accorded to the legitimate, acceptable offspring, becomes symbolically extended to include this dark side of human nature. He sets himself against the world and attempts to make the unacceptable acceptable, as he asserts himself by following the dark side of his mind. Not being able to accept both sides of his dual nature equally, he attempts to deny his own situation and thereby brings about many of the ambiguities that plague him throughout the novel.

Pierre's behavior parallels that of his father in that each flouts the traditions and precepts of society in an affair with a beautiful girl. But Pierre persists in his chosen path to the end, whereas his father eventually married a socially acceptable girl and settled into a life of complacent hypocrisy. But the unacknowledged sin of the father was visited upon the son. Pierre, in his attempt to uphold the Truth and to give Isabel an honest position in the world, paid with his life for the debt his father did not acknowledge. Thus, Pierre becomes irrevocably involved in the history the Transcendentalists would deny. He could have said, as Emerson, that "history is an impertinence and an injury if it be any thing more than a cheerful apologue or parable of my being or becoming."[89] But Melville tells us that, regardless of what man may *say*, history can become an "impertinence and an injury," and the mere act of man's denial of this fact does not make it any less a fact.

Pierre's mother, Mrs. Glendinning, represents the social world, banal conventionality, and historical ties. She, together with Mr. Falsgrave, presents a picture of "practical" religion as it is portrayed in Plinlimmon's pamphlet. Melville portrays Mr. Falsgrave with biting satire toward such an "ideal" man of God as a perfect picture of courtly gentility. He is such a fine gentleman, in fact, that "more than once Mrs. Glendinning had held him up to Pierre as a splendid example of the polishing and gentlemanizing influences of Christianity upon the mind and manners" (98). To Mrs. Glendinning, religion is important insofar as it serves its socially acceptable purpose in the community—it is an instrument through which the "righteous" should punish the "unrighteous," and is a valuable accessory to the general culture. Mr. Falsgrave is, to her, an ideal minister. He is tactful, cultured, and genteel, and, above all, he never commits the unforgivable sin of asserting himself against his "betters." When Pierre approaches Mr. Falsgrave with his problem—ostensibly concerning Delly Ulver, but actually concerning Isabel—he receives nothing but hypocritical double-talk. Later, Pierre, in his despair at the injustices of the world committed in the name of religious justice, impulsively awakens Mr. Falsgrave in the middle of the night. Melville describes the dapper little minister, who is more concerned with appearances than with realities, as "holding a candle, and invested in his very becoming student's wrapper of Scotch plaid" (163). The first part of this description contains the religious implications of candles and vestments, which heightens the satire of the mincing tone employed in the remainder of the fashion-plate description. Pierre's growing disillusion at his discovery of the "utter nothingness of good works" (137) is thoroughly confirmed in his interview with the minister. Disappointed in the inefficacy and impotence of organized Christianity, Pierre grows stronger than ever staunchly Transcendental, declaring:

> I once cherished some slight hope that thou wouldst have been able, in thy Christian character, to sincerely and honestly counsel me. But a hint from heaven assures me now, that thou hast no earnest and world-disdaining counsel for me. I must seek it direct from God Himself, whom, I now know, never delegates His holiest admonishings . . . . I think I begin to see how thy profession is unavoidably entangled by all fleshly alliances, and cannot move with godly freedom in a world of benefices. (163–164)

Pierre's attitude toward the ministry has become extremely reminiscent of that of Emerson. From this point on, Pierre never again seeks for an answer in orthodox religion, but squares himself by "the inflexible rule of holy right" (106). He forsakes the "censuses of men" and seeks the "suffrages of the god-like population of the trees," which now seem to him "a nobler race than man" (106). Pierre does not understand that in renouncing the errors of men, he is also renouncing man's potentialities, as well as his own. At this point, Melville comments:

> But Pierre, though charged with the fire of all divineness, his containing thing was made of clay. Ah muskets the gods have made to carry infinite combustions, and yet made them of clay! (107)

Pierre, though fired with the noble idealism of a god, is nevertheless a mortal, and thus subject to human limitations. Here again we have a statement of the fundamental problem as Melville sees it—the god-soul, coupled with the man-body; the infinite capacity of the spirit bound into the finite capacity of the body. Because Pierre cannot bring himself to submit to the unidealistic ways of the world, he rejects the world entirely and exiles himself into the regions of the absolute. Pierre's father, in the symbolic passage of the chair portrait, tries to warn him against just this sort of behavior: "In mature life, the world overlays and varnishes us, Pierre; . . . in youth we *are*; Pierre, but in age we *seem*" (83). In his youthful enthusiasm for absolute truth, Pierre despises the hypocritical veneer of the world, the blind conformity to unidealistic social standards, the deprivation of individualism, which is an integral part of civilization. He is intent on maintaining his own identity, even if he must forsake the world in order to do so. He refuses to *"seem"* and determines to *be*. As Melville says, he is "as yet untranquillized by long habituation to the world as it inevitably and eternally is" (166). Although Pierre suffers many moments of indecision and comes to distrust himself, he never distrusts his heart. He believes, in true Transcendental fashion, that "heaven itself has sanctified that with its blessing"; it is the "distrust of his intellect" that disturbs him (167). Pierre gives intuition precedence over reason, just as Emerson did. Although his obsession for truth-above-all is just as all-consuming as was Emerson's, his outlook on the results of Truth differs considerably. Pierre says: "On, not long will Joy abide, when Truth doth come; nor Grief her laggard be" (91). Pierre, like Adam, finds that knowledge of worldly truth brings him not freedom, but the loss of paradise. He discovers that the gold and green glitter of Saddle Meadows is but a superficial veneer beneath which lies a vast void of blackness. With his uncompromising nature, Pierre is overcome by an ambiguous world in which the "seeming" good can be the actual evil, and what appears to be evil can very possibly turn out to be good. In his immaturity he does not recognize the possibility that the gold and black threads of life are inextricably interwoven. To him, in his insistence on absolute Virtue and Truth, life instead appears as a two-sided coin—of which one side is golden and the other side black. With his standard of values completely overturned by what has occurred, Pierre now sees the golden side as the false, fraudulent, "seeming" side of the world; the blackness represents the true reality of life. With Delly and Isabel, Pierre now leaves the false Eden of Saddle Meadows at dusk, and journeys into darkness.

As he rides along in the coach, Pierre's "thoughts were very dark and wild; for a space there was rebellion and horrid anarchy and infidelity in his soul." Melville steps in at this point and tells a story that has a vital bearing on the problem he presents. He likens Pierre's situation to that of a Catholic priest who, while administering the sacrament of communion, was suddenly smitten with the possibility of the "mere moonshine of the Christian Religion." Now, to Pierre, the

"Evil One propounded the possibility of the mere moonshine of all his self-renouncing enthusiasm." The priest succeeded in vanquishing the "Evil One" by "instant and earnest prayer"; he was held to his "firm Faith's rock" by the "imperishable monument of his Holy Catholic Church; the imperishable record of his Holy Bible; the imperishable intuition of the innate truth of Christianity." But Pierre has no Church, monument, or Bible that could unequivocally say to him, "Go on; thou art in the Right; I endorse thee all over; go on." Melville sums up this parable by saying:

> So the difference between the priest and Pierre was herein:—with the priest it was a matter, whether certain bodiless thoughts of his were true or not true; but with Pierre it was a question whether certain vital acts of his were right or wrong. In this little nut lie germ-like the possible solution of some puzzling problems; and also the discovery of additional, and still more profound problems ensuing upon the solution of the former. For so true is this last, that some men refuse to solve any present problem, for fear of making still more work for themselves that way. (205)

In cutting himself off from the accepted standards of religion, society, and history, Pierre, like Taji, sets himself up, according to the doctrine of Emerson, as a standard unto himself. He no longer has recourse to any exterior source for guidance, nor can he excuse and vindicate his behavior on the basis of any precedent. Furthermore, he is putting into *action* a theoretically ideal form of behavior. "Bodiless thoughts" alone can do no harm, but "vital acts," as Melville points out, present an entirely different problem. Emerson said:

> It is only as a man puts off all foreign support and stands alone that I see him to be strong and to prevail. . . . He who knows that power is inborn, that he is weak because he has looked for good out of him and elsewhere, and, so perceiving, throws himself unhesitatingly on his thought, instantly rights himself, stands in the erect position, commands his limbs, works miracles. . . .[90]

Pierre has attempted to follow this advice explicitly, but he is not so sure that he has "worked miracles." In fact, he is so overcome by the dreadful responsibility that he has taken upon himself that he groans: "Lo! I leave corpses wherever I go! . . . Can then my conduct be right? . . . Corpses behind me, and the last sin before, how then can my conduct be right?" (206).

It is at this point, with Pierre in this mood, that Melville introduces his discourse by Plotinus Plinlimmon on the Chronometricals and Horologicals. H. M. Tomlinson has remarked that Melville could write a Christian sermon "better than any dean except Donne." He goes on to say:

> Strange that Christians should be unaware of so remarkable an apology for their faith as that of the non-benevolent Plinlimmon; but it was very like Melville to stow that sermon in a dark barque, built in the eclipse, with a bit of a gibbet post about her some-where, and a tragic figure aboard who had to brood over even unmentionable sins.[91]

Plinlimmon's pamphlet is one of the most remarkable examples of Melville's subtle satire. It has been taken by many critics as a very seri-ous statement by Melville of his own deepest convictions. Instead, it is a many-faceted discourse that succeeds in communicating much that it does not say explicitly, but implies by satire. Pierre discovers this pamphlet while he is in a "dark and wild" mood (205). He has been earnestly and conscientiously striving to do the right thing for all concerned, and has acted according to what his heart speaks as the Truth. Now, in the dark hours of the night, he begins to wonder if he has acted rashly. The coach is wrapped in silence, Delly and Isabel are sleeping, and Pierre's hand slips down upon the seat and chances to fall upon a "thin, tattered, dried-fish-like thing" (206). Thus Melville introduces the pamphlet, in terms of the Christian symbol of the fish, but this is hardly a wholesome image. He continues describing the pamphlet in deprecating terms: "mean, sleazy paper-rag"; . . . a "dried-fish-like, pamphlet-shaped rag." Having described the paper in such a derogatory way, Melville heaps up the satire by saying with mock-seriousness, "Doubtless, it was something vastly profound." Pierre tries to interest himself in the pamphlet when the sun rises, "more to force his mind away from the dark realities of things than from any other motive" (207).

Melville builds up to the disclosure of the contents of the pam-phlet in a devious, circuitous manner. First he gives a preamble con-cerning the "startling solecism" of Christianity—that it "calls upon all men to renounce this world; yet by all odds the most Mammonish part of this world—Europe and America—are owned by none but pro-fessed Christian nations, who glory in the owning" (207). When this solecism becomes apparent to the earnest youth, he institutes an intense reperusal of the Sermon on the Mount. Having done this, the youth takes another look at the world around him and is overpow-ered by a "sense of the world's downright positive falsity . . . the world seems to lie saturated and soaking with lies." Upon discovering this fact, "in the soul of the enthusiast youth two armies come to the shock; and unless he can find the talismanic secret, to reconcile this world with his own soul, then there is no peace, for him. . . ." Following this statement Melville makes one of his most direct thrusts at the Transcendentalists:

> Now without doubt this Talismanic Secret has never yet been found; and in the nature of human things it seem as though it never can be. Certain philosophers have time and again pretended to have found it; but if they do not in the end discover their own delusion, other people soon discover it for themselves, and so those philosophers and their vain philosophy are let glide away into practical oblivion. Plato, and Spinoza, and Goethe, and many more belong to this guild of self-impostors, with a preposterous rabble of Muggletonian Scots and Yankees, whose vile brogue still the more bestreaks the stripedness of their Greek or German Neoplatonical originals. (208)

This problem of reconciling the world with the soul is, of course, exactly the problem that is occupying Pierre's mind at this time. Coincidentally, that problem is just what Plinlimmon's pamphlet attempts to solve. This problem is set forth in terms of time— Chronometrical, or heavenly time, and Horological, or earthly time. The central argument is based on an extended figure of speech utilizing a sea chronometer which is set and adjusted to coincide with Greenwich time (absolute time) and is employed in reckoning the ship's position at sea in relation to the Greenwich meridian. This reckoning can be made even when the ship is anchored on the other side of the world, in a China port. But the watches and clocks of the China port are set in accordance with local time, or China time, and these local timepieces are referred to as "horologues."

The meaning and significance of these conflicting timepieces is next applied. Even as there is a distinct difference between Chronometrical time and Horological time, there is a striking contrast between the absolute time of God and the local time of human beings. Plinlimmon extends this contrast between ship's time and China time, and shows that China time is not wrong in China; indeed for local purposes in China, China time is correct and ship time is incorrect. Just so, the contrast between God's Chronometrical time and man's Horological time does not mean that man's Horological time is wrong, on earth; indeed, man's time is correct on earth, and God's time is incorrect for local purposes.

Next Plinlimmon poses the question: "But why then does God now and then send a heavenly chronometer . . . into the world . . . to give the lie to all the world's time-keepers?" The answer is that such men as Christ are sent to give man occasional testimony as to what heaven's time is really like. He warns that if a man finds that he has a chronometrical soul within himself, and if he should seek to force heavenly time upon earth, he can never succeed; and if he attempts to regulate his own daily conduct by it, "he will but array all men's earthly time-keepers against him, and thereby work himself woe and death" (212). It is his opinion that God's truth is one thing and man's truth is another. "What man who carries a heavenly soul in him has not groaned to perceive, that unless he committed a sort of suicide as to the practical things of this world, he never can hope to regulate his earthly conduct by the same heavenly soul?" The worst part of all is that "by an infallible instinct he knows, that that monitor cannot be wrong in itself" (213).

Plinlimmon's pamphlet continues with very logical, concrete applications of this theory to the practical affairs of man. The major ideas are presented in a summation near the end: "In things terrestrial a man must not be governed by ideas celestial," and "He must by no means make a complete unconditional sacrifice of himself in behalf of any other being, or any cause, or any conceit." Plinlimmon's final conclusion is that "a virtuous expediency, then, seems the highest desirable or attainable earthly excellence for the mass of men, and is the only earthly excellence that their Creator intended for them" (214). He warns of the dangers of attempting to live on any other basis. He contends that if one tries to live by an absolute moral standard, he will either become so discouraged and desperate at his inability to succeed that he will turn to all "manner of moral abandonment, self-deceit, and hypocrisy," or else he will run, "like a mad dog, into atheism" (215).

On the surface this pamphlet, as a presentation of Melville's views, would seem to be a clear indictment of Transcendental and religious idealism on the basis of practical expediency. However, Melville's views were not sufficiently narrow to permit him to take so simple a view of so complex a problem. Consideration must be given to the fact that Melville inserted a lengthy statement of apology for including this pamphlet in the novel. This satirical apology clearly conveys the half-serious, mock attitude with which Melville presents "what seems to me a very fanciful and mystical, rather than philosophical lecture, from which, I confess, that I myself can derive no conclusion." He goes on to say that for him "it seems more the excellently illustrated restatement of a problem, than the solution of the problem itself" (210).

The pamphlet does state the very problem that concerns Melville throughout the novel, but the "virtuous expediency" solution it offers was obviously distasteful to him. He was quite well aware that man cannot live by the absolute, Chronometrical truths of Transcendentalism, and he was just as thoroughly convinced that man's "heavenly" soul will not allow him to revert to simple savagery. But Plinlimmon's proposed solution to the dilemma is nothing but a clear statement of the typical "practical" religious viewpoint that Melville so bitterly satirizes in the character of Mr. Falsgrave. Obviously such a conclusion could only appear as ludicrous to Melville. His manipulation of the arguments in this pamphlet is masterly and shows the real depths of Melville's thinking. He was obviously aware of the shallowness, in their final essence, of the arguments he presents in Plinlimmon's name, and yet he logically and forcefully presents his case, leaving the reader to "skip, or read and rail for himself" (210).

Melville's use of the pamphlet at this point in the narrative serves the purpose of presenting the problem in unmistakable terms to the reader. It is also a means of offering a possible solution of his problem to Pierre, although Pierre at this point does not consciously allow himself to understand the meaning of the pamphlet. The coach reaches New York while Pierre is still deep in meditation over the pamphlet. Melville gives a symbolic description of the entry of these refugees from Paradise into the world of reality. He describes the "twinkling perspective of two long and parallel rows of lamps leading into the town . . . —lamps which seemed not so much intended to dispel the general gloom, as to show some dim path leading through it, into some gloom still deeper beyond . . ." (229). The city is presented as cold, hard-hearted, dark, and cheerless, and is symbolic of the world of reality. When the tired travelers arrive at the house that cousin Stanley has promised as a refuge, it is enshrouded in darkness and locked tight. Pierre goes to Stanley's home and is denied admittance, but forces his way in and confronts Stanley before his dinner guests. Stanley gazes coldly at Pierre and denies that he knows him, and Pierre is forcibly removed from the house. Enraged and even further disillusioned, Pierre storms back to the girls and they all find lodgings in a hotel. Later, they take up residence in an old church that has been turned into a commercial building and is being rented to tenants. The old church was named the Church of the Apostles, and so now the motley assortment of threadbare tenants who reside here are known as "the Apostles." This group of "Teleological

Theorists, and Social Reformers, and political propagandists of all manner" represents a vehicle for another of Melville's commentaries on the general movement of Transcendentalism (268). He describes the society as

> secretly suspected to have some mysterious ulterior object, vague-ly connected with the absolute overturning of Church and State, and the hasty and premature advance of some unknown great political and religious Millennium . . . yet, to say the truth, was the place, to all appearance, a very quiet and decorous one, and its occupants a company of harmless people, whose greatest reproach was efflorescent coats and crack-crowned hats all pod-ding in the sun. (269)

Among the members of this group, Pierre takes up residence. "There he sits, a strange exotic, transplanted from the delectable alcoves of the old manorial mansion, to take root in this niggard soil" (271). It is fitting that Pierre should dwell among these Transcendentalists, for he is following the doctrines they themselves live by:

> Oh, not for naught, in the time of this seeming peace, are warrior grandsires given to Pierre! For Pierre is a warrior too; Life his cam-paign, and three fierce allies, Woe and Scorn and Want, his foes. The wide world is banded against him; for lo you! he holds up the standard of Right and swears by the Eternal and True. (270)

In this place Pierre undertakes to write his great book, in which he will unveil the eternal, universal, and absolute Truths to the world. He is fired with zeal to "gospelise the world anew, and show them deeper secrets than the Apocalypse!" But, at the same time, he is torn by his mixed emotions toward Isabel. The innocent, spiritual love that he has pledged himself to feel for her mingles with a fleshly lust that he struggles to deny. Again the problem of man's duality plagues Pierre. He says, "Let the gods look after their own combustibles. If they have put powder-casks in me—let them look to it!" He is over-come by a sense of the nothingness of moral standards and the inad-equacy of man's ideals of perfection:

> Ah! now I catch glimpses, and seem to half see, somehow, that the uttermost ideal of moral perfection in man is wide of the mark. The demigods trample on trash, and Virtue and Vice are trash! (273)

It is at this point that Pierre draws the conclusion that Virtue and Vice are "two shadows cast from one nothing" (274).

As Pierre works on his book, he becomes increasingly disconnected from the mortal world. After spending several weeks in this isolation, he receives word from Saddle Meadows that his mother has died, and that Glen Stanley has inherited her estate and is Lucy's suitor. An "infinite quenchless rage and malice" takes possession of Pierre and he goes out to walk around and vent his anger before Isabel notices it (289). While in this mood, Pierre sees Plotinus Plinlimmon, author of the pamphlet. Plinlimmon lives in the tower of the old Church of the Apostles, and his face begins to haunt Pierre. Whenever he finds himself in a mood of depression and despair, or when dark thoughts of his miserable condition steal over him, and black doubts as to the integrity of his unprecedented course in life suggest themselves to him, then the "mystic-mild" face of Plinlimmon appears to him and speaks:

> Vain! vain! vain! said the face to him. Fool! fool! fool! said the face to him. Quit! quit! quit!, said the face to him. But when he mentally interrogated the face as to why it thrice said Vain! Fool! Quit! to him; there there was no response. For that face did not respond to anything. (293)

The symbolism of Plotinus Plinlimmon offers much in the way of interpretive fodder. The name Plotinus suggests the ancient ascetic philosopher who sought for metaphysical absolutes. Plotinus Plinlimmon's major characteristic is his complete withdrawal from all things human. Melville says:

> Now, anything which is thus a thing by itself never responds to any other thing. If to affirm, be to expand one's isolated self; and if to deny, be to contract one's isolated self; then to respond is a suspension of all isolation. (293)

Pierre becomes obsessed with the idea of finding the old pamphlet that he has misplaced. He searches frantically, because he senses that if he could only reread the pamphlet he might find some answer to his problems. Melville works in a Procrustean bit of coincidence, in order to point out the significance he intends for the reader to discover in this passage. It seems that the pamphlet had slipped down into the lining of Pierre's coat, and all this time he was carrying it around with him but didn't know it. Melville says that just so might Pierre have carried about with him, in his mind, the thorough under-

standing of the book, and yet not have been aware that he so understood it. Melville goes on to suggest that perhaps "some things that
men think they do not know, are . . . for all that thoroughly compre-
hended by them; and yet . . . though contained in themselves, are
kept a secret from themselves. The idea of Death seems such a thing"
(294).

As Pierre becomes more involved in his book, his cheeks become
pale and his lips become blue as he sits in his solitary room for hours
at a time. Melville describes the condition into which Pierre has fall-
en and exclaims: "Civilization, Philosophy, Ideal Virtue! behold your
victim!" (302). There is no doubt as to where Melville places the
blame for Pierre's downfall, but the best evidence he offers as to the
victimizing of Pierre is found in the excerpts he gives from Pierre's
writing. These writings can best exemplify Melville's indictment of
Transcendentalism, because they reflect the sorry state into which
Pierre has fallen in his attempt to believe in absolutes, innocence, and
a beneficent universe. The author-hero of Pierre's book, Vivia, speaks
for Pierre, and he soliloquizes thus:

> A deep-down, unutterable mournfulness is in me. Now I drop all
> humorous or indifferent disguises, and all philosophical preten-
> sions. I own myself a brother of the clod, a child of the Primeval
> Gloom. Hopelessness and despair are over me, as pall on pall.
> Away, ye chattering apes of a sophomorean Spinoza and Plato,
> who once didst all but delude me that the night was day, and
> pain only a tickle. Explain this darkness, exorcise this devil, ye
> cannot. Tell me not, thou inconceivable coxcomb of a Goethe,
> that the universe cannot spare thee and thy immortality, so long
> as—like a hired waiter—thou makest thyself 'generally useful.'
> Already the universe gets on without thee, and could still spare a
> million more of the same identical kidney. Corporations have no
> souls, and thy Pantheism, what was that? Thou were but the pre-
> tentious, heartless part of a man. Lo! I hold thee in this hand, and
> thou art crushed in it like an egg from which the meat hath been
> sucked.
>   Cast thy eye in there on Vivia; tell me why those four limbs
> should be clapped in a dismal jail—day out, day in—week out,
> week in—month out, month in—and himself the voluntary
> jailor! Is this the end of philosophy? This the larger, and spiritual
> life? This your boasted empyrean? Is it for this that a man should
> grow wise, and leave off his most excellent and calumniated
> folly?
>   Cast thy eye in there on Vivia; he, who in the pursuit of the
> highest health of virtue and truth, shows but a pallid cheek!

> Weigh his heart in thy hand, oh, thou gold-laced, virtuoso
> Goethe! and tell me whether it does not exceed thy standard
> weight!
>   Oh God, that man should spoil and rust on the stalk, and be
> wilted and threshed ere the harvest hath come! And oh God, that
> men that call themselves men should still insist on a laugh! I hate
> the world, and could trample all things of mankind as grapes,
> and heel them out of their breath, to think of the woe and the
> cant,—to think of the Truth and the Lie! (302–303)

From these comments it is obvious that Pierre is thoroughly disillusioned with Transcendentalism, and he seems to blame his present
troubles on his former idealism. He appears to be renouncing his
formed desire to live by spiritual ideals because he now owns himself
a "brother of the cold" and "child of the Primeval Gloom" (302).
Shortly after this time, Pierre receives word from Lucy that she comes
to join him and Isabel in New York. Ironically, just as Pierre begins to
turn away from his idealism, Lucy has caught the fire and set her own
feet on the path which has led Pierre to his destruction. She says,
"Thou art sacrificing thyself, and I hasten to re-tie myself to thee, that
so I may catch thy fire" (309). She promises to behave as if she were
"some nun-like cousin immovably vowed to dwell with thee in thy
strange exile." She sees Pierre as an exile from the world, dwelling in
some region of absolute Virtue and Truth: "Now I . . . shall soar up to
thee, where thou sittest in thine own calm, sublime heaven of heroism" (310). She says that she knows that the aftermath of her decision
will mean an estrangement from her mother and brothers, as well as
the whole "taunting and despising world," but "thou art my mother
and my brothers, and all the world, and all heaven, and all the universe to me," (311), she tells Pierre.

Pierre receives this letter with mixed emotions. He feels tri-
umphant that such a girl could feel so strongly toward him, that she
should "in this most tremendous of all trials, have acquitted herself
with such infinite majesty." But then the old battle resumes:

> He sunk utterly down from her, as in a bottomless gulf, and ran
> shuddering through hideous galleries of despair, in pursuit of
> some vague, white shape, and lo! two unfathomable dark eyes
> met his, and Isabel stood mutely and mournfully, yet all-
> ravishingly before him. (312)

Pierre has renounced idealism; he has accepted the dark side of his
nature and rejected Transcendental optimism. Now Lucy has renewed
the battle within him. The symbolism of the situation cannot be

overlooked. Lucy and Isabel, the two sides of Pierre's dual nature, have come together, for the first time, in the old church—which has ceased to be a place of orthodox religion and has turned into a refuge for a band of Transcendentalists. Within this building, symbolic of Pierre's own background, he finds himself caught inextricably between Lucy and Isabel. "On either hand clung to by a girl who would have laid down her life for him; Pierre, nevertheless, in his deepest, highest part, was utterly without sympathy from anything divine, human, brute, or vegetable." He is isolated from humanity more than ever: "Pierre was solitary as at the Pole" (338). Melville has used "the Pole" several times as a symbol of the barren regions of absolute truth. Pierre, in his mad search for the absolute, had finally arrived at that barren region where the compass can point no directions. Pierre has not as yet given up:

> Against the breaking heart, and the bursting head; against all the dismal lassitude, and deathful faintness and sleeplessness, and whirlingness, and craziness, still like a demi-god bore up. His soul's ship foresaw the inevitable rocks, but resolved to sail on, and make a courageous wreck. (339)

He does make a "courageous wreck," a glorious wreck. When he determines to make his last magnificent gesture and kill cousin Stanley, he makes a grand, tragic farewell speech to Lucy and Isabel. Standing between the doors of their two rooms he speaks to both: "For ye two, my most undiluted prayer is now, that from your here unseen and frozen chairs, ye may never stir alive;—the fool of Truth, the fool of Virtue, the fool of Fate, now quits ye forever!" (358). With the inevitability of a Greek tragedy, Pierre, Isabel, and Lucy meet their destruction in rapid succession.

Shortly before Pierre makes his fateful decision to kill Stanley, he has a dream, or vision, while in a "state of semi-unconsciousness, or rather trance" (342). This vision he experiences is one of the central symbols of the book. It is a further extension of the Plinlimmon passage, in which Melville has already set forth the problem of life as he sees it. In the Enceladus passage he presents a possible solution to that problem. This solution is not completely satisfactory, but it *is* attainable. In these two passages of the book, Plinlimmon's pamphlet and Enceladus, can be found a microcosm of the novel and an understanding of Melville's philosophical position at this point in his life.

The central image in this passage is the Mount of the Titans, "a singular height standing quite detached in a wide solitude not far from the grand range of dark blue hills encircling his [Pierre's] ancestral manor" (342). Most critics agree that the Saddle Meadows of the novel is representative of the home in which Melville lived at Pittsfield. From the room in which he wrote *Pierre* he had a magnificent view of Greylock, or Saddleback, Mountain, and it was to this mountain that he dedicated his novel. It is this same mountain that serves for the central image of *Pierre*.

Melville opens this passage with another rather direct gibe at the Transcendentalists. He presents a contradiction of the Emersonian view of Nature as the "universal tablet":

> Say what some poets will, Nature is not so much her own ever-sweet interpreter, as the mere supplier of that cunning alphabet, whereby selecting and combining as he pleases, each man reads his own peculiar lesson according to his own peculiar mind and mood. (342)

Having established that the meaning of an object is provided by each individual according to his own peculiar situation at the moment, like the doubloon scene in *Moby-Dick*, Melville launches into a discussion of the name attached to his symbolic mountain. It is no accident that the title "Delectable Mountain" was supplied by, specifically, "a Baptist farmer, and hereditary admirer of Bunyan and his most marvelous book." The fact that this farmer was a member of a strict religious sect and that he admired the time-honored Christian allegory, *Pilgrim's Progress*—from which came the name for the mountain—is significant in that it serves as an illustration of Melville's attitude toward the blindness of orthodox religion. It took a "high-aspiring, but most moody, disappointed bard" to see the mountain in its true light and to bestow the felicitous title of the "Mount of the Titans" (342). The significance here lies in that the poet was, like Pierre, idealistic but disillusioned. This is another example of Melville's belief that true enlightenment is found in the darkness of despair rather than in the brightness of man's optimistic moods.

The title Mount of Titans can be interpreted to have several meanings in the context of Melville's philosophical position. The Titans were a race of giants who overthrew their father and set themselves up as rulers of the world. Perhaps Melville chose this particular reference to support his feeling that orthodox religion had become an evil in the hands of mortals—that men had overthrown God and were ruling the world in their own way, but in His name. The Transcendentalists had done much the same thing. In claiming to have intuitive knowledge of the Divine Mind, which Melville believed to be inscrutable and silent, the Transcendentalists had declared themselves capable of perceiving God's will directly and therefore believed themselves to be partakers of divinity. Melville himself had no belief in either a beneficent Deity or in divine guidance. He saw man as flung into the world, and then ignored by both the world and the inscrutable gods. The mountain itself symbolizes the real, and the Titans, perhaps, represent the inscrutable gods who are the source of destiny and fate.

In describing the appearance of the mountain, Melville says that "where it fronted the old manor-house, some fifteen miles distant, the height, viewed from the piazza of a soft haze-canopied summer's noon, presented a long and beautiful, but not entirely inaccessible-looking purple precipice" (342). The old manor-house represented for both Pierre and Melville a certain stratum of society, the traditional aristocracy of mid-nineteenth-century America. The overwhelming, impenetrably mysterious truths of life, viewed from the security of the aristocratic position, appear pleasant and comfortable—but not at all terrifying or distressing. Life itself presents a "long and beautiful" panorama ending at the not-inaccessible "purple precipice" of heaven. As long as one remains comfortably ensconced on the piazza, the realities of life retain their pleasant aspects; it is only as one forsakes the artificial security of man-made aristocracy and approaches closer to actuality that he begins to perceive the true nature of things.

Melville begins to take the reader closer to the mountain. In describing the hillside pastures leading up to the mountain, Melville makes use of the amaranthine flower—which he later identifies as the "ever-encroaching appetite for God," as opposed to the catnip that he says represents "man's earthly household peace" (345). Because the amaranth is described as being destructive to the catnip and a begetter of sterility to the land, animals, and tenants, this symbolism forms another denunciation of the God-aspirations of Transcendentalism. This particular symbol plays a large part in understanding the tale of Enceladus, which will be addressed shortly.

Melville continues his description of the mountain as viewed through the eyes of a traveler who attempts to penetrate the realities of life symbolized by the mountain. As the traveler draws nearer, the mountain becomes more terrifying, "radiating with a hideous repellingness." He finally approaches close enough to see that "stark desolation; ruin, merciless and ceaseless; chills and gloom,—all here lived a hidden life, curtained by that cunning purpleness, which, from the piazza of the manor-house, so beautifully invested the mountain once called Delectable, but now styled Titanic." Reality is not at all what Pierre, and Melville, had been led to believe it would be. Outside the charmed circle of the pseudo-Eden created by society lay the stark brutalities of a not-at-all-beneficent universe. "Beaten off by such undreamed-of glooms and steeps" (344), the traveler sadly retraces his steps.

On his way back from the mountain, the traveler comes upon the natural rock formation known as Enceladus. It is most interesting at this point to note the apparently trivial anecdote Melville includes here concerning the group of college boys who, with Pierre, took their spades and attempted to excavate around Enceladus. They "bared a good part of his mighty chest, and exposed his mutilated shoulders, and the stumps of his once audacious arms . . . leaving stark naked his in vain indignant chest to the defilements of the birds" (345). It is possible that Melville was implying here that the potential danger of partial knowledge. Pierre's education had opened new doors to him, raised new questions, but had not provided the answers—it had merely left him exposed to the ravagings of many previously unrecognized evils.

As the passage continues, Enceladus becomes synonymous with Pierre, and through him becomes synonymous with mankind in general. The natural rock Enceladus is compared with the statue by Marsy, and the conclusion is that "Marsy gave arms to the eternally defenseless; but Nature, more truthful, performed an amputation, and left the impotent Titan without one serviceable ball-and-socket above the thigh." Pierre sees the armless giant, "despairing of any other mode of wreaking his immitigable hate," turning his trunk into a battering-ram and hurling himself against the mountain (342). Thus Pierre sees himself, aspiring to the heights and yet unable to free himself from his earthly nature, hurling himself vainly against the invincible fates, achieving nothing but his own destruction.

Melville steps in at this point and says that Pierre's "random knowledge" did not carry him far enough for him to understand fully the symbolism; therefore, he did not find the comfort that it held. He says Pierre "did not flog this stubborn rock as Moses his, and force even aridity itself to quench his painful thirst" (346). Melville then tells what message Pierre should have received from his vision, but the message is again presented in symbolic terms. In order to interpret the full meaning of what Melville has to say, one must amalgamate many of his preceding meanings with his final unraveling of the myth of Enceladus. A rough paraphrase of this follows:

The Enceladus figure represents Man in his indissoluble position of half-God, half-animal. The incompatibility of these two component parts places him in an impossible position. Thus, as with the amaranth-catnip symbol, the more all-consuming Man's search for the absolute truth of the God ideal becomes, the more his earthly peace is destroyed—try as he may, he cannot reconcile these two sides of his being. The passage about the collegians seems to be saying that Man tries to study Man in an effort to obtain the knowledge whereby he can solve the unsolvable problem, but "the wearied young-collegians gave over their enterprise in despair. With all their toil, they had not yet come to the girdle of Enceladus" (345). This attempt to understand and pinpoint Man into a formula is doomed to failure. Man, unable to accept his role as earthly, and yet unable to become God, batters himself into destruction "against the invulnerable steep" (346).

This much of the story Pierre was able to comprehend, but he stopped short of the final consolation, which Melville states thus:

> Wherefore whoso storms the sky gives best proof he came from thither! But whatso crawls contented in the moat before that crystal fort, shows it was born within that slime, and there forever will abide. (347)

In other words, the animal-God who is content to remain all animal does not suffer agonies of frustration, as does the animal-God who attempts to be God—but neither does he share the breath of divinity that is found in those who struggle to regain their birthright in the skies. The very desire to storm the heights, although foredoomed to failure, is in itself an affirmation of a divine spark within man. Thus in Melville's opinion, man must recognize the futility and absurdity of his position in the world, but he must not be content to crawl in the slime—rather he must continue to struggle, striving to reach the unreachable, finding the ultimate value within the struggle itself.

By the time Melville wrote *Pierre*, he had progressed to the point of realizing that symbols can no more remain static than can life itself. Many early critics found themselves frustrated by Melville's use of symbolism in *Pierre* because it defies a cut-and-dried interpretation. But it is this ungraspable quality that lends Melville's writing its quality of abstract realism—that is, in dealing with abstractions, Melville achieves, through his fluctuating symbols, a level of reality that it would be impossible to attain through the customary use of static, allegorical symbols such as are found in *Mardi*, or even through the use of an ambiguous symbol such as that of *Moby-Dick*. Melville had come to realize that a symbol has meaning only in the context of the life situation—and the meaning of the symbol must necessarily change as the situation changes. Thus Lucy, in the beginning, is symbolic of everything that is good, bright, and beautiful in Pierre's conventional life in the conventional world of conventional society; but when Pierre is suddenly plunged out of his cozy little corner in the gold and green paradise of Saddle Meadows, when his values are all overturned and his world is inverted, then Lucy and all that she symbolizes can no longer be viewed by Pierre from the same perspective. If he is to question the true value of the world of Saddle Meadows, then it is only natural that he must also question the meaning and significance of this girl who has been symbolic to him of all that is perfect in this now questionable world.

The simple problem of physical and spiritual duality of man that occupied Melville in *Mardi* has now become an extremely complex problem involving the psychological, social, and emotional aspects of man, as well as his philosophical and theological views. The simple body/soul problem that plagued the Transendentialists, the separation of the Not Me from the Me has assumed, for Melville, a much more complex and modern problem of duality—the separation of the Me from the Me. Thus the simple nineteenth-century philosophical pondering has progressed into a twentieth-century psychological probing into the depths of Being.

The irony of Melville and Pierre comes full circle with the realization that Melville, while bitterly satirizing the foolhardiness of Pierre, was himself foolhardy in much the same heroic, impractical fashion. Melville must have known at some level that he was committing literary suicide by writing a book like *Pierre*. In the chapter entitled "Pierre, as a Juvenile Author, Reconsidered," Melville traces Pierre's youthful success in the literary field—which greatly resembles his own career—and tells how Pierre considers his early work as shallow; consequently Pierre now intends to write of the great truths. Melville warns that "though the world worship Mediocrity and Commonplace, yet hath it fire and sword for all contemporary Grandeur; that though it swears that it fiercely assails all Hypocrisy, yet hath it not always an ear for Earnestness" (264). That Melville was well aware of the fickle public, and had learned his lesson painfully is evidenced in his letter to Duyckinck after his *Mardi* experience:

> I am but a poor mortal, & admit that I learn by experience & not by divine intuitions. Had I not written & published 'Mardi,' in all likelihood, I would not be as wise as I am now, or may be. For that thing was stabbed at (I do not say through)—& therefore, I am the wiser for it.[92]

Clearly Melville knew how the public would react toward a book like *Pierre*. Surely he was not too surprised when the book was condemned by the critics. The *Boston Post* said: "What the book means, we know not. To save it from almost utter worthlessness, it must be called a prose poem, and even then, it might be supposed to emanate from a lunatic hospital rather than from the quiet retreats of Berkshire."[93] *Graham's Magazine* said: "The spirit pervading the whole book is intolerably unhealthy, and the most friendly reader is obliged at the end to protest against such a provoking perversion of talent and waste of power."[94]

One cannot resist speculating as to why Melville chose to make this heroically futile gesture, while simultaneously satirizing the very futility of such behavior. Unlike the Transcendentalists, however, he realized and admitted the futility of his "storming of the heights," and whatever gratification he received for his inner self must have compensated, in his opinion, for the humiliating indignities heaped upon him by the literary world. Melville never took issue with the Transcendentalists on the basis of their idealism—as noted in his copy of Emerson's *Essays*, he accepted their aspirations as "noble." What he did take issue with was their method of achieving their ideals—their blind optimism and childlike faith in a beneficent universe, their denial of circumstance and situation, their refusal to accept the brutal aspects of reality, and their unwillingness to recognize the limitations of the human condition. What Melville satirizes in *Pierre* is not the basic vision of the Transcendentalists, but, rather, their general "sophomorean" immaturity. Apparently Melville had reached the stage of becoming what might be called a "practical" Transcendentalist.

On the surface it would appear that such a juxtaposition of terminology would be incompatible. If we consider the word "practical" to mean, as it usually seems to in its Melvillean connotations, the facing of reality without illusion, then it does, indeed, seem to be a poor adjectival choice to modify a Transcendentalist. The basic tenets of Transcendentalism—its emphasis on romantic subjectivism and the reality of ideality to the exclusion of empirical fact—would appear to negate the meaning of "practical" as defined. However, Melville evidences a merging, or integration, of the subjective and objective views—a completely realistic, disillusioned, grounded-in-reality view of the world—a thorough realization of the ineffectuality of man's subjective idealism when applied to the practical affairs of men, and yet a realization of the value *per se* of idealism. As a result of this merger he avows the spiritual necessity for a man to build his own private world of subjective values—even in the face of his own destruction. He adheres to Transcendental idealism, not because he believes that it will bring about the "best of all possible worlds," but because he finds within this idealism a basic value exclusive of any benefits he might hope to derive from it.

Contrary to his forerunners, the early members of the Transcendental Club and the Brook Farm movement, who saw Transcendental idealism as a means of procuring the brotherhood of man and the salvation of the world—the impractical Transcendentalists, the visionaries who dreamed castles-in-air from blueprints-in-heaven—Melville saw, understood, and accepted the reality of the world for what it was. He built his idealistic castle with foundations deep in the earth, fully realizing that it would be besieged by all manner of men for all manner of purposes—fully accepting the fact that it might not be able to withstand the siege and might very possibly be destroyed around him. The destruction of it was not so important, however, as was the value he had found in the building of it. Herein lies the basic difference between the Emersonian Transcendentalists and Melville.

Chapter Six

Naked Nature aboard the *San Dominick*: "Benito Cereno," Emerson, and the Gothic

URING THE WINTER AND SPRING OF 1855, MELVILLE COMPOSED "Benito Cereno," an indictment of "benign" racism that currently enjoys growing critical attention, doubtless because of heightened academic interest in issues of race, as well as gender and class.[1] Melvillians, however, have generally shied away from readings of this long short story that consider it in the context of Emersonian Transcendentalism,[2] the reason probably being that the question of slavery is at issue here and Emerson's abolitionist efforts—which are richly documented—ostensibly work against such an interpretation.[3] Nevertheless, I intend to explore this possibility by approaching the story as a reactive work of Gothic fiction that may be read as a brilliantly contrived critique of the rational, self-reliant, and highly optimistic philosophy professed by Ralph Waldo Emerson.

My approach to "Benito Cereno" focuses on the conventions and tropes of Gothic literature, which form the fabric of the story. I contest traditional assessments classifying Gothic fiction as escapist; instead, I join with critics such as Teresa A. Goddu and David Punter in arguing that Gothic narratives are intimately and inseparably connected to the cultures that produce them.[4] The Gothic aspects of "Benito Cereno" do not emerge from a cultural vacuum, but instead arise where concrete experience contradicts the dream world of social myth. While this chapter addresses several historical horrors Melville includes in this story—such as slavery, mutiny, and murder—it more specifically concerns how Melville uses them to dramatize the character Delano's misperceptions as an extreme Emersonian.

In his groundbreaking work *Nightmare on Main Street*, cultural critic Mark Edmundson indirectly offers a new route to understanding Melville's complex relationship with Transcendentalism.[5] Edmundson focuses on present-day America, which he finds characterized by the parallel cultures of the Gothic and the Transcendental. He cites numerous contemporary examples, ranging from Gothicized media renderings of the O. J. Simpson trial to facilely Transcenden-talistic New Age panaceas, inspired by the belief that self-transformation is as easy as a fairy-tale wish. Edmundson argues that these current events are rooted in the nineteenth century, as a careful examination of the Emerson-Melville relationship illustrates. In one of his few references to this time period, Edmundson writes that the

> Gothic shows the dark side, the world of cruelty, lust, perversion, and crime that, many of us at least half believe, is hidden beneath established conventions. [The] Gothic tears through censorship, explodes hypocrisies, to expose the world as the corrupted, reeking place it is. . . . Unsentimental, enraged by gentility and high-mindedness, skeptical about progress in any form, the Gothic mind is antithetical to all smiling American faiths. A nation of ideals, America has also been, not surprisingly, a nation of hard disillusionment, with a fiercely reactive Gothic imagination. Ours is the culture that produced both "Self-Reliance" and "The Fall of the House of Usher."[6]

Edmundson touches upon what Leslie Fiedler has argued in his *Love and Death in the American Novel*: that the American Gothic began as "a literature of darkness and the grotesque in a land of light and affirmation."[7] In its initial wave, the literary Gothic proliferated in Europe as the literature of revolution, specifically the revolution in France that dominated European consciousness in the last decade of the eighteenth century. The best examples of this genre served the important function of rousing its readers from smug self-assurance induced by enlightenment rationalism. The Gothic was a reaction against the sanitized empirical philosophies of an age. In the Gothic novel readers discovered, or rediscovered, the irrational and the repressed; they met up with the fears and desires that enlightened reason had attempted to banish.

This mirrors the pattern of the Gothic in mid-nineteenth-century America, which was on the brink of Civil War. This period in the United States was simultaneously one of realization and disillusionment. In a period marked by a profound belief in man's ability to improve his world, some societal groups inevitably realized the negative aspects that called for reform, and began to search for ways to implement positive change. Espousing his aphoristic wisdom regard-

ing methods for man's self-improvement, Emerson and the philosophy he stood for reflected the spirit of positive change that pervaded
society at this time. America was accomplishing new things—building a new civilization—but as critics such as Fiedler and Carolyn L.
Karcher have been quick to point out, there was a "shadow over the
promised land," which was, in part, the same "shadow" that Don
Benito observes has darkened his own situation.[8] National guilt over
the institutionalized oppression of slavery and the genocide of Native
Americans contradicted the American myth that Emerson so poeti-
cally articulated.

This is not to say that Melville necessarily had Emerson or any
other Transcendentalist specifically in mind when he shaped
Delano's character. However, the possibility exists that Melville was
reacting fiercely against certain assumptions of American culture at
this historical moment, many of which found expression in
American Transcendentalism. The Gothic—a manifestation of what
Rosemary Jackson refers to as "the literature of subversion"—enabled
Melville, in "Benito Cereno" more so than in any other work, to articulate rifts between ideology and actuality in imagined worlds that
were produced within, and determined by, their social context.[9]
Harold Bloom once observed that "self-reliance, the Emersonian
answer to original Sin, does not exist in the Poe cosmos, where you
start out damned, doomed and dismal."[10] This observation is equally
applicable to the cosmos of Herman Melville. As seen in my discussion of *Pierre*, the later fiction of Melville's career persistently engages
many of the same questions raised by the Transcendentalists, but his
answers to those questions are radically different. Emerson and
Melville, then, may be seen as two sides of the same cultural coin,
and "Benito Cereno" may be read as an example of Melville's specifically Gothic critique of the Transcendental hypothesis.

Melville's adaptation of the *Narrative of Voyages and Travels in the
Northern and Southern Hemispheres*, published in 1817 by Captain
Amasa Delano, an ancestor of Franklin D. Roosevelt, opens as the
captain of an American sealer discerns a mysterious ship that, from
afar, resembles a floating monastery. When the Yankee captain boards
the ship, he discovers that the strange vessel is a Spanish slaver and
that the dark figures that resemble cowled Black Friars, or
Dominicans, are actually enslaved Africans. The slaver's captain, a
young Spaniard named Don Benito Cereno, tells Delano that most of
his crew was wiped out by a plague that also killed the ship's owner,
his friend Don Alexandro Aranda, so the Africans must help with the
running of the ship. As Don Benito tells his story to Delano, he faints
repeatedly, and his faithful black servant, Babo, supports him with his

arm. The "liberal" Delano, a "Massachusetts man" who assumes that
Africans are jolly primitives who love bright colors and have a special
talent for waiting on white people, constantly compares the "fun-
loving" Africans to animals. Boasting that he takes to Negroes "not
philanthropically, but genially, just as other men to Newfound dogs,"
he offers to buy Babo from Don Benito by way of complimenting the
black for being such an excellent body servant.[11] Despite misgivings
prompted by the provocative behavior of several of the remaining
Spanish sailors and various other unsettling events, Delano cannot
fathom what is really going on aboard the ship.

Melville builds suspense by limiting his third-person narrative to
Delano's point of view until the moment at which Delano himself
realizes, with a Melvillian "shock of recognition," that the Africans
have taken over the ship and slaughtered most of the whites, and that
Babo has woven an elaborate web of deception enabled by the
American's own prejudices and naïveté.[12] By the end of the story,
Melville has drawn those readers who have adopted Delano's view of
the *San Dominick* into the same entangling web.

In this tough-minded story, Melville indicts slavery without sen-
timentalizing either the blacks or the whites. He makes it clear that
Don Alexandro Aranda's having allowed the Africans to move around
the decks unfettered does not change the fact that he considered
them his property and planned to reshackle and sell them as soon as
the ship reached port. Aranda's leniency in keeping his "cargo" on
deck, where fresh air and water would insure a higher survival rate,
can be seen as purely self-serving, since better health meant fewer
deaths, and fewer deaths meant more profit for the slave owner.
Moreover, freedom within the confines of a slave ship did not protect
the women against rape and sexual abuse; in fact, cleaning them up
and letting them roam the deck instead of leaving them crammed in
a filthy hold made them more accessible to the lustful crew.[13] After
Aranda's death, the women, whom Delano imagines to be as docile
and sweet as does with their fawns, shave Aranda's bones clean with
their hatchets, then hang his skeleton over the carved figurehead of
Cristobal Colón as a warning to the surviving Spaniards, covering it
with a cloth when another ship draws near.[14]

Melville deconstructs "niceness" as a moral category at the end of
the story; when the Americans board the ship, finally having realized
the mutiny that has occurred, they restrain themselves from maim-
ing or killing the Africans not because they are kind, but because they
plan to claim the "cargo" and want it to be undamaged. The willingness of the American Captain to continue the slave trade parallels the

willingness of the "enlightened" founding fathers to bring the slavery of the old world into the new.

After Delano and his men overpower the Africans and take
control of the ship, the narrative switches to a legal deposition that
purports to establish the "facts" of the case—which, of course, means
from the Spaniard's point of view. Failing to grasp Melville's reason
for including a dry legal document, *Putnam's* editor George William
Curtis assumed that the placing of the deposition at the end of the
story was laziness on Melville's part, and he complained that Melville
did everything "too hurriedly."[15] The deposition, however, actually
frames the story to form a mutilated triptych, with the implied third
panel being the "voiceless" Babo's version of the story. The legalistic
language obscures the moral issues and nullifies the Africans' point of
view, as history written by colonizers always does.

Ironically, Delano's blindness nearly costs him his life and the life
of Don Benito, yet he learns nothing from his experience or the
Spanish Captain's ordeal, and less about the suffering of the blacks.
In a coda following the conclusion of the trial, Delano blithely suggests that Don Benito can forget his harrowing ordeal, but the
Spaniard remains haunted by the shadow of "the Negro." Like
Charles V, the Holy Roman Emperor who ordered the first Africans
shipped to Santo Domingo to replace the Indians who had been
worked to death by Columbus and his men, Don Benito retires to a
monastery. In the end, Babo's point of view comes across wordlessly
and lingers in the reader's mind. The story closes with the image of
Babo's head, "that hive of subtlety," impaled on a pole in the Plaza by
the "civilized" Spaniards. The "unabashed gaze" of Babo stares down
the long corridors of history in accusation and defiance, a challenge
to a nation heading inexorably toward civil war.[16]

The reader of "Benito Cereno," caught up in the same mystery
that Captain Delano cannot penetrate, longs for a final release of the
suspense—a solution to the surreal puzzle. At the core of this narrative, then, lies a quest for a concealed truth. In his introduction to
The Castle of Otranto, E. F. Bleiler argues that "the Gothic novel is a
primitive detective story in which God or Fate is the detective."[17]
While "Benito Cereno" is very much a "detective story," it is not
quite a narrative in which "God or Fate is the detective," as the
omniscient narration of the story superficially suggests. Instead,
Melville holds the reader until the flash of illumination in the climax
by using Delano's consciousness as a lens through which characters,
scenes, and actions are experienced. Despite its title, "Benito Cereno"
is actually Delano's story because the narrator focuses on the impact

of the events on him, concealing the truth until Delano finally discovers it himself.

The reader's revelation is delayed by its dependence on Delano's character, whom the narrator describes in the opening pages of the story as

> a person of a singularly distrustful good nature, not liable, except on extraordinary and repeated incentives, and hardly then, to indulge in personal alarms, any way involving the imputation of malign evil in man. Whether, in view of what humanity is capable, such a trait implies, along with a benevolent heart, more than ordinary quickness and accuracy of intellectual perception, may be left to the wise to determine." (47)

Delano's behavior remains constant throughout the story; his blithely optimistic and self-assured disposition does not change. No matter what confronts him, he sees nothing but the "benign" aspect of nature. But in describing Delano's personality, this passage raises serious questions about the limitations of his Emersonian epistemological perspective. The narrator's ironic statement about Delano's lack of awareness points to the story's central theme: the dangers of an isolated, idealistic perspective untempered by an Ishmaelesque flexibility. Melville thus critiques Transcendentalism by implying that it can lead into danger those who lack sufficient awareness to moderate its application. In *Moby-Dick,* he shows that Transcendentalism is not for self-reliant extremists like Ahab; in *Pierre,* he shows its limitations as a worldview and behavioral guide; and in "Benito Cereno," he illustrates its problems for the hyper-näive Delano. Unlike Ahab, Delano emerges from his horrific trials and their aftermath unscathed, much less disfigured or annihilated. But Delano's obvious failure to understand or to learn from his experiences nevertheless binds him to Ahab with the stoutest of monkey-ropes. While Ahab's unwillingness to compromise or to tolerate any other perspective that his own ultimately destroys him, Delano's unchanging self-satisfied view of the world intimates his own possibilities for destruction, for it is by sheer accident alone that he survives his sojourn aboard the *San Dominick.* Delano's unquestioning nature blinds him to the facts of human history, which are largely written in blood. In effect, he misapplies Emerson's epigram to "Self-Reliance," which encapsulates its theme: "Ne to quaesiveris extra"—literally, do not seek outside yourself and/or do not ask any opinion but your own. This is exactly the position that Delano dramatizes, for it is his own self-assured insularity that finally defines him. For Melville, true identity lies not in

Emerson's suprahistorical self-reliance, but, paradoxically, in a highly individuated identification of self with history.

As the narrator suggests, Delano fails to recognize his situation for what it is, even with extraordinary and repeated incentives. While there are no haunted castles in "Benito Cereno," the *San Dominick* is described as "battered and mouldy, the castellated forecastle seemed some ancient turret, long ago taken by assault and then left to decay" (48). A Gothic atmosphere of ruin permeates the ship, yet Delano sees only "the mild sun . . . of his own good nature" (65). Onboard, psychologically shocking incidents pile up within the story: the knife blow to the cabin boy's bloody head, the shaving incident giving the impression of a headsman and his victim, Don Alexandro Aranda's ghastly skeleton riveted to the *San Dominick*'s prow—these images heighten the Gothic suspense of the story, and prove to be a Gordian knot Delano cannot even see, much less unravel or cut. Don Benito must do this for him, with his desperate leap into the *Rover.* Consider Delano's reaction to the Gothic events onboard the ship with the following passage from Emerson's *Nature:*

> Build therefore your own world. As fast as you conform your life to the pure idea in your mind, that will unfold its great proportions. A corresponding revolution in things will attend the influx of spirit. So fast will disagreeable appearances, swine, spiders, snakes, pests, mad-houses, prisons, enemies, vanish; they are temporary and shall no more be seen. The sordor and filths of nature, the sun shall dry up and the wind exhale.[18]

Delano appears to heed a similar directive, yet in a superficial manner. This suggests "Benito Cereno"'s fundamental irony: apparent virtues—innocence, idealism, and self-reliance—can become defects in the wrong combination; they lead the Captain to misapprehension after misapprehension. Thus, as E. F. Carlisle notes in "Captain Amasa Delano: Melville's American Fool,"

> Melville seems to have placed the extreme of Emersonian affirmation and hope for the future in the mind of a sea Captain. In *Moby-Dick* Ahab dramatizes self-reliance gone mad; in "Benito Cereno" Delano reveals affirmation become foolish and blind. Instead of an American hero, who reveals the triumph of American innocence, benevolence, and good will, then, Melville's tale presents the American fool.[19]

Indeed, Delano typifies the extreme of Emersonian affirmation to the point of absurdity. Through Delano, Melville shows that some are simply ill equipped to "build their own worlds" by following the Transcendental plan.

As mentioned in previous chapters, the historical facts of Melville's exposure to Emerson are substantial and documented in several sources, including John Williams's 1991 *White Fire: The Influence of Emerson on Melville* and volume one of Hershel Parker's recent Melville biography.[20] That Melville was impressed with Emerson after hearing him lecture on February 5, 1849 emerges from his previously mentioned correspondence later that month with Evert Duyckinick in which he wrote: "I have heard Emerson since I have been here. Say what they will, he's a great man."[21] Yet one week later, he responded to Emerson more fully and more critically:

> I could readily see in Emerson, notwithstanding his merit, a gap-ing flaw. It was, the insinuation, that had he lived in those days when the world was made, he might have offered some valuable suggestions. These men are all cracked right across the bow. And never will the pullers-down be able to cope with the builders up.[22]

Melville found a "gaping flaw" in Emerson that could not be obscured by his other admirable qualities. Melville saw Emerson as deeply presumptuous in his implicit belief that had Emerson been around when the world was created, he could have given God some constructive suggestions. Nothing in Melville's impression conflicts with the ideas of Emerson, who held that everyone was divine because all physical reality partakes of the divine spirit.

For Melville, thinkers like Emerson "are all cracked right across the bow," including Amasa Delano. Melville identifies with "the builders-up," for "the pullers-down" like Emerson always project the dangerous results of their own values onto the universe. The skepti-cal irony of the "the builders-up" is the only possible stance for Melville. The tension in "Benito Cereno" is between another such "builder-up," Don Benito, and Delano, a "puller-down." Don Benito is a "builder-up" because he sees horrific things as they really are, having lived through them; he faces reality without projecting his own values upon it. By the story's close, Cereno's unflinching engage-ment with things as they are finally leads him to the symbolically named Mount Agonia, where within three months' time death over-takes him, destroyed by the nightmare of his experiences. Delano, however, is a "puller-down." He comes to his perception of the world with his mind already made up; he sees the real world through the lens of his own preconceived ideas. In this, he is an extreme example of the detached insularity characterizing the Emersonian individualist.

In the famous letter to Hawthorne penned just before the publication of *Moby-Dick,* Melville outlines a problem inherent in Emersonian Transcendentalism by describing how slippery language can be:

> We incline to think that God cannot explain his own secrets, and that he would like a little more information upon certain points himself. We mortals astonish him as much as he us. But it is this Being of the matter; there lies the knot with which we choke ourselves. As soon as you say *Me*, a *God*, a *Nature*, so soon you jump off from the stool and hang from the beam. Yes, that word is the hangman.[23]

For Melville, imposing any kind of a mental construct upon the universe is ultimately destructive. In this way, Melville shows that Emerson's famous line from *Nature*, "Words are signs of natural facts,"[24] has potentially grave implications. Melville believes instead that the "word is the hangman"—that by rigidly categorizing any area of the world we limit our ability to see, and this is a kind of philosophical suicide. As Michael J. Hoffman observes,

> The only important measure of value is the accuracy with which the individual sees the world. Value lies in the confrontation, not in either the perceiver or the object, and the attempt to find value in the world or to see physical entities as symbols or retainers of meaning is a great mistake, a deadly mistake. . . . Avoid giving things names at all, if possible, and if not avoid letting names bestow finality of "significance" on the object. For names have nothing to do with "Being"; categories are antithetical to process, and the life process is the only reality.[25]

One reason Melville warns against such categorization is because of men like Amasa Delano. Certain types of people tend to become dangerously comfortable with labels and with the reduction of life's complexities to schemata. Indeed, failing to read Emerson's maxim "Nature always wears the colors of the spirit" by moonlight, Delano becomes the quintessential literal reader—in effect, Melville's "sub-sub librarian."[26] He accepts what he sees as truth; he benignly equates the apparent with the actual. Delano's misapprehensions may be read as ironic commentary on the following previously cited passage from Emerson, which bears repeating:

Standing on the bare ground,—my head bathed by the blithe air, and uplifted into infinite space,—all mean egotism vanishes. I become a transparent eye-ball; I am nothing; I see all; the currents of the Universal Being circulate through me; I am part or particle of God."[27]

But far from seeing all, Delano has a real problem with perception. In fact, "Benito Cereno" can be viewed as an allegory of misreading, with Delano as the bumbling naïf who blunders through treacherous circumstances, but who somehow always ends up, ironically, safe in the end. His misapprehensions recur throughout the story, from his mistaking the *San Dominick's* crew for "a ship-load of monks" (48), to his opinion of Babo as "less a servant than a devoted companion" (52), to Don Benito. Yet despite his misplaced confidence in his own viewpoint, blind luck sees Delano through.

After reading one rationalization after another, one begins to sense that the American does not merely understand slowly, but that he actively fights awareness. The point after which only a truly foolish American innocent would misread the signs seems to occur when Delano dwells on his incorrect suspicion about Don Benito. Cereno has just asked a series of suspicious questions about the American's ship, ending with "Your ships generally go—go more or less armed, I believe, Señor?" Delano answers all of the questions—questions that might suggest to the reader that Cereno is considering an attack. The Captain, with characteristic "intrepid indifference," volunteers all to Cereno, including that he has silver coin on board the *Bachelor's Delight* and twenty-five men, some of whom would be going on a fishing party that night (66). Not only does the American fail to recognize Don Benito's desperate attempt to assess his ability to retake the slaves, but he also does not appreciate the potential risk of providing this information. Here Delano's confident self-reliance, which blinds him to the true circumstances of his situation, puts himself and his crew in danger.

So far this chapter suggests that Captain Delano embodies Emersonian affirmation taken to the point of absurdity. The pattern of action, the ironic point of view, the frequent misperceived signs and subsequent rationalizations by the American Captain provide some support for this view. But it is not yet enough. No one denies Delano's trusting good nature or that he does not understand, nor does anyone deny that the reader perceives a great deal more that the generous American. Upon examining Delano's attitudes and thoughts, however, one discovers that rather then being just a bit obtuse, the Captain holds profound misconceptions that not only mislead him, but make him an utter failure at understanding and dealing with life. He may, in the end, sail confidently away into "yon bright sun," but he does so only by sheer accident.

Delano's optimistic, "benevolent" outlook, as the reader has seen, causes him to misread life. For example, although he believes himself to be fair and republican in his dealings, he knows nothing about the slaves, and he easily accepts their oppression. He has a distorted idea of them as noble savages. At one point, as he wanders about the ship observing the seamen and the Negroes, he notices "a slumbering negress . . . lying like a doe in the shade of a woodland rock." The woman is sleeping with her child, "her wide-awake faun" at her breast. She wakes to find Delano looking at her and immediately begins to play the part of mother. Delano's reaction is typical; the specific language and the point of view emphasize the extreme misconception involved. He thinks, "There's naked nature, now; pure tenderness and love" (73). The narrator goes on to explain Delano's reaction:

> This incident prompted him to remark to the other negresses more particularly than before. He was gratified with their manners; like most uncivilized women, they seemed at once tender of heart and rough of constitution; equally ready to die for their infants or fight for them. Unsophisticated as leopardesses; loving as doves. Ah! thought Captain Delano, these, perhaps, are some of the very women whom Ledyard saw in Africa, and gave such a noble account of. (73)

What he is wrong about is *not* their potential for violence (he recognizes that, viewing them as brute animals) but their ability to carry out a sophisticated plan. By the story's close, we are well aware that Babo understands irony far better than Delano ever does.

Later, walking around the deck, he tries to analyze the strange behavior of Benito Cereno. He speculates about possible complicity about Benito and the blacks for some unimagined end. He muses to himself:

> But if the whites have some dark secret concerning Don Benito, could then Don Benito be in any way in complicity with the blacks? But they were too stupid. Besides, who has ever heard of a white so far a renegade as to apostatize from his very species almost, be leaguing in against it with negroes? (75)

Delano's sense of the Negroes' inferiority and of the necessary separation of the races becomes obvious from this passage. He reveals the same belief when he thinks about the negro's fitness as servant. As he watches Babo shave Bentio Cereno, the Captain observes,

> There is something in the negro which, in a peculiar way, fits him for avocations about one's person. Most negroes are natural valets and hairdressers; taking to the comb and brush congenially as castanets, and flourishing them with almost equal satisfaction. (83)

Delano believes that negroes are "naturally" more musical than whites; he even attributes to them "the great gift of good humor . . . a certain easy cheerfulness, harmonious in every glance and gesture; as though God has set the whole negro to some pleasant tune" (83). Babo's intellect and the scheme produced by it soundly refute both of Delano's absurd beliefs.

Babo's very existence—his intelligence and control of the ship— suggest, of course, that there are more ways of looking at reality than Delano ever imagined. Thus Babo's point of view, although oversimplified (he is too often dismissed as some form of masked depravity), invalidates Delano's point of view.

Rather than merely a deceived innocent, Delano is a fool. The narrator passes rather severe judgment on the American by making him the butt of jokes, ridiculing him. Delano furrows his brow in a comical attempt to discern the purpose of the knot the old sailor throws at him:

> "What are you knotting there, my man?"
> "The knot," was the brief reply, without looking up.
> "So it seems; but what is it for?"
> "For someone else to undo."
> "Undo it, cut it, quick." (76)

And the narrator next famously observes that "knot in hand, and knot in head, Captain Delano stood mute." Thus the sailor's clue is completely lost on the Captain. One can argue that Delano's very innocence saves him, for if he had suspected rightly and betrayed this knowledge he would have immediately been killed. Had he not jumped and had Delano made it back to the ship before Benito Cereno leapt into his boat, he would have been as safe and as unwise and as ignorant as he has always been. He would have remained untouched by knowledge of evil. As a result, his understanding of life and his ability to cope with complexity and ambiguity—constants in human experience—would remain the same. The ironies and complexities of the tale, however, raise more that merely a question of safety and apparent success.

One must not forget, however, that Delano "saves the day" by reinstating order to the *San Dominick*; he seems to deal successfully with moral ambiguity. Although he may deal with it practically, he uses force to overwhelm a complexity that he fails to comprehend. His innocence ironically saves him; brute force makes him a success. But, as Carlisle observes, "his innocence is ignorance rather than divine innocence, and therefore it is inadequate."[28] The reader cannot have any faith that a big stick and lots of good luck are sufficient for safe passage through life's unhospitable waters. Perhaps the American does win, for a moment; the victory, however, does not change the basic condition that exists, nor does it change Delano—he still knows nothing. Thus his victory is hollow and superficial at best: at the worst, it is meaningless and deceptive. He has advanced no further toward knowledge than when he first appeared in the story. Even when he knows what has happened to him and to Don Benito, he does not really understand, for Benito's retreat from life lies beyond the American's comprehension. At the end Delano's prevailing optimism asserts itself in a future of blue skies and blue seas:

> You generalize, Don Benito, and mournfully enough. But the past is passed; why moralize upon it? Forget it. See, yon bright sun has forgotten it all, and the blue sea, and the blue sky; these have turned over new leaves. (116)

The reality that Melville portrays is far more complex than Delano's conclusion suggests, for in an important sense the reality remains unchanged—the world does not turn over a new leaf. Rather than learning from his experiences, Delano fails to reflect upon what has happened; he does not learn. He sees instead that the natural world appears unaffected by human experiences and resolves to remain unaffected himself. Through Delano's stubborn blindness, Melville shows the dangers of taking things at face value—of building up each day from that morning's sunrise instead of tearing them down from unrealistic and unattainable ideals. The Transcendentalist position was to see the divine in man, to see the nobility inherent in the human condition. Melville, deep thought-diver he was, could not accept a viewpoint that fails to account for the Gothic truth that humanity has its weaknesses and the human condition its ambiguities. In Melville's paradigm, for one to overlook these facts is risky at best.

Chapter Seven

The Endless, Winding Way: Melville's Engagement with Emerson in *The Whale*'s Wake

P ERHAPS MELVILLE'S MOST SUCCESSFUL ANTI-TRANSCENDENTAL STORY IS "Bartleby, the Scrivener," first published in *Putnam's Monthly Magazine* for November and December 1853.[1] The story ridicules total self-reliance in the character of an inactive office worker. Bartleby's humorously pathetic assertion of independence—his constant refrain is "I would prefer not to"—amounts to a complete withdrawal from the routines of living. In contrast, in "The American Scholar" Emerson advocated a life of action for the self-reliant scholar, who also is influenced by nature and books. "The one thing of value," Emerson said, "is the active soul."[2] Even Thoreau, who withdrew from all social routines at Walden Pond, studied nature, read the classics, and hoed beans. In addition to the apparent satire, Melville may have designed this story at least in part as a self-portrait. Like Bartleby, who had worked in the Dead Letter Office, Melville also withdrew into himself, embittered by his apparent failure as an author.

Despite the merit of individual stories, *The Piazza Tales* was not a financial success. Still in poor health, though somewhat improved, Melville concluded his professional career as a novelist in 1857 with publication of *The Confidence-Man*, a comprehensive though ineffective satire on the optimism of the age. If *Pierre* marks that point in Melville's career at which he rejects the idea of a moral order in nature that governs the affairs of men, *The Confidence-Man* portrays the logical consequence that there is no basis for trust in human relationships. In contrast to the tragic melodrama of *Pierre*, the mood of *The Confidence-Man* is bitter satire that recalls neoclassical attacks on optimism in Voltaire's *Candide* and Samuel Johnson's *Rasselas*, both of which, however, amount to defenses of reason and common sense.

Melville's last novel to be published during his lifetime portrays confidence as a masquerade of the foolish, the fearful, and the selfish in a series of loosely related episodes aboard the whitewashed Mississippi steamer, *Fidèle*. Perhaps because Melville was not familiar with his materials, this mock world-ship is hardly more than a stage setting for the conversations of the characters, who are presented as static types rather than as developing individuals. In the opening chapter, Melville establishes a sardonic tone in his description of a mute with a lamb-like appearance, who boards the vessel on April Fool's Day and irritates passengers by holding up a slate on which he has written a series of texts from I Corinthians, chapter XIII: "Charity thinketh no evil. Charity suffereth long and is kind. Charity endureth all things. Charity believeth all Things. Charity never faileth."[3] Regarded as a lunatic, the stranger settles down eventually at the foot of a ladder leading to a deck above and falls asleep, while the ship's barber hangs out his ironically inoffensive sign, which suggests the theme of the novel—"No Trust" (5).

In succeeding chapters, Melville introduces a variety of apparently confident men representing all levels of society and points of view, from Negro beggar to philosopher. Each in turn is exposed as a sham. Melville ridicules in particular the cold intellectuality of the metaphysic and ethic of Transcendentalism in the characters of Winsome and Eggbert, a mystic and his practical disciple, who suggest Emerson and perhaps Thoreau. Winsome, for example, is easily trapped by inconsistencies in his argument with another confidence man identified merely as "the Cosmopolitan," but he blandly defends himself with a paraphrase of "Self-Reliance":

> Yes, but what of that? I seldom care to be consistent. In a philosophical view, consistency is a certain level at all time, maintained in all the thoughts of one's mind. But, since nature is nearly all hill and dale, how can one keep naturally advancing in knowledge without submitting to the natural inequalities in the progress? (193)

The Cosmopolitan rejects Winsome's philosophy as "moonshiny" in theory but heartless in practice: "Why wrinkle the brow and waste the oil both of life and lamp," he tells Egbert, "to turn out a head kept cool by the under ice of the heart? What your illustrious magian has taught you, any poor old broken-down, heart-shrunken dandy might have lisped. Pray, leave me, and with you take the last dregs of your inhuman philosophy" (223).

Despite this show of righteous indignation, the Cosmopolitan is himself a masquerader. He enters into an agreement to repay the barber for any loss "that may come from trusting mankind, in the way of his vocation, for the residue of his trip," provided that the barber keep out of sight his sign, "No Trust"; then the Cosmopolitan departs from the barber shop without paying for his shave. "Look at your agreement," he tells the skeptical barber. "You must trust" (237). The novel concludes abruptly with a conversation between the Cosmopolitan and an old man, whose loss of faith is suggested as the confidence man leads him into the dark, "money belt in hand, and life-preserver under arm" (251).

In perspective, Melville's professional career as a novelist falls into two major phases corresponding to the growth and shift in his art. In the developmental phase, from 1845 to 1851, Melville wrote his six Transcendental novels of the sea, in which he defended self-reliance, attacked conformity, and learned to employ Transcendental symbols of increasing complexity. This phase culminates in *Moby-Dick* with its presentation of Transcendental idealism and its simultaneous subversion, under the influence of Hawthorne. After the departure of Hawthorne in the winter of 1851, Melville endeavored to find new ways to express himself, but with the exception of his short fiction failed to develop successful techniques of his own to dramatize the moral deserts he chose to explore. In this period of transition, from 1852 to 1857, he wrote anti-Transcendental fiction attacking self-reliance as well as conformity and substituting nihilism and the Gothic for Emersonian compensation. In terms of representative characters, the two phases are as different from each other as buoyant Jack Chase of *White-Jacket* is from inert Bartleby, both of whom are portraits of self-reliance.

Melville's weakened health, financial insecurity, and natural rebelliousness of temper help to account for his reaction against Transcendental idealism. Eleanor Melville Metcalf best summarizes Melville's condition at the time he completed *The Confidence-Man*:

> While Samuel Shaw was studying in Berlin and enjoying theatre and ballet and *The Confidence-Man* was making its way through the press, Melville was on the ocean bound for Glasgow. He had recovered from severe attacks of rheumatism and sciatica, but his plight had become so desperate (and in consequence, the plight of his family, who had begun to suffer not only from insufficient funds for daily needs, but far more from his bursts of nervous anger and attacks of morose conscience) that his father-in-law provided the means for escape—a third Atlantic crossing.[4]

In the fall of 1857, after his return from an extended tour of Europe and the Middle East during which he visited Hawthorne in Liverpool, Melville tried lecturing, as Emerson and others had done, but with no great success.[5] When he embarked on still another cruise in May of 1860 aboard a merchant ship with his brother Thomas as captain, Melville left behind a manuscript volume of poetry with instructions to his family for publication.[6]

Melville's last work of fiction, the short novel *Billy Budd*, composed in the year of his death (1891), returns to the characteristic dramatic situation of the early novels—the Transcendental sailor aboard a world-ship. In this unfinished work, which was not published until 1922, Melville again matches Transcendental idealism with a tragic plot as in *Moby-Dick* and "Benito Cereno." Setting his tale aboard a British warship of Nelson's time, Melville focuses his narrative on the plight of Billy Budd, the "handsome sailor," impressed for service aboard *H.M.S. Indomitable* from the merchantman *Rights of Man* during the war with France in 1797.

Billy is a recrudescence of such independent sailor types as Jack Chase, to whom the novel is dedicated, and Steelkilt of "The Town-Ho's Story" in *Moby-Dick*. He also is the epitome of the innocent, intuitive "Adam before the fall" that Emerson characterized as the essential man in this passage from Nature:

> All that Adam had, all that Caesar could, you have and can do. Adam called his house, heaven and earth; Caesar called his house, Rome; you perhaps call yours, a cobbler's trade; a hundred acres of ploughed land; or a scholar's garret. Yet line for line and point for point your dominion is as great as theirs, though without fine names. Build, therefore, your own world.[7]

Billy, who attempts to build his own world aboard the *Indomitable*, is popular with his messmates but lacks the wisdom of the serpent. "By his original constitution aided by the cooperating influences of his lot," Melville writes, "Billy in many respects was little more than an upright barbarian, much such perhaps as Adam presumably might have been ere the urbane Serpent wriggled himself into his company."[8] Billy's inability to perceive evil, like Captain Delano's innocence in "Benito Cereno," corresponds, however, to the criticism of Transcendental optimism which Melville made with reference to Emerson's essay "Prudence." In his copy of *Essays, First Series*, which he purchased in 1862, Melville checked Emerson's sentence, "Trust men, and they will be true to you; treat them greatly, and they will show themselves great, though they make an exception in your favor to all their rules of trade." In the margin, he commented, "God help the poor fellow who squares his life according to this."[9]

Furthermore, Billy's speech impediment, his single defect, is a characteristic which Emerson associated with the Transcendental poet—a child of music, not merely a lyrist.[10] In "The American Scholar," for example, Emerson writes that "Man Thinking" influenced primarily by nature "must stammer in his speech, often forego the living for the dead" in order to perform his duties of inspiring and guiding men.[11] In "The Poet," Emerson challenges the poet to speak out:

> Doubt not, O poet, but persist. Say "It is in me, and shall out."
> Stand there, balked and dumb, stuttering and stammering,
> hissed and hooted, stand and strive, until at last rage draw out of
> thee that dream-power which every night shows thee is thine
> own.[12]

Billy, who acquires the nickname "Baby Budd," has the gift of poetry, though he is illiterate. "He could not read," Melville writes, "but he could sing, and like the illiterate nightingale was sometimes the composer of his own song" (649). Of Billy's impediment, Melville observes:

> Though our Handsome Sailor had as much of masculine beauty
> as one can expect anywhere to see, nevertheless, like the beauti-
> ful woman in one of Hawthorne's minor tales, there was just one
> thing amiss in him. No visible blemish, indeed, as with the lady;
> no, but an occasional liability to a vocal defect. Though in the
> hour of elemental uproar or peril, he was everything that a sailor
> should be, yet under sudden provocation of strong heart-feeling
> his voice, otherwise singularly musical, as if expressive of the har-
> mony within, was apt to develop an organic hesitancy, in fact
> more or less of a stutter or even worse. (650)

Like the stammer of Emerson's poet, Billy's stutter is organically related to "the harmony within." In addition, his overall "masculine beauty" corresponds to his purity of spirit in the sense that Emerson describes in *Nature*: "Beauty is the mark God sets upon virtue. Every natural action is graceful. Every heroic act is also decent and causes the place and the bystanders to shine."[13] In "The Transcendentalist," Emerson acknowledges that there are no pure Transcendentalists: "I mean we have yet no man who has leaned entirely on his character, and eaten angels' food. . . . Only in the instinct of the lower animals we find the suggestion of the methods of it, and something higher than our understanding."[14] Melville, however, portrays in the character of Billy the ideal innocence of the Transcendental poet in relation to the knowledge of evil that characterizes civilized society. Melville writes,

> Billy Budd's position aboard the seventy-four was something analogous to that of a rustic beauty transplanted from the provinces and brought into competition with the high-born dames of the court. But of this change of circumstances he scarce noted. (647)

Aboard the *Indomitable*, Billy is involved with three characters who represent worldly alternatives to the rigid impersonal conformity imposed by custom and the Articles of War on the ship society. Claggart, the master-at-arms, whose duty is to enforce the law, exploits the evil inherent in conventions, which serve to conceal and protect his natural depravity. Though Emerson denies the existence of such an evil principle in his published writings—in "The Divinity School Address" he says, "Good is positive. Evil is entirely privative, not absolute: it is like cold, which is the privation of heat"—he nevertheless acknowledges the practical reality of mortal imperfection. "All evil," he continues, "is so much death or nonentity."[15]

Both Melville and Emerson, however, conceive of malevolence as an outcome of static rules and regulations, which debase the individual and punish his nonconformity. Of natural depravity, Melville writes, "Civilization, especially if of the austerer sort, is auspicious to it. It folds itself in the mantle of respectability" (674–675).

In contrast to Claggart, who uses the law for his own irrational purposes, Captain Vere is a prisoner of the Articles of War and his own logic, which are in conflict with his higher instincts. The skipper of the *Indomitable* is perhaps Melville's most realistic tragic character. More like Benito Cereno than unregenerate Ahab, Captain Vere represents the plight of the civilized conformist, who sacrifices his individuality to preserve the traditions and conventions that comprise the structure of society. As a man who lives with books, he subordinates the heart to the head. Melville writes:

> He had a marked leaning toward everything intellectual. He loved books, never going to sea without a newly replenished library, compact but of the best. The isolated leisure, in some cases so wearisome, falling at intervals to commanders even during a war cruise, never was tedious to Captain Vere. (660)

Though inconspicuous in appearance and meditative—his nickname is "starry Vere"—the skipper also is a man of decisive action. "This unobtrusiveness of demeanor," Melville observes, "may have proceeded from a certain unaffected modesty of manhood sometimes accompanying a resolute nature . . . and which shown in any rank of life suggests a virtue aristocratic in kind" (658). In this, Vere suggests Emerson's ideal "Man Thinking," who is influenced primarily by nature and secondarily by books and action. Billy, on the other hand, lacking an education, also is less than a whole person. The relation of Billy's innocence to Vere's worldly experience illustrates two contrasting kinds of tragic imbalance that characterize the human condition: with no sense of evil, Billy as a child of nature is the victim of a society fraught with mantraps; Vere as an agent of society dedicated to preserve its inflexible code is out of harmony with his private conscience.

Aboard the world-ship, the character of the Dansker, an old sailor from the tragic warship *Agamemnon*, best represents a "healthy" balanced perspective. Melville describes him as "long anglicized in the service, of few words, many wrinkles, and some honorable scars" (668). He is "the old Merlin" and "salt seer" who befriends Billy and warns him of Claggart's malevolence (668–669). Like Ahab, the Dansker has a crack in his nature represented by "a long pale scar like a streak of dawn's light falling athwart the dark visage"; but he has not lost his perspective on either the inner or the outer world (668). In contrast to Billy, an unscarred young Saxon, the Dansker has a knowledge of evil derived from experience; this tragic wisdom is "the dawn's light" that cuts across "the dark visage," tanned by a Platonic sun. On the other hand, in contrast to Captain Vere, the Dansker retains his individuality and essential humanity despite the pressures of the conforming society. While the conformists aboard the *Indomitable* regard the Dansker as an eccentric, Billy "revering him as a salt hero, would make advances, never passing the old *Agamemnon* man without a salutation marked by that respect which is seldom lost on the aged however crabbed at times or whatever their station in life" (669).

Of the four principal characters, the Dansker alone is detached from the dramatic conflict, which begins when Claggart falsely accuses Billy of fomenting a mutiny. Billy, who cannot find words to speak in his defense, answers impulsively with his fist, killing the master-at-arms. Condemned to death by a court-martial only after Captain Vere points out the responsibility of the officers to uphold the law, Billy in the climactic scene as he is about to hang stuns the captain and crew with his clearly spoken last words: "God bless Captain Vere" (729).

Melville describes the poetry of Billy's language: "Syllables, too, delivered in the clear melody of a singing-bird on the point of launch-
ing from the twig, had a phenomenal effect, not unenhanced by the
rare personal beauty of the young sailor spiritualized now through
late experiences so poignantly profound" (729). Shortly after Billy's
execution, Captain Vere is fatally wounded in an engagement with
the French warship *Athéiste* and dies murmuring "Billy Budd, Billy
Budd" (736). Although the official record of the trial and execution
portrays Billy as a depraved criminal and Claggart as a "respectable
and discreet" petty-officer, the crew preserve the memory of Billy's
humanity in their folk song, "Billy in the Darbies," their sentimental
farewell to "the handsome sailor" (737–738).

In *Billy Budd*, subtitled "An Inside Narrative," Melville's most
sympathetic characters are Billy and Captain Vere, who represent the
polarities of intuition and logic comprising the Transcendental world
of the mind. In the admirable character of the Dansker, however,
Melville portrays the indomitable human spirit, which endures in
spite of the hardships of war, savage nature, and the regulations of
society that, as Emerson said, conspires against the manhood of the
individual. Glued on the inside of Melville's writing box containing
the manuscript of *Billy Budd* and his last poems was a motto suggesting the author's identification with the early Transcendental phase of
his career: "Keep true to the dreams of thy youth."[16]

The impact of Transcendentalism on Melville's fiction from *Typee*
through *Billy Budd* is so pervasive that it suggests new dimensions in
the art of both Emerson and Melville. It was F. O. Matthiessen's
attempt in *American Renaissance* to determine Emerson's "prevailing
tone" and then to compare it with Melville's that led to his key assertion: "How an age in which Emerson's was the most articulate voice
could also have given birth to *Moby-Dick* can be accounted for only
through reaction."[17]

Melville, however, was not one to take Emerson or any other
writer whole, as a less independent author would be inclined to do;
like Emerson, Melville realized that imitation cannot rise above its
model. Melville's genius was to take the best of Emerson's thinking
and to make these ideas peculiarly his own.

The Emerson-Melville Relationship: An Annotated Secondary Bibliography

I.

THIS APPENDIX COMPRISES AN ANNOTATED LISTING OF THE SEVENTY-FOUR modern biographical and cultural studies directly considering the Emerson-Melville relationship, from the earliest in 1937 to the present. It does not include references to Emerson and Melville contained in contemporary reviews, encyclopedias, general literary histories, or biographical dictionaries. It also excludes items written in languages other than English. Reprints are not included unless significantly revised, and I have included only those introductions to primary texts that constitute substantial contributions to the area.

While allusions to Emerson and Melville appear in nearly every biography or critical study of each writer and his milieu, most of these accounts restate factual information about Melville's attendance at an Emerson lecture in February of 1849 and his self-documented reaction to it, offering little or no analysis of these facts.[1] It is the purpose of this bibliography to obviate such fruitless exploration. I list only substantial contributions to the body of scholarship that directly link the two men and/or their writings.

Items in this bibliography are listed chronologically to reveal critical trends during specific time periods. The entries are listed under each year in the following order: book publications (alphabetically by author), annual journals (alphabetically by title), and journal articles arranged by date of publication (alphabetically by title when specific dates are the same).

My intention in annotating this bibliography was to record as objectively as possible the approach, theories, applications, and texts employed by each author. In each instance I endeavored to gloss the essential argument of the given work, quoting it directly whenever possible for the sake of fidelity. Fair assessment of these studies can, of course, only arise from considering them in their entirety. Above all, this bibliography offers a point of departure for critical inquiry into the Emerson-Melville relationship—not an end.

II.

Consideration of the various approaches applied to Emerson-Melville studies over time enables certain meaningful observations. While no single argument has dominated the output, especially in more recent decades, there are particular assertions that nevertheless consistently recur. In this section I consider individual studies from the context of the criticism as a whole to make general observations about critical trends. I have constructed year ranges to facilitate this end.

1937–1959

Interest in the Emerson-Melville began during this time period. It is significant, however, that the first study of Emerson and Melville does not take place until over fifteen years after the Melville revival catalyzed by the 1921 publication of Raymond Weaver's *Herman Melville, Mariner and Mystic*. Between 1937 and 1959, Melville's induction to the American literary canon inspired Jay Leyda's *The Melville Log* (5), which still remains the standard work of its kind in Melville scholarship until Hershel Parker's *New Melville Log* becomes available.[2] This period is marked by studies arguing that Melville was satirizing Emerson and Transcendentalism in his fiction, especially in *Moby-Dick* and *The Confidence-Man*. This argument was first made by William Braswell in his "Melville as a Critic of Emerson of Emerson" (1) and given book-length treatment in Howard P. Vincent's *The Trying-Out of Moby-Dick* (4). Egbert Oliver's "Melville's Picture of Emerson and Thoreau in *The Confidence-Man*" (3) identifies Mark Winsome as a satiric portrait of Emerson, an assertion that gains popularity over subsequent decades.

1960–1969

The 1960s was an expansive period for the study of the Emerson-Melville relationship. In this decade, more works were written than in the previous three combined (fifteen as opposed to eight). Equally expansive was the range of topics that scholars dealing with this relationship drew upon: Edgar Allan Poe, the sphinx, allegory, the quest motif, and the American Gothic.

Sidney Moss argues against claims of previous studies that Melville was anti-Emerson (20), while Allen Austin (16) and Michael Hoffman (23) maintain that *Moby-Dick* is anti-Transcendental. This period also saw the publication of Merton Sealts's *Melville's Reading* (17), which documents for the first time the copies of Emerson's works Melville owned and borrowed.

1970–1979

The scholarly output of the 1970s increased marginally over the standard that the 1960s established, with seventeen treatments published as opposed to the fifteen of the previous decade. Many new studies appear that deal with Emerson's influence on Melville and Melville's satire of Emerson, including William Sanders's "Emerson and Melville: The Oversoul and the Underworld" (31). In addition, several other kinds of work were published: David Leverenz offered the first psychoanalytical reading of the Emerson-Melville relationship in his "Anger and Individualism" (35); Victor J. Vintanza in "Melville's *Redburn* and Emerson's 'General Education of the Eye'" (36) examines the motif of the eye in the two works; and Larzer Ziff considers in his "Shakespeare and Melville's America" (39) Emerson's and Melville's differing debts to Shakespeare. With these more heterogeneous interpretations, we can perceive a trend toward increased diversity in critical approach.

1980–1984

The early 1980s yielded more items treating the Emerson-Melville relationship per year than any other period—sixteen treatments within five years. The increase encompassed a proportional proliferation of journal articles and book-length studies.

The diversification trend of the previous decade continues in this period, with the introduction of studies considering epistemology (53), theology (44, 55), aesthetic (47) and language theory (43, 49), and Nathaniel Hawthorne (45). Studies considering Melville's satire of Emerson (46, 48, 54) remain a constant alongside these different approaches.

1985–1989

Scholarly output waned slightly from the efflux of the early eighties, consisting of twelve works during the second half of the decade. A sequence of valuable research tools emerged from this period, including John Bryant's *A Companion to Melville Studies* (58), Mary Bercaw's *Melville's Sources* (60), Walter Cowen's *Melville's Marginalia* (61), and

Howard C. Horsford's newly edited edition of Melville's *Journals* (68).

Interest in *The Confidence-Man* continued with Helen Trimpi's *Melville's Confidence-Men and American Politics in the 1850s* (62), which builds on the "Mark Winsome-as-Emerson" argument introduced forty years earlier by Egbert Oliver (3).

1990–PRESENT

The final range of scholarship treating the Emerson-Melville relationship consists of a mere eight entries. The major event of this period in relation to the Emerson-Melville relationship was clearly the publication of John Williams's *White Fire* (70), the first book-length study of Emerson's influence on Melville, to which Sealts published a response (72), as well as his essay collection, *Beyond the Classroom* (75). Lynn Horth's volume of Melville's collected correspondence (73) supplements and updates *The Letters of Herman Melville* (9). Melville studies generally, of course, advanced greatly during this period with the publication of Hershel Parker's magnum opus two-volume biographical treatment of Melville's (74 and 76). Disappointingly, however, Parker does not investigate the Emerson-Melville relationship to any significant extent in either volume.

BIBLIOGRAPHY

1937

1   Braswell, William. "Melville as a Critic of Emerson." *American Literature* 9 (November 1937): 317–334.

Thorough discussion of Melville's written commentary on Emerson. While Melville agreed with Emerson's belief that man should follow his own particular calling, he opposed the view that a man's ambition and his powers are necessarily commensurate.

1939

2   Forsythe, Robert S. "Emerson and *Moby-Dick*." *Notes and Queries* 177 (December 1939): 457–458.

Quotes Emerson's 19 February 1854 journal entry on the white whale "Old Tom." The story Emerson heard from a seaman he met "would seem to show that when he was a boy in Albany, New York, the legend of the vengeful white whale had already taken shape."

1946

3   Oliver, Egbert. "Melville's Picture of Emerson and Thoreau in *The Confidence-Man.*" *College English* 8 (November 1946): 61–72.

Finds that Melville modeled Mark Winsome of *The Confidence-Man* on Emerson, asserting that Winsome's conversation bears a relationship, in general and in many particulars, to the ideas and phrasing of Emerson's Nature.

1949

4   Vincent, Howard P. *The Trying-Out of* Moby-Dick. Boston: Houghton Mifflin, 1949.

Interprets *Moby-Dick* as a response to Emersonian Transcendentalism (passim).

1951

5   Leyda, Jay, ed. *The Melville Log: A Documentary Life of Herman Melville, 1819–1891.* 2 vols. New York: Harcourt Brace and Company, 1951.

Provides a useful chronology of Melville's life and reprints Melville's marginalia in his copies of Emerson's books (passim). [Reprinted and supplemented in 1969 (22).]

1954

6   Melville, Herman. *The Confidence-Man: His Masquerade.* Ed. by Elizabeth S. Foster. New York: Hendricks House, 1954.

In her introduction and notes, Foster maintains that Mark Winsome is a satiric representation of Emerson (lxxiii–lxxxii and 351–357).

1955

7   Rosenberry, Edward H. *Melville and the Comic Spirit.* Cambridge, MA: Harvard UP, 1955.

Maintains that Melville's opinion of Emerson "was suspicious, sometimes indignant, or incredulous" but "not contemptuous or even altogether antagonistic" (166–170).

1957

8   Stern, Milton R. *The Fine Hammered Steel of Herman Melville.* Urbana, IL: U of Illinois P, 1957.

Unlike the Transcendentalists, Melville subordinated the ideal to the facts of material history by utilizing "the plight of the very pronounced individuals in his books to achieve a constant formula: idealistic vision results in personal vision; personal vision results in separation of self and community; separation results in monomania; monomania results in a sterilizing and frantic quest for the attainment of vision according to the dictates of self; the quest results in obliteration of self and murder." For Melville, "true identity lies not in Emerson's suprahistorical self-reliance, but, paradoxically, in a highly-individuated identification of self with history" (11–13 and passim).

1960

9   Melville, Herman. *The Letters of Herman Melville*. Ed. by Merrell R. Davis and William H. Gilman. New Haven, CT: Yale UP, 1960.

Contains Melville's letters of 24 February and 3 March 1849 to Evert A. Duyckinck, which record Melville's responses to hearing Emerson lecture (77–79). [See Lynn Horth's edition (73) for a newly revised and annotated text.]

10   Cameron, Kenneth Walter. "Emerson and Melville Lecture in New Haven (1856–1857)." *Emerson Society Quarterly* 19 (2d Quarter 1960): 85–96.

Reprints advertisements and items regarding Emerson's and Melville's lectures as they were recorded in contemporary newspapers.

1961

11   Griffith, Clark. "'Emersonianism' and 'Poeism': Some Versions of the Romantic Sensibility." *Modern Language Quarterly* 22 (June 1961): 125–134.

"Emersonianism" is "completely metaphysical," it "enunciates a doctrine of symbolism," and is "characterized by strangely contradictory attitudes toward language." "Poeism" withholds "from making blanket pronouncements about symbolism" and has "an abiding faith in language." Melville's work is categorized under "Emersonianism" and Hawthorne's under "Poeism."

1962

12   Lyndenberg, John. "Emerson and the Dark Tradition." *Critical Quarterly* 4 (Winter 1962): 352–358.

After the 1830s, Emerson's emphasis shifted gradually from the "glorious potentialities" of freedom to the "note of horror" that characterizes the dark tradition of Poe and Melville.

1963

13 Rose, E. J. "Melville, Emerson, and the Sphinx." *New England Quarterly* 36 (June 1963): 249–258.

Citing "The Sphinx" and *Moby-Dick*, Rose maintains that "Emerson's treatment of the sphinx reveals his characteristic confidence in the explicability of the 'all' as well as his confidence in the justice and goodness inherent in existence once the enigma is solved. Melville's treatment of the symbol, once again characteristically, reveals his belief in the inexplicability of the 'all' and his skeptical views about any possible inherent justice or goodness in what appears to be a hostile universe."

1964

14 Strauch, Carl F. "The Problem of Time and the Romantic Mode in Hawthorne, Melville, and Emerson." *Emerson Society Quarterly* 35 (2d Quarter 1964): 50–60.

Focuses primarily on Emerson but does link him to Melville by discussing their mutual belief in "the necessity, for survival, of the will to believe and the therapeutic value of art." They differ in that Emerson represents the Apollonian and Melville the Dionysian in Nietzsche's dialectic.

1965

15 Ehrlich, Heyward. "A Note on Melville's 'Men Who Dive.'" *Bulletin of the New York Public Library* 69 (1965): 661–664.

Argues that Emerson is not one of "the men who dive" mentioned in Melville's 3 March 1849 letter to Evert Duyckinick by considering Melville's relationship to Duyckinick and his own explicit denial.

16 Austin, Allen. "The Three-Stranded Allegory of *Moby-Dick*." *College English* 26 (February 1965): 344–349.

One of the allegorical strands of *Moby-Dick* is a satire of Emersonian Transcendentalism, including the related doctrine of individualism.

1966

17 Sealts, Merton M., Jr. *Melville's Reading: A Check List of Books Owned and Borrowed.* Madison, Wisconsin: U of Wisconsin P, 1966.

Lists the copies of Emerson's works Melville owned and borrowed (p. 59). [Substantially updated and revised with a new introduction in 1988 (65).]

18 Drummond, C. Q. "Nature: Meek Ass of White Whale?" *Sage* [University of Wyoming] 1 (Spring 1966): 71–84.

"The two halves of Emerson's divided attitude toward nature are respect and awe on the one hand and disdain and contempt on the other. What Melville does in *Moby-Dick* is to seize Emersonianism at this crucial point, pull the two halves apart, identify one as the whale and the other as Ahab, and allow them to war against one another."

1967

19 Cowan, S. A. "In Praise of Self-Reliance: The Role of Bulkington in Moby-Dick." *American Literature* 38 (January 1967): 547–556.

Finds in Bulkington the virtuous self-reliance and dedication to the solitary search for truth that Melville admired in Transcendentalism.

1968

20 Moss, Sidney P. "'Cock-A-Doodle-Doo!' and Some Legends in Melville Scholarship." *American Literature* 40 (May 1968): 192–210.

Argues against the belief that Melville was anti-Transcendentalist, and especially anti-Emersonian, a mistake "that has lead to inaccurate reading of his later novels," most importantly *Pierre* and *The Confidence-Man.* Also contends that Melville's "Cock-A-Doodle-Doo!" is not a satire of Emerson, Thoreau, or Transcendentalism, but that it is a companion piece to "Bartleby." [For a rejoinder, see (24).]

21 Van Nostrand, A. D. *Everyman His Own Poet: Romantic Gospels in American Literature.* New York: McGraw-Hill, 1968.

"Ahab and Ishmael are versions of the self-seeking mind that Emerson defined and Thoreau dramatized" (passim).

1969

22 Leyda, Jay. *The Melville Log: A Documentary Life of Herman Melville, 1819–1891*. 2 vols. 1951. New York: Harcourt, Brace, 1969.

Provides a useful chronology of Melville's life and reprints Melville's marginalia in his copies of Emerson's books (passim). [A reprint of the 1951 edition (5) with a new supplement by Hershel Parker.]

23 Hoffman, Michael J. "The Anti-Transcendentalism of *Moby-Dick*." *Georgia Review* 23 (Spring 1969): 3–16.

Moby-Dick is a "totally ironic" novel in that, though "anti-Transcendental," it is written in the "Transcendental style." Argues that Ahab is Emerson "carried to the extreme — and the irony of his building up is that it leads to another kind of pulling down: the pulling down of the Pequod to the bottom of the sea."

1970

24 Parker, Hershel. "Melville's Satire of Emerson and Thoreau: An Evaluation of the Evidence." *American Transcendental Quarterly* 7 (Summer 1970): 61–67.

Prompted by Sidney P. Moss's article on "Cock-A-Doodle-Doo" (20), Parker's argues that identifications of Emerson as a subject of satire in Melville's work are exaggerated. Also maintains that "Melville may have been a good deal more interested in Thoreau than in Emerson and might have wanted to satirize him, since he evidently linked him with Emersonian optimism." [See also Parker's "Melville's Satire of Emerson and Thoreau: Corrections" (25).]

1971

25 Parker, Hershel. "Melville's Satire of Emerson and Thoreau: Corrections." *American Transcendental Quarterly* 9 (Winter 1971): 70.

[Corrects manuscript changes Parker did not approve in the copyediting of his "Melville's Satire of Emerson and Thoreau: An Evaluation of the Evidence" (24).]

1972

26 Kaplan, Harold. *Democratic Humanism and American Literature.* Chicago, IL: U of Chicago P, 1972.

Sees Ahab as a Transcendentalist and Democrat "gone berserk" (57–59).

27   Travis, Mildred K. "Echoes of Emerson in Plinlimmon."
     American Transcendental Quarterly 14 (1972): 47–48.

Plotinus Plinlimmon in *Pierre* is modeled on Emerson, whom Melville satirizes for his philosophical ideas as well as his personal history.

28   Shurr, William H. "Melville and Emerson." *Extracts* 11 (1972): 2.

Emerson's "The Transcendentalist" provides Melville with the inspiration for the character of Timoleon. This psychological type is central in many of Melville's late poems and develops into a "controlling concept" in the characterization of Billy Budd, Claggart, and Vere, and also "sheds light backward to clarify analyses that begin with the main characters of *Pierre* and *Mardi*."

1973

29   Aaron, Daniel. *The Unwritten War: American Writers and the Civil War*. New York: Knopf, 1973.

In Melville's *Battle-Pieces*, John Brown is not "Emerson's Christ" but instead "the dark Anarch branded with a literal and emblematic 'cut' who is at once a symbol and creature of fate" (80–83).

30   Portnoy, Howard N. "Emerson, Melville, and 'The Poet.'"
     Junction [Brooklyn College] 1 (1972): 172–175.

Melville derived many of his ideas from the philosophy of Emerson.

31   Sanders, William. "Emerson and Melville: The Oversoul and the Underworld." *Junction* [Brooklyn College] 2 (1973): 25–29.

Argues that Melville and Emerson were alike in ways not generally acknowledged. Both tried to reform nineteenth-century America by pointing out its "qualities to be refined." Also, "the 'Nature' that Emerson preached a return to included human nature, the humane nature Melville preached a return to by satirizing the inhumanity of mankind."

1974

32   Henderson, Harry B., III. *Versions of the Past: The Historical Imagination in American Fiction*. New York: Oxford UP, 1974.

Representative Men is "a source of direct inspiration, if not parody," for Israel Potter (144–146).

33 Wiley, Margaret Leonore. *Studies in American Literature: Creative Skepticism in Emerson, Melville, and Henry James.* Folcraft, PA: Folcraft Library Editions, 1974.

Melville "learned from the Transcendentalists . . . a technique of insight which he then used to criticize the Transcendentalist position with respect to the problem of evil, a problem which he took much more to heart than the Transcendentalists" (19–30).

34 Sten, Christopher W. "Bartleby the Transcendentalist: Melville's Dead Letter to Emerson." *Modern Language Quarterly* 35 (1974): 30–44.

Melville drew upon "The Transcendentalist" for "Bartleby," with Bartleby himself based on Emerson's idealist and the narrator modeled after Emerson's materialist. Maintains that "Bartleby" is not only a critique of Emerson's Transcendentalism but also a critique of materialism.

1975

35 Leverenz, David. "Anger and Individualism." *Psychoanalytic Review* 62 (1975): 407–428.

Contrasts Emerson's "ebullient narcissism" to Melville's "paranoid fatalism." Argues that in both cases "their disdain for social authority blocks their awareness of interpersonal anger and transforms the more complex anger of frustrated needs into the simple anger of dismissive rebellion."

36 Vitanza, Victor J. "Melville's *Redburn* and Emerson's 'General Education of the Eye.'" *ESQ: A Journal of the American Renaissance* 21 (1st Quarter 1975): 40–45.

Considers the "motif of image of the eye" in *Redburn* and finds that, though "Melville might be expected to satirize the Emersonian ideal vision as he does in later novels . . . there is no sense of irony or satire in the treatment of Carlo. In *Redburn*, Melville was able to compromise with Transcendentalism, as he could not in his mature works."

1976

37 Rubinstein, Annette T. "Henry James, American Novelist, or: Isabel Archer, Emerson's Grand-Daughter," *Weapons of Criticism: Marxism in America and the Literary Tradition.* Ed. by Norman Rudich. Palo Alto, CA: Ramparts, 1976, pp. 311–326.

Argues that James's *The Portrait of a Lady* "poses the question of perfect freedom" earlier considered in one way by Emerson and

Thoreau, and examined in another by Melville (319–321).

1977

38   Monteiro, George. "The Pilot-God Trope in Nineteenth-
Century American Texts." *Modern Language Studies* 7:2 (1977):
42–51.

Considers the "Pilot-God trope" in Emerson's poem "Terminus"
and *Moby-Dick*, finding Emerson's application of this device to
be far more ironic than Melville's.

1978

39   Ziff, Larzer. "Shakespeare and Melville's America," *New
Perspectives on Melville*. Ed. by Faith Pullin. Edinburgh:
Edinburgh UP, 1978, pp. 54–67.

While Emerson drew from Shakespeare's entire canon, Melville
derived his intensity from a narrowed focus on "Shakespeare's
blackness" (61–63).

40   Beidler, Philip D. "Billy Budd: Melville's Valedictory to
Emerson." *ESQ: A Journal of the American Renaissance* 24 (1978):
215–228.

Maintains that *Billy Budd* is an explicit critique of Transcen-den-
talist ideas and that Melville frames the novel in markedly
Emersonian terms. "Its formal development is founded . . . on a
series of carefully articulated challenges to the dictum that
Beauty . . . can achieve that perfect state whereby it becomes at
once a repository of both absolute moral virtue and ultimate
philosophical truth."

1980

41   Irwin, John T. *American Hieroglyphics: The Symbol of the Egyptian
Hieroglyphics in the American Renaissance*. New Haven, CT: Yale
UP, 1980.

"Melville's satirizing of Emerson and Thoreau in the characters
of Mark Winsome and Egbert is based on his perception of them
as authors who, in dramatizing themselves in their writings,
have presented false characters to the world" (313 and passim).

42   Sealts, Merton M., Jr. "Melville and Emerson's Rainbow." *ESQ:
A Journal of the American Renaissance* 26 (2d Quarter 1980):
53–78.

Examines in detail the facts concerning Melville's response to
Emerson and concludes, quoting Melville himself, that "for all

Melville's reservations about Emerson, he continued to respect the man's 'noble' writing, which, like his own, proceeded 'from noble thinking, and a natural sympathy with greatness.'"

1981

43 Gura, Philip F. *The Wisdom of Words: Language, Theology, and Literature in the New England Renaissance*. Middletown, CT: Wesleyan UP, 1981.

Cites *Moby-Dick*, *Pierre*, and especially *The Confidence-Man* to argue that Melville "directly attacked the problem of meaning in a world in which language is manipulated primarily toward selfish ends and not to express the timeless truths of the natural and moral worlds, as Emerson . . . had suggested it could" (148–154 and 169–170).

44 Moseley, James G. *A Cultural History of Religion in America*. Westport, CT: Greenwood, 1981.

Moby-Dick realizes Emerson's vision in Nature by its creation of "an entire world of experience" (67–82).

45 Shurr, Willliam H. "Eve's Bower: Hawthorne's Transition from Public Doctrines to Private Truths," *Ruined Eden of the Present: Hawthorne, Melville, Poe*. Ed. by Virgil L. Lokke and G. R. Thompson. West Lafayette, IN: Purdue UP, 1981, pp. 283–302.

Draws upon a wide range of Hawthorne's fiction to support the claim that his work occupies a middle ground in its treatment of evil between the extremes of Emerson and Melville.

46 Lang, Hans-Joachim, and Benjamin Lease. "Melville and 'The Practical Disciple': George William Curtis in *The Confidence-Man*." *Amerikanstudien/American Studies* 26 (1981): 181–191.

Affirms that the character of Mark Winsome in *The Confidence-Man* was indeed modeled on Emerson while arguing that Egbert's character was not based on Thoreau, as has been commonly believed, but instead on Brook Farmer George William Curtis.

47 Berthold, Dennis. "A Transcendentalist Aesthetics of Imperfection." *American Transcendental Quarterly* 50 (Spring 1981): 139–148.

Considers the Romantic "philosophy of the imperfect" and details its presence and significance in the works of Emerson and Melville, as well as those of Hawthorne. Finds that Emerson shared with Melville a belief in the "diversitarian" view of nature and the organic theory of art.

48 Graulich, Melody. "Melville's Most Fascinating Confidence

Man." *American Transcendental Quarterly* 52 (Fall 1981): 229–236.

Argues that the rattlesnake debate between Mark Winsome and the Cosmopolitan in *The Confidence-Man* is a satire on both Emerson and Transcendentalism, asserting that Melville's use of the rattlesnake implies a metaphorical criticism of them: "Both bewitch man into giving way to the archetypal dream of unity, of integration into a world of beauty, harmony, and peace."

49   Kronick, Joseph. "Emerson and the Question of Reading/Writing." *Genre* 14:3 (Fall 1981): 363–381.

Emerson's comments on representation and the absence of truth historicize what Melville suggests is the permanent condition of man. Their "intellectual affinity" extends beyond some common ground as "proto-symbolists." Both agree that "nothing is original, that there is only quotation."

1982

50   Watts, Emily Stipes. *The Businessman in American Literature.* Athens, GA: University of Georgia Press, 1982.

Identifies Emerson as the "rogue" Mark Winsome in Melville's *The Confidence Man* (43–44 and passim).

51   Lopez, Michael. "Transcendental Failure: 'The Palace of Spiritual Power,'" *Emerson: Prospect and Retrospect.* Ed. by Joel Porte. Cambridge, MA: Harvard UP, 1982, pp. 121–153.

Maintains that failure is a major theme not only in the psychology of Melville but also in his Transcendentalist contemporaries. "Emerson, Melville, and Thoreau were each keenly aware—and took as the basis of some of their greatest works and passages—the always latent impulse in Transcendentalism toward self-willed defeat, self-annihilation, and the universal refuge of Silence."

52   Raghavacharyulu, D. V. K. "The Emerson Tradition: An Approach." *Literary Criterion* 17 (1982): 22–29.

There is a refraction and inversion of the "genuine Emersonian man" in Melville because he has explored the extreme possibilities of isolation and alienation resulting from the self-reliance and nonconforming individualism of the Transcendentalist, leading to "tragic hubris" and "cognitive dissonance." In *Moby-Dick*, Melville is not so much "decreating the Emersonian myth and persona as bringing them into a vital, dramatic tension with opposites for purposes of allegory and meta-narrative fabulation"—in this, Melville affirms the need and the possibility of the Transcendental hypothesis.

53   Marovitz, Sanford E. "Melville's Problematic 'Being.'" *ESQ: A Journal of the American Renaissance* 28 (1st Quarter 1982): 11–23.

Contrasts Emerson's and Melville's differing philosophical perspectives on Being.

1983

54   Duban, James. *Melville's Major Fiction: Politics, Theology, and Imagination*. DeKalb, IL: Northern Illinois UP, 1983.

Argues that *Pierre* should be read as a rejection of Emersonian Transcendentalism (149–191).

55   Buell, Lawrence. "Literature and Scripture in New England between the Revolution and the Civil War." *Religion and Literature* 15:2 (Spring 1983): 1–29.

Moby-Dick as an analysis-revision of the story of Jonah and of other "sacred" narratives reconceived as myth "reflects the view of the most radical conception during the period of the literary appropriation of the scripture—the Emersonian view that writing, literally as well as etymologically should be scripture—that the poet's job is to write the ultimate bible that has never yet been written."

1984

56   Clarke, Graham. "The Poet as Archaeologist: Charles Olson's Letters of Origin," *Modern American Poetry*. Ed. by R. W. Herbie Butterfield. London and Totowa, NJ: Vision and Barnes & Noble, 1984, pp. 158–172.

The poetry of Charles Olson is "quite essentially Emersonian" in theme, but in it he seeks after the "original letters of his condition," like Melville.

1985

57   Bluestein, Gene. "Ahab's Sin." *Arizona Quarterly* 41:2 (Summer 1985): 101–116.

Like Hawthorne, Melville was "thoroughly repelled" by Emerson's politics but nevertheless attracted to his aesthetic sensibility, which is grounded in a theology "very close to Calvinism." Melville draws upon "Emerson's symbolist theory of language, which identifies human nature in the framework of our loss of direct communication with God as a consequence of the fall."

1986

58   Bryant, John, ed. *A Companion to Melville Studies*. Westport, CT: Greenwood, 1986.

Collects bibliographical essays treating Emerson's influence on Melville in addition to criticism that compares their work (passim).

59   Newman, Lea Bertani Vozar. *A Reader's Guide to the Short Stories of Herman Melville*. Boston, MA: G. K. Hall, 1986.

Surveys the criticism that addresses Emerson's influence on Melville's short fiction (passim).

1987

60   Bercaw, Mary K. *Melville's Sources*. Evanston, IL: Northwestern University Press, 1987.

Lists all of Melville's sources and allusions relating to Emerson, relying not only on evidence of possession but also on direct references and parallel passages (79–80).

61   Cowen, Walter. *Melville's Marginalia*. 2 vols. New York and London: Garland, 1987.

Reprints Melville's marginalia in his copies of Emerson's *Conduct of Life* (1:518–520), *Essays* (1:521–523), *Essays, Second Series* (1:524–528), and *Poems* (1:529–533).

62   Trimpi, Helen P. *Melville's Confidence Men and American Politics in the 1850s*. Hamden, CT: Archon, 1987.

Identifies Mark Winsome in *The Confidence-Man* as a satiric representation of Emerson (200–208 and passim).

63   Steele, Jeffrey. "Emerson, Hawthorne, Melville, and the Unconscious." *University of Mississippi Studies in English* n.s. 5 (1984–1987): 39–50.

Suggests that the "shifting visions" of the unconscious from Emerson to Hawthorne to Melville represent a growing suspicion of "intuitive models based upon an Idealist model of the psyche . . . . Hawthorne and Melville self-consciously examine their relationship to creative energy in terms which undercut Emerson's early idealism."

64   Young, Philip. "Small World: Emerson, Longfellow, and Melville's Secret Sister." *New England Quarterly* 60 (September 1987): 382–402.

Maintains that Melville had an illegitimate half-sister, Ann

Tracy, whom Emerson knew lived with her mother in 1834.

1988

65   Sealts, Merton M., Jr. *Melville's Reading: A Check List of Books Owned and Borrowed.* Columbia, SC: U of South Carolina P, 1988 [1966].

Lists the copies of Emerson's books Melville owned and borrowed (passim). [Substantially updated and revised from the 1966 (17) edition with a new introduction.]

66   Foster, Edward Halsey. "William Bronk's The Brother in Elysium: The Authority of Form." *Sagetrieb* 7:3 (Winter 1988): 109–117.

Argues that William Bronk's point of view, in both his poetry and prose, is closer to Melville's recognition of silence as divine language than Emerson's doctrine of correspondence as set forth in *Nature*.

67   Saunder, Brian. "Melville's Sea Change: From Irving to Emerson." *Studies in the Novel* 20 (Winter 1988): 374–388.

Cites *Redburn* to argue that Melville sees Washington Irving and Emerson as "provincials and sentimentalists in Truth." Both ignore those "fatal" limits of the natural world not easily assimilated into a "genteel sketch or a transcendental vision." Glosses *Nature* and considers "Circles" in depth.

1989

68   Melville, Herman. *Journals.* Ed. by Howard C. Horsford with Lynn Horth. Evanston, IL: Northwestern UP and the Newberry Library, 1989.

Publishes Melville's note to Lemuel Shaw on 10 September 1849, which mentions Emerson (614).

1990

69   Kier, Kathleen E. *A Melville Encyclopedia: The Novels.* 2 vols. Troy, NY: Whitston, 1990.

Lists Melville's annotations to Emerson's work with helpful commentary, as well as biographical information relevant to Emerson's relationship with Melville (1:327–328).

1991

70 Williams, John B. *White Fire: The Influence of Emerson on Melville.* Long Beach, California: California State UP, 1991.

Draws upon Emerson's unpublished lectures of 1848–1850 and the reviews of those lectures by the Boston and New York press to show how Melville "encounter[ed] Emerson's ideas [and] responded to them in his early novels."

71 Quigley, Peter. "Rethinking Resistance: Nature Opposed to Power in Emerson and Melville." *Philological Papers* [West Virginia University] 37 (1991): 39–51.

A poststructuralist reading of Emerson's essays alongside *Moby-Dick* which posits that these works "can be seen as a focal point for a philosophical and political debate about the primacy of consciousness and the legitimacy of power." Finds Melville's Ahab an "obvious" outgrowth of Emerson's implementation of will taken to the extreme.

1992

72 Sealts, Merton M., Jr. Review of *White Fire. Extracts* 91 (1992): 17–19.

Argues against Williams's contention in *White Fire* (70) that Emerson's influence on Melville outweighed that of any other single figure.

1993

73 Melville, Herman. *Correspondence*, ed. Lynn Horth. Evanston, IL: Northwestern UP and the Newberry Library, 1993.

Revises, supplements, and annotates Merrell R. Davis and William H. Gilman's 1960 edition of Melville's collected letters (9)—specifically those of 24 February and 3 March 1849 to Evert A. Duyckinck, after Melville heard Emerson lecture (119–122).

1996

74 Parker, Hershel. *Herman Melville: A Biography.* Vol. 1, 1819–1851. Baltimore, MD: Johns Hopkins UP, 1996.

Parker's biography—the first half of a two-volume set—meticulously charts Melville's early life and career through a painstaking collation of letters, diaries, newspaper accounts, and other evidence. Parker concentrates on Melville's adventures as a sailor and his subsequent transformation of his experiences into prose, closing the volume with the publication of *Moby-Dick* and a detailed exploration of the Hawthorne-Melville friendship as well as touching on Melville's relationship with Emerson and Transcendentalism (614 and 617).

75 Sealts, Merton, Jr. *Beyond the Classroom: Essays on American Authors*. Columbia, MO, and London: U of Missouri P, 1996.

Various essays that touch generally on the Emerson-Melville relationship, especially with regard to Melville's reading (passim). Melville is also connected to Walt Whitman, with brief mention of Emerson (15–20).

2002

76 Parker, Hershel. *Herman Melville: A Biography.* Vol.e 2, *1851–1891*. Baltimore, MD: Johns Hopkins UP, 2002.

Beginning where the first volume of this incredibly comprehensive biography left off, this second volume opens with American readers' hostile reaction to *Moby-Dick* for not being like his earlier successes, particularly *Typee* and *Omoo*, and details the subsequent years of Melville's life concluding with his descent into literary obscurity and subsequent death. Parker passingly references Melville, Emerson, and Transcendentalism (passim).

Notes

NOTES TO THE INTRODUCTION

1. In Jay Leyda, *The Melville Log: A Documentary Life of Herman Melville, 1819–1891* (New York: Harcourt Brace and Company, 1951), vol. 1, p. 299.

2. Leyda, *The Melville Log*, vol. 1, p. 437.

3. Leyda, *The Melville Log*, vol. 1, p. 439.

4. Leyda, *The Melville Log*, vol. 1, p. 430.

5. Leyda, *The Melville Log*, vol. 1, p. 444.

6. Eleanor Melville Metcalf, *Herman Melville: Cycle and Epicycle* (Cambridge, MA: Harvard UP, 1953), p. 124.

7. Melville began *Pierre* in late autumn, 1851. He sent a set of proofs of the new novel to Richard Bentley, the London publisher, on April 16, 1852 (Leyda, *The Melville Log*, vol. 1, p. 449).

8. Metcalf, *Herman Melville*, p. 135.

9. Of the ten surviving letters of Melville to Hawthorne, the first six were written between January 29, 1851 and November 17, 1851. The remaining four were written between July 17, 1852 and December 13, 1852. Herman Melville, *Correspondence*, ed. by Lynn Horth (Evanston and Chicago: Northwestern UP and the Newberry Library, 1993), pp. 175–242.

10. Letter of November [17?] 1851. Melville, *Correspondence*, p. 213.

11. Leyda, *The Melville Log*, vol. 1, p. 358.

12. Randall Stewart, *Nathaniel Hawthorne: A Biography* (New Haven: Yale UP, 1948), pp. 118–119.

13. Letter of July 17, 1852. Melville, *Correspondence*, pp. 230–231. Melville's three remaining letters to Hawthorne, dated August 13, October 25, and between December 3 and 13, 1852, concern the

"Agatha" story, which Melville offered to Hawthorne, who decided not to write it. Although Melville may have written other letters, the tone of these three suggests a friendly professional discussion lacking the intense personal quality of the letters written in 1851. Melville visited Hawthorne in late November 1856, in Liverpool (Leyda, *The Melville Log*, vol. 1, p. 464; vol. 2, pp. 527–529).

14. Letter of January 8, 1852. Melville, *Correspondence*, p. 219.

15. Letter of January 8, 1852. Melville, *Correspondence*, pp. 219–220.

16. Letter of January 8, 1852. Melville, *Correspondence*, p. 220.

17. Leyda, *The Melville Log*, vol. 1, p. 441.

18. Leyda, *The Melville Log*, vol. 1, p. 448.

19. Letter of January 8, 1852. Melville, *Correspondence*, p. 219.

20. Herman Melville, *Moby-Dick; or, The Whale*, ed. by Harrison Hayford, Hershel Parker, and G. Thomas Tanselle (Evanston and Chicago: Northwestern UP and the Newberry Library, 1988), p. 164.

21. Henry A. Murray, "Introduction," *Pierre; or, The Ambiguities* (New York: Hendricks House, 1949), p. xciii.

22. Hugh W. Hetherington, *Melville's Reviewers* (Chapel Hill, NC: U of North Carolina P, 1961), p. 238.

23. John B. Williams, *White Fire: The Influence of Emerson on Melville* (Long Beach, CA: California State UP, 1991).

NOTES TO CHAPTER ONE

1. Jay Leyda, *The Melville Log* (New York: Harcourt Brace, 1951), vol. 1, pp. 70.

2. Bliss Perry, "Emerson's Most Famous Speech," *The Praise of Folly and Other Papers* (New York: Houghton Mifflin, 1923), p. 86. In his reconstruction of the occasion, Perry writes, "Among the Fellows of the Harvard Corporation, you will note two of the foremost lawyers of the Commonwealth, Joseph Story and Lemuel Shaw."

3. Oliver Wendell Holmes, *Ralph Waldo Emerson* (Boston & New York: Houghton Mifflin, 1884), p. 115.

4. Perry, "Emerson's Most Famous Speech," pp. 97–99.

5. Ralph Waldo Emerson, *Emerson: Essays & Lectures*, ed. by Joel Porte (New York: The Library of America, 1983), p. 58. All references to Emerson's speeches, essays, and books derive from this edition.

6. Emerson, "The American Scholar," p. 62.

7. The phrase is from *Moby-Dick; or, The Whale*, ed. by Harrison Hayford, Hershel Parker, and G. Thomas Tanselle (Evanston and Chicago: Northwestern UP and the Newberry Library, 1988), p. 112. In an autobiographical reference, Melville has his narrator, Ishmael, comment, "If, at my death, my executors, for more properly my cred-

itors, find any precious MSS, in my desk, then here I prospectively ascribe all the honor and glory to whaling; for a whale-ship was my Yale College and my Harvard." The whale-ship *Pequod* in the novel is based in part on the vessels, *Acushnet, Lucy Ann,* and *Charles and Henry.* Melville returned from his travels as a sailor aboard the frigate *U.S.S. United States.*

8. F. O. Matthiessen titles his introductory section on Melville, "Out of unhandselled savage nature," in *American Renaissance* (New York: Oxford, 1941), pp. 371–376.

9. The phrase is Melville's description of his own reputation in a letter to Nathaniel Hawthorne in early June [1?] 1851. See Herman Melville, *Correspondence*, ed. by Lynn Horth (Evanston and Chicago: Northwestern UP and the Newberry Library, 1993), p. 193.

10. Henry A. Murray, "Introduction," *Pierre*, ed. by Murray (New York: Hendricks House, 1949), p. v.

11. Emerson, "The American Scholar," p. 62.

12. In *Selected Poems of Herman Melville*, ed. Hennig Cohen (Garden City, NY: Doubleday, 1964), p. 140.

13. John B. Williams, *White Fire: The Influence of Emerson on Melville.* Long Beach, CA: California State UP, 1991.

14. Raymond Weaver, *Herman Melville, Mariner and Mystic* (New York: G. H. Doran, 1921).

15. Vernon L. Parrington, *Main Currents of American Thought* (New York: Harcourt, Brace, 1927), vol. 2, pp. 264.

16. Matthiessen, *American Renaissance*, p. 180.

17. Matthiessen, *American Renaissance*, p. xii.

18. Matthiessen, *American Renaissance*, pp. xiii-xv.

19. Charles Feidelson, Jr., *Symbolism in American Literature* (Chicago and London: U of Chicago P, 1953), p. 120.

20. Robert A. Spiller, *Literary History of the United States* (New York: Macmillan, 1953), p. 346.

21. Spiller, *Literary History of the United States*, pp. 351–355.

22. Perry Miller, "Melville and Transcendentalism," *The Virginia Quarterly Review* 29 (Autumn 1953): 564.

23. Letter of November [17?] 1851. Melville, *Correspondence*, p. 212.

24. Melville, *Correspondence*, p. 212.

25. Melville, *Correspondence*, p. 213.

26. Melville, *Correspondence*, p. 213.

27. Emerson, "Self-Reliance," p. 265.

28. Emerson, "Self-Reliance," p. 266.

29. William R. Hutchinson, *The Transcendental Ministers* (New Haven: Yale UP, 1959), pp. 22–23.

30. Hutchinson points out that the "elder statesmen of Unitarianism"—James Walker, Nathaniel Frothingham, and Dr. Channing—were invited but did not become regular members of the club. His account of the first meeting and the membership of the group is on pp. 30–31.

31. Perry Miller, "From Edwards to Emerson," *Interpretations of American Literature*, ed. by Charles Feidelson, Jr. and Paul Brodtkorb, Jr. (New York: Oxford UP, 1959), pp. 119–120.

32. Hutchinson, *The Transcendental Ministers*, p. 28.

33. Hutchinson, *The Transcendental Ministers*, p. 29.

34. Hutchinson, *The Transcendental Ministers*, p. 29.

35. Dagobert D. Runes, ed., *Dictionary of Philosophy* (Ames, IA: Littlefield, Adams and Co., 1959), p. 320.

36. Quoted from Harold Clarke Goddard, *Studies in New England Transcendentalism* (New York: Hilary House, 1960), p. 165.

37. Letter of March 3, 1849. Melville, *Correspondence*, p. 121.

38. Immanuel Kant, *Critique of Pure Reason*, trans. by F. Max Muller (New York: Macmillan, 1924), p. 9.

39. Frank Thilly and Ledger Wood, *A History of Philosophy* (New York: Henry Holt, 1951), pp. 412–424.

40. Immanuel Kant, *Critique of Practical Reason*, trans. by Thomas K. Abbott (New York: Longman's, Green, 1909), pp. 131–132, 138. See also, "Transcendent," *Oxford English Dictionary* (Oxford: Clarendon Press, 1933), vol. 11, p. 233. Runes, *Dictionary of Philosophy*, p. 319.

41. Thilly and Wood, *A History of Philosophy*, p. 451.

42. Thilly and Wood, *A History of Philosophy*, pp. 447, 448.

43. Thilly and Wood, *A History of Philosophy*, pp. 450–478; Alban G. Widgery, "Classical German Idealism," *A History of Philosophical Systems*, ed. by Vergilius Ferm (New York: Philosophical Library, 1950), pp. 291–298.

44. The quotation of Hegel's is in Thilly and Wood, *A History of Philosophy*, p. 478.

45. Thilly and Wood, *A History of Philosophy*, pp. 476–489.

46. Kenneth W. Cameron, *Ralph Waldo Emerson's Reading* (Raleigh, NC: Thistle Press, 1941), pp. 47, 18, 23.

47. Stanley M. Vogel, *German Influences on the American Transcendentalists* (New Haven: Yale, 1955), pp. 173–175.

48. Vogel, *German Influences on the American Transcendentalists*, p. 90.

49. Vogel, *German Influences on the American Transcendentalists*, pp. 74–75.

50. Vogel, *German Influences on the American Transcendentalists*, p. xiv.

51. In *The Complete Works of Samuel Taylor Coleridge*, ed. by W. G. T. Shedd (New York: Harper, 1854), vol. 3, p. 374.

52. Kenneth W. Cameron, *Emerson the Essayist* (Raleigh, NC: Thistle Press, 1945), vol. 1, p. 78.

53. *The Works of Thomas Carlyle* (New York: Charles Scribner's Sons, 1896), vol. 1, p. 150.

54. Emerson, "The Transcendentalist," pp. 198–199.

55. Kant, *Critique of Practical Reason*, pp. 131–132, 138.

56. Emerson, "The Transcendentalist," p. 198.

57. Emerson, "The Transcendentalist," p. 196.

58. The letter, written on May 21, 1840, is quoted from Perry Miller, ed., *The Transcendentalists* (Cambridge, Massachusetts: 1950), p. 255. Of Ripley's resignation, Emerson wrote to Margaret Fuller, "What a brave thing Mr. Ripley has done. He stands now at the head of the Church militant and his step cannot be without an important sequel" (251).

59. Vogel, *German Influences on the American Transcendentalists*, p. 104.

60. In *Journals of Ralph Waldo Emerson*, ed. by Edward Waldo Emerson and Waldo Emerson Forbes (Boston: Houghton Mifflin, 1912), vol. 7, pp. 532–533.

61. O. B. Frothingham, *Transcendentalism in New England* (New York: Harper, 1959), p. 105.

62. Hutchinson, *The Transcendental Ministers*, p. 30. He refers to estimates given in George W. Cooke, *An Historical and Biographical Introduction to Accompany* The Dial (Cleveland: The Rowfant Club, 1902), vol. 1, pp. 51, 55.

63. Charles R. Metzger, *Emerson and Greenough* (Berkeley: U of California P, 1954), pp. 5–6.

64. Plato, *The Republic*, trans. by Francis MacDonald Cornford (New York: Oxford UP, 1945), pp. 183, 201, 221.

65. Frothingham, *Transcendentalism in New England*, p. 181.

66. Hutchinson, *The Transcendental Ministers*, pp. 29, 34.

67. Harold Clarke Goddard makes this point in his discussion of the lecture in his book *Studies in New England Transcendentalism* (New York: Hilary House, 1960), p. 167.

NOTES TO CHAPTER TWO

1. F. O. Mathiessen, *American Renaissance* (New York: Oxford UP, 1941), p. ix.

2. Ralph Waldo Emerson, *Nature, Emerson: Essays & Lectures*, ed. by Joel Porte (New York: The Library of America, 1983), p. 7. All ref-

erences to Emerson's speeches, essays, and books derive from this edition.

3. Emerson, *Nature*, p. 7.

4. Herbert W. Edwards and Rod W. Horton, *Backgrounds of American Literary Thought* (New York: Appleton-Century-Crofts, Inc., 1958), p. 112.

5. Wilhelm Windelband, *A History of Philosophy* (New York: Harper & Brothers, 1958), vol. 2, p. 450.

6. Edwards and Horton, *Backgrounds of American Literary Thought*, p. 113.

7. Henry David Thoreau, *Walden, Thoreau: A Week on the Concord and Merrimack Rivers; Walden, The Maine Woods; Cape Cod*, ed. by Robert F. Sayre (New York: The Library of America, 1985), p. 394.

8. James Russell Lowell, "Thoreau," *American Literature Survey: The American Romantics, 1800–1860*, ed. by Seymour L. Gross and Milton R. Stern (New York: The Viking Press, 1962), vol. 2, p. 500.

9. Lowell, "Thoreau," p. 500.

10. Lowell, "Thoreau," p. 501.

11. Lowell, "Thoreau," p. 503.

12. Edwards and Horton, *Background of American Literary Thought*, p. 113.

13. Edwards and Horton, *Background of American Literary Thought*, pp. 108–109.

14. Edwards and Horton, *Background of American Literary Thought*, p. 110.

15. Edwards and Horton, *Background of American Literary Thought*, pp. 110–111.

16. In a his September 10, 1849 letter to Lemuel Shaw, Melville requested a note of introduction for himself from Emerson to Carlyle, but the favor was not granted by Emerson. See Herman Melville, *Correspondence*, ed. by Lynn Horth (Evanston and Chicago: Northwestern UP and the Newberry Library, 1993), pp. 136–137.

17. Emerson, *Essays: Second Series*, "Nature," p. 544.

18. Emerson, *Essays: Second Series*, "Nature," p. 544.

19. Emerson, *Essays: Second Series*, "Nature," p. 547.

20. Emerson, *Nature*, p. 11. All subsequent primary quotations from Emerson will be cited parenthetically within the text.

21. Tremaine McDowell, "Foreword," *The Complete Essays and Other Writings of Ralph Waldo Emerson*, ed. by Brooks Atkinson (New York: Random House, 1950), p. xvi.

22. Lowell, "Thoreau," p. 498.

23. Oliver Wendell Holmes, *Ralph Waldo Emerson* (Boston & New York: Houghton Mifflin, 1884), p. 115.

24. Edwards and Horton, *Background of American Literary Thought*, p. 116.

25. Emerson, *The Complete Works of Ralph Waldo Emerson*, Centenary edition (Boston & New York: Houghton, Mifflin, and Company, 1903–1904), vol. 2, p. 380.

26. Edwards and Horton, *Background of American Literary Thought*, p. 119.

NOTES TO CHAPTER THREE

1. Jay Leyda, ed., *The Melville Log: A Documentary Life of Herman Melville, 1819–1891* (New York, Harcourt Brace and Company, 1951), vol. 1, p. 305.

2. Leyda, *The Melville Log*, vol. 1, p. 295.

3. Leyda, *The Melville Log*, vol. 1, p. 464.

4. Leyda, *The Melville Log*, vol. 1, p. 466.

5. Leyda, *The Melville Log*, vol. 1, p. 460.

6. Leyda, *The Melville Log*, vol. 1, p. 300.

7. Letter of December 14, 1849, in Herman Melville, *Correspondence*, ed. by Lynn Horth (Evanston and Chicago: Northwestern UP and the Newberry Library, 1993), p. 149.

8. Letter of June 5, 1849. Melville, *Correspondence*, p. 132.

9. In Eleanor Melville Metcalf, *Herman Melville: Cycle and Epicycle* (Cambridge, MA: Harvard UP, 1953), p. 71.

10. Metcalf, *Herman Melville*, p. 71.

11. Metcalf, *Herman Melville*, p. 71.

12. Metcalf, *Herman Melville*, p. 71.

13. Leyda, *The Melville Log*, vol. 1, p. 316.

14. Letter of June [1?] 1851. Melville, *Correspondence*, p. 191.

15. Herman Melville, *Pierre; or, The Ambiguities*, ed. by Harrison Hayford, Hershel Parker, and G. Thomas Tanselle (Evanston and Chicago: Northwestern UP and the Newberry Library, 1971), p. 244.

16. Leyda, *The Melville Log*, vol. 1, p. 300.

17. Ronald Mason, *The Spirit Above the Dust: A Study of Herman Melville* (London: John Lehmann, 1951), p. 109.

18. Louise Hall Tharp, *The Peabody Sisters of Salem* (Boston: Little, Brown, and Company, 1950), p. 133.

19. Lewis Mumford, *Herman Melville* (New York: The Literary Guild of America, 1929), p. 143.

20. In Mumford, *Herman Melville*, p. 138.

21. Metcalf, *Herman Melville*, p. 99.

22. William Braswell, "Melville as a Critic of Emerson," *American Literature* 9 (November 1937): 317–320.

23. In *Journals of Ralph Waldo Emerson*, ed. by Edward Waldo Emerson and Waldo Emerson Forbes (Boston: Houghton Mifflin, 1912), vol. 5, p. 210.

24. Melville, *Pierre*, p. 403.

25. In Leyda, *The Melville Log*, vol. 1, p. 529.

26. Metcalf, *Herman Melville*, p. 105.

27. Ralph Waldo Emerson, *Nature, Emerson: Essays & Lectures*, ed. by Joel Porte (New York: The Library of America, 1983), p. 5.

28. Richard Chase, *Herman Melville: A Critical Study* (New York: MacMillan, 1949), pp. 28–29.

29. Chase, *Herman Melville*, pp. 32–34.

30. Lawrance Thompson, *Melville's Quarrel With God*. Princeton: Princeton UP, 1952), p. 425.

31. R. W. B. Lewis, *The American Adam: Innocence, Tragedy, and Tradition in the Nineteenth Century* (Chicago: U of Chicago P, 1955), p. 133.

32. Lewis, *The American Adam*, p. 129.

33. Lewis, *The American Adam*, p. 129.

34. Lewis, *The American Adam*, p. 7.

35. Melville, *Pierre*, p. 208.

36. Melville, *Pierre*, p. 141.

37. Melville, *Pierre*, p. 284.

38. Metcalf, *Herman Melville*, p. 110.

NOTES TO CHAPTER FOUR

1. In *The Portable Melville*, ed. by Jay Leyda (New York: Viking, 1952), p. 410.

2. Ralph Waldo Emerson, *Representative Men*. In *Ralph Waldo Emerson: Essays & Lectures*, ed. by Joel Porte (New York: The Library of America, 1983), p. 616. All references to Emerson's books, addresses, and essays derive from this edition.

3. Melville, "Hawthorne and His Mosses," p. 413.

4. Ralph Waldo Emerson, "The American Scholar," p. 70. Perry Miller describes in detail the controversy over America's literary future among mid-nineteenth-century writers in *The Raven and the Whale: The War of Words and Wits in the Era of Poe and Melville* (New York: Harcourt, Brace, and Company, 1956). In presenting the variety of conflicting viewpoints, however, Miller overlooks the parallels in Emerson's and Melville's attitudes on literary nationalism.

5. Melville's idea that for an American to write like a man he must reject European conventions also parallels Emerson's precept in "Self-Reliance": "Whoso would be a man must be a nonconformist" (261).

6. Melville, "Hawthorne and His Mosses," p. 413.

7. Emerson, "Self-Reliance," pp. 265, 278.

8. Melville, "Hawthorne and His Mosses," p. 406.

9. Emerson, "Compensation," p. 283.

10. Melville's references to gray mists, as in the "grey imperfect misty dawn" when Ishmael and Queequeg board the *Pequod*, suggest the mystery and complexity of imperfect perception [In *Moby-Dick; or, The Whale*, ed. by Harrison Hayford, Hershel Parker, and G. Thomas Tanselle (Evanston and Chicago: Northwestern UP and the Newberry Library), 1988, p. 98]. All subsequent passages derive from this edition and will be cited parenthetically within the text.] Similarly, in the opening lines of "Benito Cereno," Melville establishes an ominous tone with his description of the slave ship *San Dominick* drifting aimlessly through "troubled gray vapors" over a leaden-hued sea. "Shadows present," Melville comments, "foreshadowing deeper shadows to come" [*The Piazza Tales and Other Prose Pieces: 1839–1860*, ed. by Harrison Hayford, Alma A. McDougall, and G. Thomas Tanselle (Evanston and Chicago: Northwestern UP and the Newberry Library, 1987), p. 46.]

11. Jay Leyda, ed., *The Melville Log: A Documentary Life of Herman Melville, 1819–1891* (New York, Harcourt Brace and Company, 1951), vol. 1, p. 70.

12. Emerson, *Nature*, p. 20.

13. Emerson, "The Poet," p. 457.

14. Leyda, *The Melville Log*, vol. 1, p. 378.

15. Letter of June 27, 1850. Melville, *Correspondence*, ed. by Lynn Horth (Evanston and Chicago: Northwestern UP and the Newberry Library, 1993), p. 163.

16. Melville, *The Portable Melville*, p. 423.

17. Nathaniel Hawthorne, *The House of the Seven Gables*, *Hawthorne: Novels* (New York: The Library of America, 1983), p. 351.

18. Nathaniel Hawthorne, "The Artist of the Beautiful," *Hawthorne: Tales and Sketches* (New York: The Library of America, 1982), p. 918.

19. Leyda, *The Melville Log*, vol. 1, pp. 379, 389.

20. B. R. McElderry, Jr., "The Transcendental Hawthorne," *Midwest Quarterly* 2 (Summer 1961): 318–319.

21. Emerson, "The Poet," p. 467.

22. Melville, *The Portable Melville*, p. 400. Melville is quoting the last sentence of Hawthorne's story. See also Hawthorne, *Hawthorne: Tales and Sketches*, pp. 930–931.

23. William R. Hutchinson, *The Transcendental Ministers* (New Haven: Yale UP, 1959), p. 32.

24. Eleanor Melville Metcalf, *Herman Melville: Cycle and Epicycle* (Cambridge, MA: Harvard UP, 1953), p. 91. Melville's description of Hawthorne suggests a knowledge of physiognomy, a pseudo-science aimed at discerning character or disposition through the study of the face or the form of the body. At the time of Mrs. Hawthorne's letter, Hawthorne was writing *The House of the Seven Gables*, whose hero, the daguerrotypist Holgrave, judges the inner traits of his photographic subjects by studying their portraits.

25. Emerson, "The Poet," p. 448.

26. In Julian Hawthorne, *Nathaniel Hawthorne and His Wife* (Boston: Ticknor, 1884), vol. 1, p. 382. Details of Hawthorne's return to Concord in 1852 derive from this work.

27. Hawthorne, *Nathaniel Hawthorne and His Wife*, vol. 2, pp. 347–348.

28. In Hawthorne, "The Old Manse," *Hawthorne: Tales and Sketches*, p. 1146.

29. Letter of March 3, 1849. Melville, *Correspondence*, p. 121.

30. In *The Complete Works of Nathaniel Hawthorne*, ed. G. P. Lathrop (New York: Houghton, Mifflin, 1882), vol 1, p. 16. Hawthorne's reference to his stories as sketches recalls Washington Irving's use of the term in his famous collection of tales and essays, *The Sketch Book* (1819–1820). In comparing the two writers after reading *Twice-Told Tales*, Melville wrote to Evert Duyckinck: "Irving is a grasshopper to him—putting the souls of the two men together, I mean" (Letter of February 12, 1851. Melville, *Correspondence*, p. 181).

31. Melville, *Correspondence*, p. 191.

32. Letter of November [17?] 1851. Melville, *Correspondence*, p. 211.

33. Herman Melville, *Mardi and a Voyage Thither*, ed. by Harrison Hayford, Hershel Parker, and G. Thomas Tanselle (Evanston and Chicago: Northwestern UP and the Newberry Library, 1970), p. 595.

34. "For spite of all the Indian-summer sunlight on the hither side of Hawthorne's soul, the other side—like the dark half of the physical sphere—is shrouded in a blackness, ten times black. But this darkness but gives more effect to the evermoving dawn, that forever advances through it, and cirumnavigates his world. Whether Hawthorne has simply availed himself of this mystical blackness as a means to the wondrous effects he makes it to produce in his lights and shades; or whether there really lurks in him, perhaps unknown to himself, a touch of Puritanic gloom,—this, I cannot altogether tell. Certain it is, however, that this great power of blackness in him derives its force from its appeals to that Calvinistic sense of Innate Depravity and Original Sin, from whose visitations, in some shape or

other, no deeply thinking mind is always and wholly free. For, in certain moods, no man can weigh this world, without throwing in something, somehow like Original Sin, to strike the uneven balance. At all events, perhaps no writer has ever wielded this terrific thought with greater terror than this same harmless Hawthorne. Still more: this black conceit pervades him, through and through. You may be witched by his sunlight,—transported by the bright gildings in the skies he builds over you;—but there is the blackness of darkness beyond; and even his bright gildings but fringe, and play upon the edges of thunder-clouds. . . . [I]t is that blackness in Hawthorne, of which I have spoken, that so fixes and fascinates me." In Melville, "Hawthorne and His Mosses," pp. 406–407. For a comprehensive discussion of Hawthorne's blackness and its influence on Melville, see Harry Levin, *The Power of Blackness: Hawthorne, Poe, Melville* (New York: Vintage Books, 1960), pp. 3–35.

35. Letter of March 25, 1848. Melville, *Correspondence*, p. 106.

36. Letter of June 27, 1850. Melville, *Correspondence*, p. 163.

37. Emerson, "The Poet," pp. 459–460.

38. Fedallah, who is Ahab's demoniac harpooner, is a Parsee, a believer in the pre-Moslem cult of Zoroastrianism. The ancient Persians adhering to this faith conceived of two gods: Ahura Mazda, the god of moral and natural order who is "the full of light," and Ahriman, the god of darkness. The two moons of Melville's description suggest the dualism of the Parsee's faith. On the other hand, Fedallah's satanism, which reflects the Zoroastrian sense of evil, contrasts with the religious significance of his braided white hair, the color of Mohammed's. See John B. Noss, *Man's Religions* (New York: Macmillan, 1963), pp. 464–493.

39. Emerson, "Compensation," p. 287.

40. Emerson, "Compensation," p. 292.

41. Letter of April [16?], 1851. Melville, *Correspondence*, pp. 186–187.

42. Melville, *Correspondence*, p. 192.

43. See Emerson's essay, "Compensation," pp. 283–302.

44. Melville, *Correspondence*, pp. 193–194.

45. Melville, *Correspondence*, pp. 194.

46. Ahab appears in the Quarter-Deck scene (161) "with bent head and half-slouched hat" in a manner paralleling Father Mapple's description of the defiant Jonah before he is swallowed by the whale: "Miserable man! Oh! most contemptible and worthy of all scorn; with slouched hat and guilty eye, skulking from his God" (43).

47. Emerson, "The Poet," p. 453.

48. Emerson, "The American Scholar," p. 60.

49. Emerson, "Compensation," p. 294.

50. Paul W. Miller in "Sun and Fire Worship in Melville's *Moby-Dick*," *Nineteenth-Century Fiction* 13 (September 1958): 139–144, points out the Zoroastrian worship of sun and fire, which helps to explain Ahab's hatred of the sun. His interpretation, however, does not take into account the pervasive Emersonian and Platonic associations of the sun as a symbol of Transcendental reality. In *Nature*, Emerson said, "Most people do not see the sun" (10).

51. Emerson, "Circles," p. 403.

52. Emerson, *Nature*, p. 10.

53. Emerson, *Nature*, p. 24.

54. Emerson, "Compensation," p. 294. Emerson's interest in whaling goes back at least to 1833, when following his return from Europe he preached often at New Bedford and lectured at Nantucket. His journal entry for February 19, 1834 refers to a story he heard about a white whale named Old Tom, which rushed attacking boats and sank them (Leyda, *The Melville Log*, vol. 1, pp. 61–62). In May of 1847, he wrote to his daughter Ellen about the Essex disaster, an event which provides the factual basis for the sinking of the *Pequod* (in *The Complete Works of Ralph Waldo Emerson* [Boston & New York: Houghton Mifflin, 1903–1904], vol. 2, p. 244).

55. Emerson, "Compensation," p. 297.

56. That Ahab is destroyed by his own line almost exactly in the manner Emerson describes in "Compensation" is crucial evidence against the assertion of Harry Levin in *The Power of Blackness* (New York: Vintage Books, 1960), p. 198: "The booming hope that all is for the best, the Emersonian doctrine of compensation, is grimly answered by Melville's cult of revenge . . ."

57. Kenneth W. Cameron, in "Etymological Significance of Melville's *Pequod*," *Emerson Society Quarterly* 29 (Winter 1962): 3–4, notes that in Hebrew and Chaldee dictionaries the term "Pequod" denotes "to strike upon or against," "to be in trepidation," "to hasten," "to go in search of," "to fall upon," "to punish," "to be punished," "to muster," also "fear, terror, punishment," also "to terrify." These meanings suggest the tragic fate of the vessel governed by Ahab's inflexible will.

58. Emerson, "Self-Reliance," p. 261

59. Emerson, "Self-Reliance," p. 274.

60. Emerson, "Self-Reliance," p. 275.

61. Emerson, "Self-Reliance," p. 274.

62. He actually didn't acquire his own copy until March 22, 1862. See Walker Cowen, *Melville's Marginalia*, vol. 1 (New York & London: Garland, 1987), pp. 521–523.

63. Merton Sealts, Jr., *Melville's Reading* (Columbia, SC: South Carolina UP, 1988), p. 56.

64. Recall that Ishmael says in chapter 10 that he and Queequeg are "a cosy, loving pair . . . [on their] hearts' honeymoon" (52).

65. Emerson, "Self-Reliance," p. 257.

66. Van Wyck Brooks characterizes Father Taylor as a "halleluja Methodist" and the greatest natural orator in Boston. See *The Flowering of New England* (New York: E. P. Dutton, 1940), p. 269.

67. Emerson, "Self-Reliance," p. 261.

68. See Hutchinson's *The Transcendental Ministers*, pp. 68–97 for analysis of Norton's *Discourse on the Latest Form of Infidelity* and other reactions to Emerson's controversial address.

69. Ahab defies not only physical and spiritual nature as represented by Moby Dick but also the owners of the *Pequod*, who had commissioned him to sail for the purpose of catching whales for a profit.

70. Flask's mistake in arithmetic—at two cents a cigar, he can buy eight hundred cigars, rather than nine hundred and sixty—underscores his limited comprehension.

71. Emerson in his poem "The Sphynx" suggests that the commonplaces of nature provide the answer to the riddle of the universe. Ahab's meditation, on the other hand, serves in part to indicate the extent of his disillusionment with nature. Addressing a whale head as the Sphynx, the skipper says: "O head! thou hast seen enough to split the planets and make an infidel of Abraham, and not one syllable is thine" (312).

72. Emerson, "The American Scholar," p. 60.

73. Melville, *Moby-Dick*, p. 237. "An enraged man is a lion," Emerson said in *Nature* (20).

74. Melville, *Moby-Dick*, p. 352. James Dean Young provides the low German translation of "die Deern" in "The Nine Gams of the *Pequod*," in *Discussions of Moby-Dick*, ed. by Milton R. Stern (Boston: Heath, 1960), p. 102.

75. Melville, *Moby-Dick*, p. 441. The doctor's account of the whale contrasts with the portrayals of the whale as an instrument of divine justice in "The Town Ho's Story" and Father Mapple's sermon about Jonah.

76. Emerson, "Compensation," p. 292.

77. Owen Chase, *Shipwreck of the Whaleship Essex*, ed. by B. R. McEldery, Jr. (New York: Corinth Books, Inc., 1963), pp. 17–22.

78. Chase, *Shipwreck of the Whaleship Essex*, p. xv.

79. Chase, *Shipwreck of the Whaleship Essex*, p. xv.

80. Chase, *Shipwreck of the Whaleship Essex*, p. 22.

81. Chase, *Shipwreck of the Whaleship Essex*, p. 24.

NOTES TO CHAPTER FIVE

1. Melville, *Pierre; or, The Ambiguities*, ed. by Harrison Hayford, Hershel Parker, and G. Thomas Tanselle (Evanston and Chicago: Northwestern UP and the Newberry Library, 1971), p. 296. All subsequent passages derive from this edition and will be cited parenthetically within the text.

2. Ralph Waldo Emerson, "The American Scholar," *Emerson: Essays & Lectures*, ed. by Joel Porte (New York: The Library of America, 1983), p. 64. All references to Emerson's books, addresses, and essays derive from this edition.

3. R. W. B. Lewis, *The American Adam: Innocence, Tragedy, and Tradition in the Nineteenth Century* (Chicago: U of Chicago P, 1955), p. 9.

4. Melville's embittered disillusion at the incompatibility of the ideal "Truth" with the reality of the nineteenth-century American world is apparent in his letter to Hawthorne on July 29, 1851: "But Truth is the silliest thing under the sun. Try to get a living by the Truth—and go to the Soup Societies. Heavens! Let any clergyman try to preach the Truth from its very stronghold, the pulpit, and they would ride him out of his church on his own pulpit bannister. . . . Though I wrote the Gospels in this century, I should die in the gutter." Herman Melville, *Correspondence*, ed. by Lynn Horth (Evanston and Chicago: Northwestern UP and the Newberry Library, 1993), pp. 191, 192.

5. Emerson, "Self-Reliance," p. 265.

6. Emerson says in "Experience": "I am thankful for small mercies. I compared notes with one of my friends who expects everything of the universe and is disappointed when anything is less than the best, and I found I begin at the other extreme, expecting nothing, and am always full of thanks for moderate goods" (479–480).

7. Emerson, *Nature*, p. 39.

8. Emerson, "Divinity School Address," p. 76.

9. Emerson, "Self-Reliance," p. 270.

10. Emerson, "Compensation," p. 298.

11. Emerson, "Spiritual Laws," p. 307.

12. Emerson, *Nature*, p. 41.

13. Emerson, "Divinity School Address," p. 75–76.

14. Emerson, "Self-Reliance," p. 270.

15. Emerson, "The Over-Soul," p. 392.

16. "Although, as we have said, there is no pure Transcendentalist, yet the tendency to respect the intuitions, and to

give them, at least in our creed, all authority over our experience, has deeply colored the conversation and poetry of the present day; and the history of genius and of religion in these times, though impure, and as yet not incarnated in any powerful individual, will be the history of this tendency." Emerson, "The Transcendentalist," p. 199.

17. Emerson, "Self-Reliance," p. 274.

18. Emerson, "Self-Reliance," p. 275.

19. Emerson, "Compensation," pp. 299–300.

20. "And still deeper the meaning of that story of Narcissus, who because he could not grasp the tormenting, mild image he saw in the fountain, plunged into it and was drowned. But that same image, we ourselves see in all rivers and oceans. It is the image of the ungraspable phantom of life; and this is the key to it all." Herman Melville, *Moby-Dick; or, The Whale*, ed. by Harrison Hayford, Hershel Parker, and G. Thomas Tanselle (Evanston and Chicago: Northwestern UP and the Newberry Library), 1988, p. 5.

21. Emerson, "The American Scholar," p. 25.

22. Emerson, "Divinity School Address," p. 88.

23. Emerson, "Self-Reliance," p. 259.

24. Emerson, "Spiritual Laws," p. 305.

25. Emerson, *Nature*, p. 48.

26. Emerson, *Nature*, p. 39.

27. Emerson, "Compensation," p. 300.

28. Emerson, "Compensation," p. 289.

29. Emerson, "Compensation," p. 289.

30. Emerson, "Compensation," p. 297.

31. Emerson, "The Transcendentalist," p. 198.

32. Karl H. Sundermann, *Herman Melville's Gedankengut; eine kritische Untersuchung seiner weltanschaulichen Grundideen* (Berlin: A. Collignon, 1937), p. 105.

33. Emerson, "The Poet," pp. 460–461.

34. Letter of March 3, 1849. Melville, *Correspondence*, p. 121.

35. Emerson, "Spiritual Laws," p. 313.

36. William Braswell, "Melville as a Critic of Emerson," *American Literature* 9 (November 1937): 320.

37. Emerson, "Spiritual Laws," p. 310.

38. Emerson, "Spiritual Laws," p. 310.

39. Letter of December 13, 1850. Melville, *Correspondence*, p. 174.

40. Emerson, "The Poet," p. 460.

41. Braswell, "Melville as a Critic of Emerson," p. 322.

42. Letter of March 3, 1849. Melville, *Correspondence*, p. 122.

43. Letter of June [1?] 1851. Melville, *Correspondence*, pp. 191–192.

44. Emerson, "The Poet," p. 455.
45. Braswell, "Melville as a Critic of Emerson," p. 324.
46. Emerson, "The Poet," p. 456.
47. Braswell, "Melville as a Critic of Emerson," p. 324.
48. Emerson, "The Poet," p. 461.
49. Emerson, "Heroism," p. 373.
50. Braswell, "Melville as a Critic of Emerson," p. 327.
51. Emerson, "Illusions," p. 1122.
52. Braswell, "Melville as a Critic of Emerson," p. 328.
53. Emerson, "Spiritual Laws," p. 314.
54. Braswell, "Melville as a Critic of Emerson," p. 328.
55. Emerson, "Divinity School Address," p. 77.
56. Emerson, "The Poet," p. 455.
57. Braswell, "Melville as a Critic of Emerson," p. 330.
58. Emerson, "Spiritual Laws," p. 314.
59. Braswell, "Melville as a Critic of Emerson," p. 330.
60. Emerson, "Considerations by the Way," p. 1083.
61. Braswell, "Melville as a Critic of Emerson," p. 330.
62. Emerson, "The Poet," p. 457.
63. Braswell, "Melville as a Critic of Emerson," p. 331.
64. Braswell, "Melville as a Critic of Emerson," p. 325.
65. Braswell, "Melville as a Critic of Emerson," p. 326.
66. Braswell, "Melville as a Critic of Emerson," p. 330.
67. Emerson, *Nature*, p. 39.
68. Emerson, "Nature," *Essays: Second Series*, p. 541.
69. Emerson, Nature," *Essays: Second Series*, p. 543.
70. Emerson, "Heroism," p. 380.
71. Emerson, "Heroism," p. 376.
72. Emerson, "Prudence," p. 362.
73. Emerson, "Friendship," p. 354.
74. Emerson, "Love," p. 331.
75. Emerson, "Love," p. 331.
76. Emerson, "Culture," pp. 1033–1034.
77. Emerson, "Spiritual Laws," p. 311.
78. Emerson, "Spiritual Laws," p. 314.
79. Emerson, "Spiritual Laws," p. 305.
80. Emerson, "Divinity School Address," p. 76.
81. Emerson, "Heroism," p. 374.
82. Emerson, "Heroism," p. 374.
83. Emerson, "Heroism," p. 374.
84. Emerson, "Heroism," p. 375.
85. Emerson, "Heroism," p. 379.
86. Emerson, "Self-Reliance," p. 312.

87. Emerson, "Self-Reliance," p. 274.
88. Emerson, "Heroism," p. 375.
89. Emerson, "Self-Reliance," p. 270.
90. Emerson, "Self-Reliance," p. 282.
91. H. M. Tomlinson, Preface, *Pierre; or, The Ambiguities*, Herman Melville (New York: E. P. Dutton and Company, Inc., 1929), p. xvii.
92. Letter of December 14, 1849. Melville, *Correspondence*, p. 149.
93. Jay Leyda, ed., *The Melville Log: A Documentary Life of Herman Melville, 1819–1891* (New York, Harcourt Brace and Company, 1951), vol. 1, p. 456.
94. Leyda, *The Melville Log*, vol. 1, p. 462.

NOTES TO CHAPTER SIX

1. Melville's long short story is an adaptation of the *Narrative of Voyages and Travels in the Northern and Southern Hemispheres*, published in 1817 by Captain Amasa Delano, an ancestor of Franklin D. Roosevelt. These differences are significant in understanding the artistic ends Melville's sought to achieve. He changed the date, and he changed the names of the two ships from the actual *Perseverance* and *Tryal* to the symbolic *Bachelor's Delight* and *San Dominick*. For further information about Melville's adaptation, see Shoh Yamamoto, "The Source and Structure of 'Benito Cereno,'" *Studies in English Literature*, 162 (1973): 189–191 and William T. Pilkington, "Melville's 'Benito Cereno': Source and Technique," *Studies in Short Fiction* 2 (1965): 247–255.
2. John B. Williams is a notable exception. In *White Fire: The Influence of Emerson on Melville*, he passingly reads "Benito Cereno" against Emerson's "Fugitive Slave Law Address." See Williams, *White Fire* (Long Beach, CA: California State UP, 1991), pp. 169–170.
3. See Emerson's address on "The Fugitive Slave Law," which he delivered at the Tabernacle in New York City, March 4, 1854. In a vigorous attack on Daniel Webster for backing the law, Emerson points out his position on the issue of slavery: "I have lived all my life without suffering any known inconveniences from American Slavery. I never saw it; I never heard the whip I never felt the check on my free speech and action, until, the other day, when Mr. Webster, by his personal influence, brought the Fugitive Slave Law on the country. . . . The new Bill made it operative, required me to hunt slaves, and it found citizens in Massachusetts willing to act as judges and captors. Moreover, it discloses the secret of the new times, that Slavery was no longer mendicant, but was become aggressive and dangerous." In *The Complete Works of Ralph Waldo Emerson*, ed. by Edward Waldo Emerson (New York: Houghton Mifflin, 1903–1921), vol. 11, pp. 219,

228–229. See also *Emerson's Antislavery Writings*, ed. by Len Gougeon and Joel Myerson (New Haven, CT: Yale UP, 1995), Albert J. Von Frank's *The Trials of Anthony Burns: Freedom and Slavery in Emerson's Boston* (Cambridge, MA: Harvard UP, 1998), and Len Gougeon's *Virtue's Hero: Emerson, Antislavery, and Reform* (Athens, GA: U of Georgia P, 1990).

4. See Teresa Goddu, *Gothic America: Narrative, History, and Nation* (New York: Columbia UP, 1997) and David Punter, *Gothic Pathologies: The Text, the Body, and the Law* (New York: St. Martin's Press, 1998).

5. Mark Edmundson, *Nightmare on Main Street: Angels, Sadomasochism, and the Culture of the Gothic* (Cambridge. MA: Harvard UP, 1997).

6. Edmundson, *Nightmare on Main Street*, pp. 4–5.

7. Leslie Fiedler, *Love and Death in the American Novel* (New York: Stein and Day, 1982), p. 4.

8. Carolyn L. Karcher, *Shadow Over the Promised Land: Slavery, Race, and Violence in Melville's America* (Baton Rouge, Louisiana and London: Louisiana State UP, 1980).

9. Rosemary Jackson, *Fantasy: The Literature of Subversion* (London and New York: Methuen, 1981).

10. Harold Bloom, *The Poetics of Influence* (New Haven: Schwab, 1988), p. 284.

11. Herman Melville, "Benito Cereno," *The Piazza Tales and Other Prose Pieces: 1839–1860*, ed. by Harrison Hayford, Alma A. McDougall, and G. Thomas Tanselle (Evanston and Chicago: Northwestern UP and the Newberry Library, 1987), p. 84. Subsequent quotations will be cited parenthetically with the text.

12. "For genius, all over the world, stands hand in hand, and one shock of recognition runs the whole circle round." In "Hawthorne and His Mosses," *The Portable Melville*, ed. by Jay Leyda (New York: Viking, 1952), p. 410.

13. See Carolyn L. Karcher, "The Riddle of the Sphinx: Melville's 'Benito Cereno' and the *Amistad* Case," *Critical Essays on Melville's Benito Cereno*, ed. by Robert Burkholder (Boston: G. K. Hall, 1992), pp. 217–218.

14. Sterling Stuckey elucidates the unspecified gristly details in the chapter on cannibalism and "Benito Cereno" in *Going Through the Storm: The Influence of African American Art in History* (New York and Oxford: Oxford UP, 1994), pp. 171–186.

15. Letter of April 20, 1855. In *The Melville Log: A Documentary Life of Herman Melville, 1819–1891*, ed. Jay Leyda (New York: Harcourt Brace and Company, 1951), vol. 2, p. 501.

16. References to the Spanish Empire and the Inquisition suggest that Melville was drawing an analogy between the Holy Roman Empire, the Spanish empire in the New World, and the burgeoning American empire. For more on this relationship see H. Bruce Franklin, "'Apparent Symbol of Despotic Command': Melville's 'Benito Cereno,'" *New England Quarterly* 34 (1961): 462–477 and Eric J. Sundquist, "*Benito Cereno* and New World Slavery," in *Reconstructing American Literary History*, ed. Sacvan Bercovitch (Cambridge: Harvard UP, 1986), 93–122.

17. E. F. Bleiler, Introduction, *Three Gothic Novels*, ed. by Bleiler (New York: Dover, 1966), p. xv.

18. Ralph Waldo Emerson, *Nature*, *Emerson: Essays & Lectures*, ed. by Joel Porte (New York: The Library of America, 1983), pp. 48–49. All references to Emerson's books, addresses, and essays derive from this edition.

19. E. F. Carlisle, "Captain Amasa Delano: Melville's American Fool," *Criticism* 7:4 (Fall 1965): 350.

20. Hershel Parker, *Herman Melville: A Biography* (Baltimore, Maryland: Johns Hopkins UP, 1996).

21. Letter of February 24, 1849. In Herman Melville, *Correspondence* (Evanston and Chicago: Northwestern UP and the Newberry Library, 1993), p. 119.

22. Letter of March 3, 1849. Melville, *Correspondence*, p. 121.

23. Letter of April 16, 1851. Melville, *Correspondence*, p. 186.

24. Emerson, *Nature*, p. 20.

25. Michael J. Hoffman, "The Anti-Transcendentalism of *Moby-Dick*," *Georgia Review* 23:1 (Spring 1959): 6–7.

26. See "Extracts," *Moby-Dick; or, The Whale*, ed. by Harrison Hayford, Hershel Parker, and G. Thomas Tanselle (Evanston and Chicago: Northwestern UP and the Newberry Library, 1988), p. xvii.

27. Emerson, *Nature*, p. 10.

28. Carlisle, "Captain Amasa Delano," p. 357.

NOTES TO CHAPTER SEVEN

1. Herman Melville, *The Piazza Tales and Other Prose Pieces: 1839–1860*, ed. by Harrison Hayford, Alma A. McDougall, and G. Thomas Tanselle (Evanston and Chicago: Northwestern UP and the Newberry Library, 1987), p. 572.

2. Ralph Waldo Emerson, *Nature*. In *Emerson: Essays & Lectures*, ed. by Joel Porte (New York: The Library of America, 1983), p. 57. All references to Emerson's books, addresses, and essays derive from this edition.

3. Herman Melville, *The Confidence-Man: His Masquerade*, ed. by Harrison Hayford, Hershel Parker, and G. Thomas Tanselle (Evanston and Chicago: Northwestern UP and the Newberry Library, 1984), pp. 4–5. Subsequent quotations will be cited parenthetically within the text.

4. Eleanor Melville Metcalf, *Herman Melville, Cycle and Epicycle* (Cambridge, Massachusetts: Harvard UP, 1953), p. 159.

5. Jay Leyda, ed., *The Melville Log: A Documentary Life of Herman Melville, 1819–1891* (New York: Harcourt, Brace and Company, 1951), vol. 2, p. 496.

6. Leyda, *The Melville Log, 1819–1891*, vol. 2, p. 612.

7. Emerson, *Nature*, p. 48.

8. Herman Melville, *Billy Budd, Sailor*. In *The Portable Melville*, ed. by Jay Leyda (New York: Viking, 1952), p. 649. Subsequent quotations will be cited parenthetically within the text.

9. Leyda, *The Melville Log, 1819–1891*, vol. 2, p. 648.

10. In "The Poet," Emerson contrasts the writer of verses with the Transcendental poet: "Our poets [i.e., lyrists] are men of talents who sing, and not the children of music" (450).

11. Emerson, "The American Scholar," p. 63.

12. Emerson, "The Poet," pp. 466–467.

13. Emerson, *Nature*, p. 16.

14. Emerson, "The Transcendentalist," 197–198.

15. Emerson, "The Divinity School Address," p. 77.

16. In *The Portable Melville*, p. 740.

17. F. O. Matthiessen, *American Renaissance* (New York: Oxford UP, 1941), p. 184. Matthiessen observes, "Many texts could be cited from Emerson to prove that he was not unconscious that evil existed, but, as always with him the significant thing to determine is the prevailing tone" (181).

NOTES TO THE APPENDIX

1. For a brief summary of this, see Jay Leyda, *The Melville Log: A Documentary Life of Herman Melville, 1819–1891* (New York: Harcourt Brace and Company, 1951), vol. 1, p. 287.

2. Hershel Parker, Jay Leyda's designated heir, originally intended to release the *New Melville Log* in time for the centennial of Melville's death in 1991. As Julian Markels points out in "The *Moby-Dick* White Elephant" [*American Literature* 66:1 (March 1994): 105–122], the delay has been frustrating to Melville scholars.

Bibliography

Bleiler, E. F. "Introduction," *Three Gothic Novels*. Ed. by Bleiler. New York: Dover, 1966, pp. i–xl.

Bloom, Harold. *The Poetics of Influence*. New Haven: Schwab, 1988.

Brooks, Van Wyck. *The Flowering of New England*. New York: E. P. Dutton, 1940.

Braswell, William. "Melville as a Critic of Emerson." *American Literature* 9 (November 1937): 317–334.

Burkholder, Robert E., and Joel Myerson. *Emerson: An Annotated Secondary Bibliography*. Pittsburgh: U of Pittsburgh P, 1985.

———. *Ralph Waldo Emerson: An Annotated Bibliography of Criticism, 1980–1991*. Westport, CT: Greenwood, 1994.

Cameron, Kenneth W. *Emerson the Essayist*. 2 vols. Raleigh, NC: Thistle Press, 1945.

———. "Etymological Significance of Melville's *Pequod*." *Emerson Society Quarterly* 29 (Winter 1962): 3–4.

———. *Ralph Waldo Emerson's Reading*. Raleigh, NC: Thistle Press, 1941.

Carlisle, E. F. "Captain Amasa Delano: Melville's American Fool." *Criticism* 7:4 (Fall 1965): 349–362.

Chase, Owen. *Shipwreck of the Whaleship Essex*. Ed. by B. R. McEldery, Jr. New York: Corinth Books, Inc., 1963.

Chase, Richard. *Herman Melville: A Critical Study*. New York: MacMillan, 1949.

Coleridge, Samuel Taylor. *The Complete Works of Samuel Taylor Coleridge*. 7 vols. Ed. by W. G. T. Shedd. New York: Harper, 1854.

Cooke, George W. *An Historical and Biographical Introduction to Accompany* The Dial. 2 vols. Cleveland: The Rowfant Club, 1902.

Cowen, Walker. *Melville's Marginalia.* 2 vols. New York & London: Garland, 1987.

Edmundson, Mark. *Nightmare on Main Street: Angels, Sadomasochism, and the Culture of the Gothic.* Cambridge, MA: Harvard UP, 1997.

Edwards, Herbert W., and Rod W. Horton. *Backgrounds of American Literary Thought.* New York: Appleton-Century-Crofts, Inc., 1958.

Emerson, Ralph Waldo. *The Complete Works of Ralph Waldo Emerson.* 12 vols. Ed. by Edward Waldo Emerson. New York: Houghton Mifflin, 1903–1921.

———. *Emerson: Essays & Lectures.* Ed. by Joel Porte. New York: The Library of America, 1983.

———. *Emerson's Antislavery Writings.* Ed. by Len Gougeon and Joel Myerson. New Haven: Yale UP, 1995.

———. *Journals of Ralph Waldo Emerson.* 10 vols. Ed. by Edward Waldo Emerson and Waldo Emerson Forbes. Boston: Houghton Mifflin, 1912.

Feidelson, Charles, Jr. *Symbolism in American Literature.* Chicago and London: U of Chicago P, 1953.

Fiedler, Leslie. *Love and Death in the American Novel.* New York: Stein and Day, 1982.

Franklin, H. Bruce. "'Apparent Symbol of Despotic Command': Melville's 'Benito Cereno.'" *New England Quarterly* 34 (1961): 462–477.

Frothingham, O. B. *Transcendentalism in New England.* New York: Harper, 1959.

Goddard, Harold Clarke. *Studies in New England Transcendentalism.* New York: Hilary House, 1960.

Goddu, Teresa. *Gothic America: Narrative, History, and Nation.* New York: Columbia UP, 1997.

Gougeon, Len. *Virtue's Hero: Emerson, Antislavery, and Reform.* Athens, GA: U of Georgia P, 1990.

Hawthorne, Julian. *Nathaniel Hawthorne and Wife.* 2 vols. Boston: Ticknor, 1884.

Hawthorne, Nathaniel. *The Complete Works of Nathaniel Hawthorne.* 12 vols. Ed. by G. P. Lathrop. New York: Houghton Mifflin, 1882.

———. *Hawthorne: Novels.* New York: The Library of America, 1983.

———. *Hawthorne: Tales and Sketches.* New York: The Library of America, 1982.

Hetherington, Hugh W. *Melville's Reviewers.* Chapel Hill, NC: U of North Carolina P, 1961.

Hoffman, Michael J. "The Anti-Transcendentalism of *Moby-Dick.*" *Georgia Review* 23:1 (Spring 1959): 3–16.

Holmes, Oliver Wendell. *Ralph Waldo Emerson.* Boston & New York: Houghton Mifflin, 1884.

Hutchinson, William R. *The Transcendental Ministers.* New Haven: Yale UP, 1959.

Jackson, Rosemary. *Fantasy: The Literature of Subversion.* London and New York: Methuen, 1981.

Kant, Immanuel. *Critique of Practical Reason.* Trans. by Thomas K. Abbott. New York: Longman's, Green, 1909.

———. *Critique of Pure Reason.* Trans. by F. Max Muller. New York: Macmillan, 1924.

Karcher, Carolyn L. "The Riddle of the Sphinx: Melville's 'Benito Cereno' and the *Amistad* Case," *Critical Essays on Melville's* Benito Cereno. Ed. by Robert Burkholder. Boston: G. K. Hall, 1992, pp. 196–229.

———. *Shadow Over the Promised Land: Slavery, Race, and Violence in Melville's America.* Baton Rouge, LA and London: Louisiana State UP, 1980.

Levin, Harry. *The Power of Blackness: Hawthorne, Poe, Melville.* New York: Vintage Books, 1960.

Lewis, R. W. B. *The American Adam: Innocence, Tragedy, and Tradition in the Nineteenth Century.* Chicago: U of Chicago P, 1955.

Leyda, Jay, ed. *The Melville Log: A Documentary Life of Herman Melville, 1819–1891.* 2 vols. New York: Harcourt Brace and Company, 1951.

Lowell, James Russell. "Thoreau," *American Literature Survey: The American Romantics, 1800–1860.* 4 vols. Ed. by Seymour L. Gross and Milton R. Stern. New York: The Viking Press, 1962.

Markels, Julian. "The *Moby-Dick* White Elephant." *American Literature* 66:1 (March 1994): 105–122.

Mason, Ronald. *The Spirit Above the Dust: A Study of Herman Melville.* London: John Lehmann, 1951.

Matthiessen, F. O. *American Renaissance.* New York: Oxford UP, 1941.

McDowell, Tremaine. "Foreword," *The Complete Essays and Other Writings of Ralph Waldo Emerson.* Ed. by Brooks Atkinson. New York: Random House, 1950, pp. i–xxvii.

McElderry, B. R., Jr. "The Transcendental Hawthorne." *Midwest Quarterly* 2 (Summer 1961): 307–323.

Melville, Herman. *The Confidence-Man: His Masquerade.* Ed. by Harrison Hayford, Hershel Parker, and G. Thomas Tanselle. Evanston and Chicago: Northwestern UP and the Newberry Library, 1984.

———. *Correspondence.* Ed. by Lynn Horth. Evanston and Chicago: Northwestern UP and the Newberry Library, 1993.

———. *Mardi and a Voyage Thither*. Ed. by Harrison Hayford, Hershel Parker, and G. Thomas Tanselle. Evanston and Chicago: Northwestern UP and the Newberry Library, 1970.

———. *Moby-Dick; or, The Whale*. Ed. by Harrison Hayford, Hershel Parker, and G. Thomas Tanselle. Evanston and Chicago: Northwestern UP and the Newberry Library, 1988.

———. *The Piazza Tales and Other Prose Pieces: 1839–1860*. Ed. by Harrison Hayford, Alma A. McDougall, and G. Thomas Tanselle. Evanston and Chicago: Northwestern UP and the Newberry Library, 1987.

———. *Pierre; or, The Ambiguities*. Ed. by Harrison Hayford, Hershel Parker, and G. Thomas Tanselle. Evanston and Chicago: Northwestern UP and the Newberry Library, 1971.

———. *The Portable Melville*. Ed. by Jay Leyda. New York: Viking, 1952.

———. *Selected Poems of Herman Melville*. Ed. by Hennig Cohen. Garden City, NY: Doubleday, 1964.

Metcalf, Eleanor Melville. *Herman Melville: Cycle and Epicycle*. Cambridge, MA: Harvard UP, 1953.

Metzger, Charles R. *Emerson and Greenough*. Berkeley, CA: U of California P, 1954.

Miller, Paul W. "Sun and Fire Worship in Melville's *Moby-Dick*." *Nineteenth-Century Fiction* 13 (September 1958): 139–144.

Miller, Perry. "From Edwards to Emerson," *Interpretations of American Literature*. Ed. by Charles Feidelson, Jr. and Paul Brodtkorb, Jr. New York: Oxford UP, 1959, pp. 114–136.

———. "Melville and Transcendentalism." *The Virginia Quarterly Review* 29 (Autumn 1953): 556–575.

———. *The Raven and the Whale: The War of Words and Wits in the Era of Poe and Melville*. New York: Harcourt, Brace, and Company, 1956.

———, ed. *The Transcendentalists*. Cambridge, MA: Harvard UP, 1950.

Mumford, Lewis. *Herman Melville*. New York: The Literary Guild of America, 1929.

Murray, Henry A. "Introduction," *Pierre; or, The Ambiguities*. Ed. by Murray. New York: Hendricks House, 1949, pp. i–xxi.

Noss, John B. *Man's Religions*. New York: Macmillan, 1963.

Parker, Hershel. *Herman Melville: A Biography. Volume 1, 1819–1851*. Baltimore, MD: Johns Hopkins UP, 1996.

———. *Herman Melville: A Biography. Volume 2, 1851–1891*. Baltimore, MD: Johns Hopkins UP, 2002.

Parrington, Vernon L. *Main Currents of American Thought*. 2 vols. New York: Harcourt, Brace, 1927.

Perry, Bliss. "Emerson's Most Famous Speech," *The Praise of Folly and Other Papers*. New York: Houghton Mifflin, 1923.

Pilkington, William T. "Melville's 'Benito Cereno': Source and Technique." *Studies in Short Fiction* 2 (1965): 247–255.

Plato. *The Republic*. Trans. by Francis MacDonald Cornford. New York: Oxford, 1945.

Punter, David. *Gothic Pathologies: The Text, the Body and the Law*. New York: St. Martin's Press, 1998.

Runes, Dagobert D., ed. *Dictionary of Philosophy*. Ames, IA: Littlefield, Adams and Co., 1959.

Sealts, Merton, Jr. *Melville's Reading*. Columbia: South Carolina UP, 1988.

Spiller, Robert A. *Literary History of the United States*. New York: Macmillan, 1953.

Stewart, Randall. *Nathaniel Hawthorne: A Biography*. New Haven: Yale UP, 1948.

Stuckey, Sterling. *Going Through the Storm: The Influence of African-American Art in History*. New York and Oxford: Oxford UP, 1994.

Sundermann, Karl H. *Herman Melville's Gedankengut; eine kritische Untersuchung seiner weltanschaulichen Grundideen*. Berlin: A. Collignon, 1937.

Sundquist, Eric J. "*Benito Cereno* and New World Slavery," *Reconstructing American Literary History*. Ed. by Sacvan Bercovitch. Cambridge: Harvard UP, 1986.

Tharp, Louise Hall. *The Peabody Sisters of Salem*. Boston: Little, Brown, and Company, 1950.

Thilly, Frank, and Ledger Wood. *A History of Philosophy*. New York: Henry Holt, 1951.

Thompson, Lawrance. *Melville's Quarrel with God*. Princeton: Princeton UP, 1952.

Thoreau, Henry David. *Thoreau: A Week on the Concord and Merrimack Rivers; Walden, The Maine Woods; Cape Cod*. Ed. by Robert F. Sayre. New York: The Library of America, 1985.

Tomlinson, H. M. "Preface," *Pierre; or, The Ambiguities*. Herman Melville. New York: E. P. Dutton and Company, Inc., 1929, pp. vii–xxvii.

"Transcendent," *Oxford English Dictionary*. Oxford, England: Clarendon Press, 1933, vol. xi, p. 233.

Von Frank, Albert J. *The Trials of Anthony Burns: Freedom and Slavery in Emerson's Boston*. Cambridge, MA: Harvard UP, 1998.

Vogel, Stanley M. *German Influences on the American Transcendentalists*. New Haven: Yale UP, 1955.

Weaver, Raymond. *Herman Melville, Mariner and Mystic*. New York: G.
    H. Doran, 1921.
Widgery, Alban G. "Classical German Idealism," *A History of
    Philosophical Systems*. Ed. by Vergilius Ferm. New York:
    Philosophical Library, 1950.
Williams, John B. *White Fire: The Influence of Emerson on Melville*. Long
    Beach, CA: California State UP, 1991.
Windelband, Wilhelm. *A History of Philosophy*. 2 vols. New York:
    Harper & Brothers, 1958.
Yamamoto, Shoh. "The Source and Structure of 'Benito Cereno.'"
    Studies in English Literature 162: 189–191.
Young, James Dean. "The Nine Gams of the *Pequod*," *Discussions of
    Moby-Dick*. Ed. by Milton R. Stern. Boston: Heath, 1960, pp.
    98–106.

Index